WRITTEN SKILLS FOR LAWYERS

WRITTEN SKILLS FOR LAWYERS
SECOND EDITION

Katherine Blow and Jacqueline Kempton

Second edition published 2023 by
The University of Law,
2 Bunhill Row
London EC1Y 8HQ

© The University of Law 2023

Contains public sector information licensed under the Open Government Licence v3.0

First edition published 2021

British Library Cataloguing in Publication Data

A catalogue record for this book is available from the British Library.

ISBN 978 1 915698 64 3

Preface

The Solicitors Qualifying Examination (SQE) is the new assessment for all aspiring solicitors in England and Wales. They will have to pass both stages of the SQE assessment: SQE1 which focuses on Functioning Legal Knowledge (FLK) and SQE2 which tests practical legal skills and knowledge. This is one of two study manuals that have been specifically designed to support the reader to achieve the SQE2 Assessment Specification. Each manual aims to provide the reader with a thorough knowledge and understanding of the practical legal skills assessed in SQE2.

This study manual covers the Solicitors Regulation Authority (SRA)'s syllabus for the SQE2 assessments in Legal Writing, Legal Drafting, Legal Research and Case and Matter Analysis. It offers practical guidance on each skill accompanied by realistic examples and/or handy templates. While this manual focuses on mastering the SQE2 written skills and passing the SQE2 assessments, it also offers some more general advice on developing those skills in professional legal practice.

This manual has been compiled from the version of the SRA's SQE2 Assessment Specification current at the time of writing. The manual is not intended to constitute legal advice. The publisher and writers are not responsible or liable for the results of any person acting (or omitting to act) on the basis of information contained within this publication.

For those readers who are students at The University of Law, this study manual is used alongside other learning resources to best prepare students not only for the SQE2 assessments, but also for a future life in professional legal practice.

We hope you find this manual supportive of your preparation for SQE2 and we wish you every success.

The legal principles and rules contained within this manual are stated as at 1 January 2023.

Author acknowledgements

The authors would like to thank their colleagues at The University of Law for their invaluable help in the preparation of this manual.

Extracts from the SRA's SQE2 Assessment Specification are reproduced with kind permission of the SRA (see https://sqe.sra.org.uk/exam-arrangements/assessment-information).

Contents

Contents

1 Introduction to the Written Skills Assessments

SQE2 syllabus

This chapter summarises the guidance which the SRA has issued on the SQE2 written skills assessments. There is a corresponding chapter on the SQE2 oral skills assessments in The University of Law SQE2 manual *Oral Skills for Lawyers*.

While this manual focuses on mastering the SQE2 written skills and passing the SQE2 assessments, it also offers some more general guidance on developing those skills in legal practice.

1.1   Introduction

This manual looks individually at each of the SQE2 written skills, but it begins by considering themes which are common to all the written skills. This chapter examines the framework which the SRA has set out for the SQE2 written assessments. **Chapter 2** deals with written communication and **Chapter 3** with negotiation.

This chapter looks at:

- the four written skills;
- the other areas which will be tested pervasively;
- the practicalities of the assessments;
- the assessment objectives and criteria;
- how the SQE2 assessments are marked;
- the threshold standard;
- the Statement of Solicitor Competence; and
- the Functioning Legal Knowledge (FLK) required for SQE2.

IMPORTANT. The information below is taken from the SRA's SQE2 Assessment Specification and is correct at time of going to press. However, as this may be updated it is vital that you check the SRA website to view the most up-to-date specification (https://sqe.sra.org.uk/exam-arrangements/assessment-information).

1.2   The written skills

There are four written skills which will be assessed in SQE2:

- Case and Matter Analysis
- Legal Research
- Legal Writing
- Legal Drafting

There are two further aspects of a solicitor's work, negotiation and ethics and professional conduct, which will not be tested individually but will be assessed in the context of the SQE2 assessments, as per the table below.

Written skill	Negotiation may be assessed?	Ethical and professional conduct issues may arise?
Case and Matter Analysis	✓	✓
Legal Research		✓
Legal Writing	✓	✓
Legal Drafting		✓

1.2.1 Negotiation

There is no separate assessment called negotiation, but the SRA has made it clear that all deliveries of SQE2 will contain at least one assessment involving negotiation. You can read more about the skill of negotiation in the context of the SQE2 assessments in **Chapter 3**.

1.2.2 Ethics and professional conduct

Questions on ethics and professional conduct will be pervasive throughout SQE2. The SRA guidance makes it clear that ethical and professional conduct issues will not be flagged, and that candidates will need to identify any such issues and exercise judgment to resolve them honestly and with integrity. The chapters on the individual written skills in this manual discuss the types of issue which might arise.

1.2.3 The practice areas

The table below shows the practice areas in which the SQE2 written skills will be assessed and the underlying black letter law on which they may draw. The FLK required is considered in more detail at the end of this chapter.

The table also identifies the practice areas in which questions involving Taxation or Money Laundering and Financial Services may arise in the SQE2 assessments. The full details can be found in Annex 1 of the SRA's SQE2 Assessment Specification.

Practice area	Black letter law	Taxation	Money laundering and financial services
Criminal Litigation (including advising clients at the police station)	Criminal Liability		
Dispute Resolution	Contract Law and Tort		
Property Practice	Land Law	✓	
Wills and Intestacy, Probate Administration and Practice	Trusts	✓	
Business Organisations, Rules and Procedures	Contract Law	✓	✓

1.3 SQE2 written assessments – the practicalities

The SQE2 written skills will be assessed over three assessment days. You can find detailed guidance about these on the SRA website, as well as information about the assessment windows.

1.3.1 Venue

All SQE2 written assessments will take place at Pearson Vue assessment centres in the UK and internationally. More details are available on the Pearson Vue and SRA websites.

1.3.2 The assessment timetable

The SQE2 written assessments will take place over three consecutive days. You will take a total of 12 written skills assessments, as per the table below. On each day you will sit four assessments spread across two sessions. As you can see from the table, you will sit assessments in the same skills on each of the three days, but the practice areas will be different each day. The table also shows the length of each assessment.

Day One	Day Two	Day Three
Case and matter analysis (60 minutes)	Case and matter analysis (60 minutes)	Case and matter analysis (60 minutes)
Legal drafting (45 minutes)	Legal drafting (45 minutes)	Legal drafting (45 minutes)
Legal research (60 minutes)	Legal research (60 minutes)	Legal research (60 minutes)
Legal writing (30 minutes)	Legal writing (30 minutes)	Legal writing (30 minutes)
Practice areas: Two of these exercises will be in the context of Dispute Resolution and two will be in the context of Criminal Litigation.	**Practice areas:** Two of these exercises will be in the context of Property Practice and two will be in the context of Wills and Intestacy, Probate Administration and Practice.	**Practice areas:** You will sit all assessments in the context of Business Organisations, Rules and Procedures.

You may complete the assessments in a different order to that listed.

1.3.3 The form of the assessments

The SRA website provides a sample question for each of the SQE2 assessments. These include sample answers A and B, which are both at pass level but of different standards, as well as a discussion of the answer. These are a very useful resource which you can use to familiarise yourself with the way the questions may be framed, but do note the SRA's warning at the front of each sample question.

The SQE2 written assessments are all computer-based assessments, which means that your instructions and any documents will be provided electronically and there will be a 'page' for you to type your answer. You can see how these will be presented by looking at the SRA website ('SQE2 exam functionality on Pearson VUE').

Certain tools (such as spell-check) may not be available.

The SQE2 written assessments are closed book, and you may not bring any materials, such as books and notes, into the assessments or use them. If the assessment requires knowledge of an aspect of the law which a Day One solicitor would have to look up, this will be given to you in the assessment.

You will be provided with an erasable whiteboard notepad and marker pen to be used only during the assessment. These must be handed in at the end of the assessment.

You will only have a limited time to answer each question. The time limits for each assessment vary, as set out in the table above. The time limit will be rigidly enforced; indeed, there is likely to be an automatic 'time out' which prevents anything further being added to the answer once the allocated time has expired.

1.4 Assessment Objectives and Criteria

Each of the SQE2 assessments has its own Assessment Objective and Assessment Criteria. These are considered in the relevant chapters of this manual and can also be viewed on the SRA website.

1.4.1 The Assessment Objective

The Assessment Objective sets out in one sentence what the candidate can demonstrate in each assessment

SQE2 written assessment	Assessment Objective
	Candidates can demonstrate that they are able to...
Case and Matter Analysis	produce a written report to a partner giving a legal analysis of the case and client focused advice
Legal Research	conduct legal research from a variety of resources provided and produce a written report
Legal Writing	produce a letter or email as the solicitor acting in a matter
Legal Drafting	draft a legal document or parts of a legal document for a client

1.4.2 The Assessment Criteria

The Assessment Criteria set out the benchmarks against which you will be assessed in each SQE2 assessment. You will see that these are divided between skills and application of the law, which are given equal weighting in the marking.

1.4.2.1 The application of law criteria

The 'application of law' criteria are the same for all the SQE2 assessments. These require candidates to:

(1) Apply the law correctly to the client's situation.

(2) Apply the law comprehensively to the client's situation, identifying any ethical and professional conduct issues and exercising judgment to resolve them honestly and with integrity.

[NB. For Legal Drafting the criteria read:

(1) Draft a document which is legally correct.

(2) Draft a document which is legally comprehensive, identifying any ethical and professional conduct issues and exercising judgment to resolve them honestly and with integrity.]

The SRA has provided a non-exhaustive list of what applying the 'correct and comprehensive application of the law' criteria might look like, as follows:

- identifying relevant legal principles;

- applying legal principles to factual issues, so as to produce a solution which best addresses a client's needs and reflects the client's commercial or personal circumstances, including as part of a negotiation;

- interpreting, evaluating and applying the results of research;

- ensuring that advice is informed by appropriate legal analysis and identifies the consequences of different options;

- drafting documents which are legally effective;

- applying understanding, critical thinking and analysis to solve problems;

- assessing information to identify key issues and risks;

- recognising inconsistencies and gaps in information;

- evaluating the quality and reliability of information;

- using multiple sources of information to make effective judgments; and

- reaching reasoned decisions supported by relevant evidence.

You will see that some of these are clearly more appropriate to some of the SQE2 written skills: for example, 'interpreting, evaluating and applying the results of research' will clearly apply to Legal Research. Others, such as 'applying legal principles to factual issues' will apply to all the SQE2 written assessments.

The SRA has explained the distinction between 'correct' and 'comprehensive' application of the law. As you might expect, this depends on the extent to which the legal issue has been made clear in your instructions:

> The assessment criteria for application of law refer to legally correct and legally comprehensive. How each of these is interpreted will depend on an academic judgment about each assessment informed by the Statement of Solicitor Competence (Annex 3) and the Functioning Legal Knowledge for SQE2 (Annex 1). For instance, in an assessment where the candidate has to identify the legal issues, credit for this might be given under legally comprehensive. Where the legal issues are made explicit in the question, credit under legally comprehensive might be awarded for giving a comprehensive analysis of those issues, not just for identifying them.

1.4.2.2 The 'clear, precise and acceptable language' criterion

While the skills criteria are tailored to the requirements of each of the SQE2 written assessments, they all stipulate that candidates must use 'clear, precise and acceptable language'. The SRA has explained that this may include:

- using clear, succinct and accurate language and avoiding unnecessary technical terms where they are not appropriate to the recipient; and

- using an acceptable style of communication for the situation and recipient.

Chapter 2, which looks at written communication, will assist you in meeting this criterion.

1.5 Marking the SQE2 written assessments

The Assessment Criteria set out above provide the framework against which the SQE2 written assessments will be marked. The marking will be carried out by a solicitor, who will have been trained and who will assess candidates on both skills and application of law. The assessor will assess candidates' performance against the criteria using a scale from A to F and making *'global professional judgments related to the standard of competency of the assessment'*. The grading will be converted into the marks set out in the table below.

A	Superior performance: well above the competency requirements of the assessment	5
B	Clearly satisfactory: clearly meets the competency requirements of the assessment	4
C	Marginal pass: on balance, just meets the competency requirements of the assessment	3
D	Marginal fail: on balance, just fails to meet the competency requirements of the assessment	2
E	Clearly unsatisfactory: clearly does not meet the competency requirements of the assessment	1
F	Poor performance: well below the competency requirements of the assessment	0

The SRA states that in arriving at a final mark for the candidate across all assessments, skills and application of law are weighted equally and that is to make sure that adequate weighting is given to the quality of the advice provided. To pass SQE2 candidates will need to obtain the overall pass mark for SQE2.

You can find out more about how information will be given about the results of the SQE2 assessments from the 'Results and resits' page of the SRA website.

1.6 What standard will you be expected to achieve?

The standard against which you will be assessed is the 'threshold standard', which is the standard of competency of the Day One solicitor. But what does this standard mean and how will it be applied in a consistent way?

1.6.1 The threshold standard

The starting point is the Statement of Solicitor Competence (SoSC) which is a set of competencies which apply to all solicitors. To reflect the development of these competencies throughout a solicitor's career different levels of performance (from 1 to 5) apply at different stages. Candidates for SQE2 are expected to achieve level 3, which is the standard to which the competencies should be performed upon qualification as a solicitor (the 'Day One solicitor').

Annex 2 of the SQE2 Assessment Specification, which is copied below, sets out the level of performance which is expected of a level 3 solicitor in six key areas. You can read more about the threshold standard, and how it compares with the other standards, on the SRA website. You will see that, while a clear standard of competence is expected at level 3, there is also an expectation of development and improvement. For example, under the heading, 'Standard of work' you will see that a level 3 solicitor is expected to 'achieve an acceptable standard for straightforward tasks, but complex tasks may lack refinement'. By contrast, at level 4, the expectation is 'Full acceptable standard achieved routinely' and at level 5 is 'Excellence achieved with ease'.

Threshold standard

Functioning legal knowledge	Standard of work	Autonomy	Complexity	Perception of context	Innovation and originality
Identifies the legal principles relevant to the area of practice and applies them appropriately and effectively to individual cases.	Acceptable standard achieved routinely for straightforward tasks. Complex tasks may lack refinement.	Achieves most tasks and able to progress legal matters using own judgment, recognising when support is needed.	Able to deal with straightforward transactions, including occasional, unfamiliar tasks which present a range of problems and choices.	Understands the significance of individual actions in the context of the objectives of the transaction/ strategy for the case.	Uses experience to check information provided and to form judgments about possible courses of action and ways forward.

1.6.2 Statement of Solicitor Competence

So, what are the competencies? 'Competence' is defined by the SRA as 'the ability to perform the roles and tasks required by one's job to the expected standard'. In the SoSC the SRA has set out what solicitors should be able to do in these four key areas:

A. Ethics, professionalism and judgment

B. Technical legal practice

C. Working with other people

D. Managing themselves and their own work

In turn, each area is broken down into a series of propositions (A1, A2 etc.) for which examples are provided. So, for example, under the heading 'A. Ethics, professionalism and judgment' the SRA sets out the proposition 'A1. Act honestly and with integrity, in accordance with legal and regulatory requirements and the SRA Standards and Regulations'. It then provides a list of examples, beginning with:

'a. Recognising ethical issues and exercising effective judgment in addressing them.'

You can find the full SoSC at Annex 3 of the SQE2 Assessment Specification and in the appendix to this chapter.

1.6.3 The competencies mapped against the SQE2 Assessment Specification

Clearly, not all the competencies will apply to all the SQE2 written skills. The SRA has therefore mapped the relevant competencies against each one. The result can be found at Annex 4 of the SQE2 Assessment Specification, which is set out in the appendix to this chapter. You will see, for example, that SoSC C3 *'Establish and maintain effective and professional relations with other people...'*, only applies to the SQE2 Legal Writing assessments. On the other hand, all the requirements for SoSC A *'Ethics, professionalism and judgment'* apply to all the SQE2 assessments.

For each of the SQE2 assessments you should check which of the competencies the SRA has identified as being relevant, with a view to demonstrating these in the assessment. This manual provides guidance on how this can be achieved.

1.7 Functioning Legal Knowledge for SQE2

As noted above, the Assessment Criteria for each of the SQE2 written assessments have been divided between skills and application of law. In arriving at a final mark across all assessments, these are weighted equally. The SRA explains that this is to make sure that adequate weighting is given to the quality of the advice provided.

So, what law will you need to know for the SQE2 written assessments? As with SQE1, the SRA has set out the Functioning Legal Knowledge (FLK) required. This can be found at Annex 1 of the SQE2 Assessment Specification, which sets out the legal principles which candidates will be expected to know in relation to the black letter law and the five practice areas assessed in SQE2. It is described by the SRA as a 'subset' of the FLK required for SQE1.

You should refer to the SRA website for the full syllabus for each of these areas, and to your SQE1 materials for the substance of them. If you are feeling daunted by the amount of law to cover, bear in mind the guidance from the SRA below, to reassure you that the focus is not on esoteric legal points. Looking at the sample questions which the SRA has published should also reassure you that the legal points which these cover are familiar to you.

The SRA website provides the following guidance on the level of detail required:

> *In demonstrating that they have reached the standard of competency of a Day One Solicitor, candidates will need to demonstrate that they can apply fundamental legal principles in the skills based situations covered by SQE2 in a way that addresses the client's needs and concerns. They will need sufficient knowledge to make them competent to practise on the basis that they can look up detail later. Candidates will not be expected to know or address detail that a Day One Solicitor would look up, unless they have been provided with that detail as part of the assessment materials.*

It has further clarified that,

> *The questions in SQE2 are designed to test legal skills within the context of the application of fundamental legal rules and principles at the level required of a competent newly qualified Solicitor. They are not designed to test specialist practice which is unlikely to be encountered at the level of a Day One Solicitor.*

> *Questions test central areas that are clearly covered by the FLK.*

Finally, for SQE1 purposes, the SRA provided that,

> *On occasion in legal practice a case name or statutory provision, for example, is the term normally used to describe a legal principle or an area of law, or a rule or procedural step (e.g. Rylands v Fletcher, CPR Part 36, Section 25 notice). In such*

circumstances, candidates are required to know and be able to use such case names, statutory provisions etc. In all other circumstances candidates are not required to recall specific case names, or cite statutory or regulatory authorities.

The same provision arguably applies by analogy to SQE2 but remember that you may be provided with legal materials as part of an SQE2 assessment. In that case you would be expected to refer to any case names and statutory authorities which these contain, as appropriate.

APPENDIX TO CHAPTER 1

The Statement of Solicitor Competence

Annex 3 of the SQE2 Assessment Specification

A.   Ethics, professionalism and judgment

A1. Act honestly and with integrity, in accordance with legal and regulatory requirements and the SRA Standards and Regulations, including:

a.   Recognising ethical issues and exercising effective judgment in addressing them.

b.   Understanding and applying the ethical concepts which govern their role and behaviour as a lawyer.

c.   Identifying the relevant SRA principles and rules of professional conduct and following them.

d.   Resisting pressure to condone, ignore or commit unethical behaviour.

e.   Respecting diversity and acting fairly and inclusively.

A2. Maintain the level of competence and legal knowledge needed to practise effectively, taking into account changes in their role and/or practice context and developments in the law, including:

a.   Taking responsibility for personal learning and development.

b.   Reflecting on and learning from practice and learning from other people.

c.   Accurately evaluating their strengths and limitations in relation to the demands of their work.

d.   Maintaining an adequate and up-to-date understanding of relevant law, policy and practice.

e.   Adapting practice to address developments in the delivery of legal services.

A3. Work within the limits of their competence and the supervision which they need, including:

a.   Disclosing when work is beyond their personal capability.

b.   Recognising when they have made mistakes or are experiencing difficulties and taking appropriate action.

c.   Seeking and making effective use of feedback, guidance and support where needed.

d.   Knowing when to seek expert advice.

A4. Draw on a sufficient detailed knowledge and understanding of their field(s) of work and role in order to practise effectively, including:

a.   Identifying relevant legal principles.

b.   Applying legal principles to factual issues, so as to produce a solution which best addresses a client's needs and reflects the client's commercial or personal circumstances.

c.   Spotting issues that are outside their expertise and taking appropriate action, using both an awareness of a broad base of legal knowledge (insofar as relevant to their practice area) and detailed knowledge of their practice area.

A5. Apply understanding, critical thinking and analysis to solve problems, including:

    a.   Assessing information to identify key issues and risks.

    b.   Recognising inconsistencies and gaps in information.

    c.   Evaluating the quality and reliability of information.

    d.   Using multiple sources of information to make effective judgments.

    e.   Reaching reasoned decisions supported by relevant evidence.

B.   Technical legal practice

B1. Obtain relevant facts, including:

    a.   Obtaining relevant information through effective use of questioning and active listening.

    b.   Finding, analysing and assessing documents to extract relevant information.

    c.   Recognising when additional information is needed.

    d.   Interpreting and evaluating information obtained.

    e.   Recording and presenting information accurately and clearly.

B2. Undertake legal research, including:

    a.   Recognising when legal research is required.

    b.   Using appropriate methods and resources to undertake the research.

    c.   Identifying, finding and assessing the relevance of sources of law.

    d.   Interpreting, evaluating and applying the results of the research.

    e.   Recording and presenting the findings accurately and clearly.

B3. Develop and advise on relevant options, strategies and solutions, including:

    a.   Understanding and assessing a client's commercial and personal circumstances, their needs, objectives, priorities and constraints.

    b.   Ensuring that advice is informed by appropriate legal and factual analysis and identifies the consequences of different options.

B4. Draft documents which are legally effective and accurately reflect the client's instructions including:

    a.   Being able to draft documents from scratch as well as making appropriate use of precedents.

    b.   Addressing all relevant legal and factual issues.

    c.   Complying with appropriate formalities.

    d.   Using clear, accurate and succinct language.

B5. Undertake effective spoken and written advocacy, including:

    a.   Preparing effectively by identifying and mastering relevant facts and legal principles.

    b.   Organising facts to support the argument or position.

    c.   Presenting a reasoned argument in a clear, logical, succinct and persuasive way.

    d.   Making appropriate reference to legal authority.

    e.   Complying with formalities.

    f.   Dealing with witnesses appropriately.

    g.   Responding effectively to questions or opposing arguments.

    h.   Identifying strengths and weaknesses from different parties' perspectives.

B6. Negotiate solutions to clients' issues, including:

    a. Identifying all parties' interests, objectives and limits.

    b. Developing and formulating best options for meeting parties' objectives.

    c. Presenting options for compromise persuasively.

    d. Responding to options presented by the other side.

    e. Developing compromises between options or parties.

B7. Plan, manage and progress legal cases and transactions, including:

    a. Applying relevant processes and procedures to progress the matter effectively.

    b. Assessing, communicating and managing risk.

    c. Bringing the transaction or case to a conclusion.

C. Working with other people

C1. Communicate clearly and effectively, orally and in writing, including:

    a. Ensuring that communication achieves its intended objective.

    b. Responding to and addressing individual characteristics effectively and sensitively.

    c. Using the most appropriate method and style of communication for the situation and the recipient(s).

    d. Using clear, succinct and accurate language avoiding unnecessary technical terms.

    e. Using formalities appropriate to the context and purpose of the communication.

    f. Maintaining the confidentiality and security of communications.

    g. Imparting any difficult or unwelcome news clearly and sensitively.

C2. Establish and maintain effective and professional relations with clients, including:

    a. Treating clients with courtesy and respect.

    b. Providing information in a way that clients can understand, taking into account their personal circumstances and any particular vulnerability.

    c. Understanding and responding effectively to clients' particular needs, objectives, priorities and constraints.

    d. Identifying and taking reasonable steps to meet the particular service needs of all clients including those in vulnerable circumstances.

    e. Identifying possible courses of action and their consequences and assisting clients in reaching a decision.

    f. Managing clients' expectations regarding options, the range of possible outcomes, risk and timescales.

    g. Agreeing the services that are being provided and a clear basis for charging.

    h. Explaining the ethical framework within which the solicitor works.

    i. Informing clients in a timely way of key facts and issues including risks, progress towards objectives, and costs.

    j. Responding appropriately to clients' concerns and complaints.

C3. Establish and maintain effective and professional relations with other people, including:

    a. Treating others with courtesy and respect.

    b. Delegating tasks when appropriate to do so.

    c. Supervising the work of others effectively.

    d. Keeping colleagues informed of progress of work, including any risks or problems.

e. Acknowledging and engaging with others' expertise when appropriate.

f. Being supportive of colleagues and offering advice and assistance when required.

g. Being clear about expectations.

h. Identifying, selecting and, where appropriate, managing external experts or consultants.

D.   Managing themselves and their own work

D1. Initiate, plan, prioritise and manage work activities and projects to make sure that they are completed efficiently, on time and to an appropriate standard, both in relation to their own work and work that they lead or supervise, including:

a. Clarifying instructions so as to agree the scope and objectives of the work.

b. Taking into account the availability of resources in initiating work activities.

c. Meeting timescales, resource requirements and budgets.

d. Monitoring, and keeping other people informed of, progress.

e. Dealing effectively with unforeseen circumstances.

f. Paying appropriate attention to detail.

D2. Keep, use and maintain accurate, complete and clear records, including:

a. Making effective use of information management systems (whether electronic or hard copy), including storing and retrieving information.

b. Complying with confidentiality, security, data protection and file retention and destruction requirements.

D3. Apply good business practice, including:

a. Demonstrating an adequate understanding of the commercial, organisational and financial context in which they work and their role in it.

b. Understanding the contractual basis on which legal services are provided, including where appropriate how to calculate and manage costs and bill clients.

c. Applying the rules of professional conduct to accounting and financial matters.

d. Managing available resources and using them efficiently.

SQE2 skills mapping against the SQE2 Assessment Specification

Annex 4 of the SQE2 Assessment Specification

SoSC	Client interview and attendance note/legal analysis	Advocacy	Case and matter analysis	Legal writing	Legal research	Legal drafting
A. Ethics						
A1	x	x	x	x	x	x
A2	x	x	x	x	x	x
A3	x	x	x	x	x	x
A4	x	x	x	x	x	x
A5	x	x	x	x	x	x
B. Technical legal practice						
B1	x	x	x	x	x	x
B2					x	
B3	x		x	x	x	
B4						x
B5		x				
B6	x		x	x		
B7	x		x	x		
C. Working with other people						
C1	x	x	x	x	x	x
C2	x		x	x		
C3		x		x		
D. Managing themselves and their own work						
D1	x	x	x	x	x	x
D2	x					
D3	x					

2 Written Communication Skills

SQE2 syllabus

This chapter will help you to meet the SQE2 Assessment Criterion of using 'clear, precise, concise and acceptable language' in written communication.

This chapter should be read in conjunction with the chapters on Legal Writing, Legal Drafting, Case and Matter Analysis and Legal Research, as well as Chapter 5 of The University of Law SQE2 manual *Oral Skills for Lawyers*, which deals with attendance notes.

Learning outcomes

By the end of this chapter you should be able to:

- understand why clear written communication is vital to the work of a solicitor;
- identify and avoid common errors in punctuation, grammar and spelling; and
- use a written style which is clear and precise.

2.1 Introduction

It is vital for solicitors to be able to communicate clearly and accurately in writing. While clients may not be able to recognise whether what their solicitor has written is legally correct (and that is not their job) they will invariably pick up on errors of grammar, spelling and punctuation. As many solicitors have found to their cost, these avoidable mistakes can easily undermine clients' confidence in the legal advice they are receiving.

Written communication is a central part of a solicitor's practice. Solicitors need to be able to communicate clearly in writing with a range of different people, such as clients, opponents and the court. Solicitors write for a range of different purposes: to create legally enforceable documents; to negotiate with opponents; and to reassure their clients. As well as making sure that their written communication is precise and accurate, they need to communicate in a way appropriate to their audience; this is the 'tone' of the communication.

The final aspect of written communication is its style. Throughout your time in legal practice, you will develop your own style. You will also learn to recognise and adopt the written style of the partners and others for whom you are writing. Ideally, your writing should be clear, concise and a pleasure to read. It should convey your ideas to your reader as fluently as possible. While you cannot perfect your written style overnight, you can avoid some of the pitfalls which can make legal writing difficult to digest.

The traditional view may be that solicitors write in a style which is formal, even pompous, peppered with terms such as 'aforementioned', 'heretofore' and 'we refer to your letter of 20th instant'. But that is no longer the case, and this way of writing is certainly not encouraged. In this chapter you will have a chance to consider how to replace such words and phrases with simpler, more modern expressions.

If you can form good habits now, while you are preparing for the SQE2 assessments: taking care with the precision of your writing, being as succinct as possible and proofreading your work, this will stand you in good stead for your future career. A good rule of thumb is to remember that what you write may one day be read out in court: how would it withstand such scrutiny?

This chapter looks at points common to all written communication, whether for the SQE2 assessments or elsewhere. Candidates' performance in exams is often compromised by poor spelling and grammar and unclear use of language. While this chapter cannot cover these topics comprehensively, it does identify some of the common errors which candidates tend to make in their written communication and looks at how to avoid them. It provides a brief explanation of each point and some exercises which you can use to check your spelling, punctuation and grammar. The answers can be found at the end of the chapter, as well as a list of resources which you can use to refresh your understanding.

While your written style should always be courteous, your tone and vocabulary should be tailored to the recipient. Are you writing to a client who has recently been bereaved, or to your opponent in litigation? The question of using the appropriate tone will be developed in **Chapters 5** to **8**, which deal with the skills specific to the Legal Writing and Legal Drafting assessments.

This chapter looks at:

- spelling, punctuation and grammar;

- vocabulary;

- written style;

- inclusive language; and

- presentation.

2. 2   Spelling, punctuation and grammar

Poor punctuation, spelling and grammar will undermine the authority of anything that you write. Poor grammar is at best distracting and likely to leave a poor impression. At worst it may alter the meaning of a document and render it ineffective.

Remember that spellcheck and other software is unlikely to be available to assist you in the SQE2 assessments. You should therefore aim to have a sound grasp of the relevant rules.

2.2.1   Spelling

2.2.1.1   Commonly misspelt words

Some common terms are frequently spelt wrongly. Have a look at the list below and select the correct spelling of each word. The answers are in the appendix at the end of this chapter.

Exercise 1

(i)	acomodation	accommodation	accomodation
(ii)	unneccessary	unneccesary	unnecessary
(iii)	privilege	priviledge	privelige
(iv)	embarass	embarras	embarrass
(v)	professor	proffessor	profesor

2.2.1.2   Commonly confused words

Make sure that you distinguish between words which look similar but are used differently, in particular those words which often come up in a legal context.

Nouns and verbs: licence/license; practice/practise

You should write

'They have a licence to sell alcohol on the premises' ('licence' is a noun).

But

'They are licensed to sell alcohol' ('license' is a verb).

'In legal practice you will have an opportunity to practise many skills' ('practice' is a noun and 'practise' is a verb).

Nouns and adjectives: stationery/stationary

You should also distinguish between nouns and adjectives, such as 'stationery' and 'stationary'.

'Stationery' is a noun meaning paper, pencils and so on.

'Stationary' is an adjective meaning not moving: so a car might be stationary.

There/their/they're

'There' is an adverb of place, as in, 'Her desk is there'. It is also used in a sentence which is describing an indefinite person or thing, as in, 'There are two people over there'.

'Their' is a possessive adjective denoting possession: 'Their firm specialises in family law'.

'They're' is a contraction of 'they are': 'They're all asking when the meeting will start'.

Your/you're

'Your' is a possessive adjective, as in, 'Your firm has a new logo'.

'You're' is a contraction of you are, as in, 'You're working with the designer on a new logo'.

Remember that, even where spellcheck is available, it may not help you with these commonly confused words, since all the spellings above are correct. Also remember that some spellings in British English differ from American English. For example, 'license' is a verb in British English (as seen above) but a noun and a verb in American English.

2.2.2 **Punctuation**

To start with the most basic rule, sentences should begin with a capital letter and end with a full stop. Sentences can also end with a question mark (?) or an exclamation mark (!). Proper names such as 'London' or 'Sarah' should have capital letters.

Commas (,) have various uses within sentences. They should be used to separate clauses in a sentence. 'He went to the library, came home, then went to the park.' They should also be used between adjectives, 'The quick, brown fox...'. A comma should also be used before inverted commas (see below).

Colons (:) are used at the start of a list. 'These are the most popular colours: pink, blue, brown and green.' They are also used to explain or expand upon a previous clause. 'She had decided to move to a new firm: she wanted to focus on family law.'

Semicolons (;) are used to separate items on a list. 'While I was in the Dispute Resolution team I spent my time preparing bundles; drafting application notices; and contacting witnesses to check their availability.' They are also used to link two parts of a sentence which could stand as separate sentences: 'I like working as part of a team; I enjoy exchanging ideas with my colleagues.'

Apostrophes (') often cause problems. They can be used in several different ways:

- For contractions. An apostrophe is used to replace the letter 'o' in 'didn't' (did not) and 'wouldn't' (would not), and to replace 'ha' in 'could've' (could have) and so on.

  Note that there is no gap between the 'd' and the 'n' in 'didn't' or 'wouldn't'.

  An apostrophe is also used to replace the letter 'i' in 'there's' (there is), 'he's' (he is) and so on.

- To show ownership. So, Preeti's book = the book of Preeti. But how about the book of James? You can write either 'James' book' or 'James's book' (but not 'Jame's book').

  If you are writing about a group and the plural noun ends in 's', such as 'the lawyers', the apostrophe comes after the letter s: 'The lawyers' ideas are very good.'

However, if the plural form of the noun ends in a different letter, such as in the word 'children', the apostrophe comes before the 's': 'The children's interests are always paramount.'

Apostrophes should *not* be used for plurals. This is a common mistake. So, you should write 'the boys went camping' and never 'the boy's went camping'.

Inverted commas ("). These are also known as or speech marks or quotes and are used to flag up direct speech.

  She shouted, 'That's enough'.

Note that there is a comma before the inverted commas and the first word begins with a capital letter.

Inverted commas are not used in indirect speech when the speaker's actual words are not quoted.

She shouted that she'd had enough.

As in this paragraph, inverted commas are often used when providing examples. In formal writing, they are used to flag up informal words. When they are used in this way, it is not necessary to put in a comma or a capital letter.

She did not want to 'diss' him in front of his friends.

You can assess your punctuation skills by trying these exercises (answers in the appendix).

Exercise 2

Apostrophes

Add apostrophes where necessary in the following sentences:

(i) Whos likely to be delayed by a few minutes of rain?

(ii) Weve always valued both the local Gardening Institutes lectures.

(iii) Im sure he said its a ten oclock train we need to catch.

(iv) The childrens enjoyment of the fair was greater than ours.

(v) The girls football shirts hung on pegs in the cloakrooms main aisle.

Other punctuation

Add a comma or full stop beneath the *:

(i) MARY DAVENPORT WRITES WELL * HOWEVER, LUCIEN GRANT HATES WRITING.

(ii) MY PRINCIPAL AREA OF SPECIALITY IS TAX * MY SECOND SPECIALITY IS FINANCE.

Add full stops and capital letters to:

(iii) The trainee was quite clear that he needed to work harder if he wanted to get taken on it was quite possible for the firm to hire all the trainees that year his friend had already been given an indication that he would be offered a job and he had been working really long hours

Add commas to:

(iv) Edward O'Grady however always wanted to surf the Internet rather than do his work.

(v) The solicitor walked up to her office opened the door took off her coat and slumped into her chair.

(vi) For business meetings the firm offered tea coffee water fruit juices biscuits and sandwiches.

Add semicolons to:

(vii) I read the Legal Times before work every day it keeps me on top of changes in the law.

(viii) The employer wrote to the employee to complain about his time keeping workers ought to know that starting work on time is essential.

2.2.3 Grammar

Here are some points to be aware of and some common errors to avoid, to ensure that your written communication is as clear, precise and accurate as possible.

First/ second/ third person. The first person means 'I' or 'we', the second person means 'you' and the third person means 'he/she' or 'they'.

Which of these you choose will depend upon the context in which you are writing. So, for example, you would usually write a letter to a client or a memo to a partner in the first person singular, e.g. 'I have carried out the research you requested'. However, law firms usually write to each other in the first person plural, e.g. 'We have the following comments on your client's proposal'. Legal documents, such as leases, are drafted in the third person, e.g. 'The landlord will allow the tenant to park on the forecourt'.

Shall and will. 'Shall' and 'will' can cause difficulties when combined with the first, second and third person. In everyday speech they are often used interchangeably, but lawyers should be aware of their precise meanings, which are used to distinguish between things which people are going to do and things which they must do. For example,

'I/ we shall be responsible for the repairs to the roof.' In the first person this implies choice: something that I/we are going to do voluntarily. However, I/we will be responsible for the repairs to the roof suggests obligation: something I/we must do.

However, in the second or third person it is the other way round. 'You/ he/ she/ they shall be responsible for repairs to the roof' implies an obligation. 'You/ he/ she/ they will be responsible for the repairs to the roof' simply describes what is going to be done in the future.

Make sure that you consider whether an obligation is being created or not and that this is clearly reflected in what you write.

Prepositions. Sentences should not finish with prepositions. Prepositions are words which normally appear before nouns and pronouns such as 'about', 'for', 'on', 'which' and 'what'. While in everyday speech we might say, 'That's the case I told you about', in formal writing the sentence should be, 'That's the case about which I told you'.

Sticking to singular and plural. If you are writing about an individual, 'Mrs Patel' or 'the claimant', you should write in the singular, 'is', 'has', 'does' etc. For more than one person, 'Mr & Mrs Patel' or 'the Claimants', you should write in the plural, 'are', 'have', 'do' and so on. This is fairly straightforward. Problems can arise when the subject is an entity, such as a company or the SRA. While these are single entities they are made up of individuals. It can therefore feel more natural to refer to 'they' when describing what the company or the SRA should do. Either is acceptable, but it is important to decide whether to use the singular or plural and stick to it: candidates often chop and change. Check that you have been consistent when you proofread your work.

Comparative and superlative. The comparative is used to compare two different things, as the name suggests. This is done either by adding the suffix ~er to an adjective or adverb ('taller', 'quicker') or by using the word 'more' before an adjective or adverb ('more economical'; 'more skilfully'). Use either the suffix or the word more, and don't say 'more taller' or 'more quicker'.

The superlative is used to describe the most or least of a particular quality, in a group of more than two ('the largest of all the local firms', 'the smallest of the top three firms'). It is formed by adding the suffix ~est to an adjective or adverb ('tallest', 'quickest') or by using the word 'most' ('most economical'; 'most skilful'). Use either the suffix or the word most, and don't say 'the most tallest' or 'the most quickest'.

2.3 Vocabulary

Do not fall into the trap of trying to make your written communication sound more professional by using archaic and old-fashioned words or phrases such as 'crave leave' and 'hereinbefore mentioned'. Nowadays, among lawyers, there is an increasing emphasis on using clear, straightforward language. This is reflected in the SQE2 Assessment Criteria, which emphasise using clear, succinct and accurate language and avoiding unnecessary technical terms where these are not appropriate to the recipient.

When you are practising writing for the SQE2 assessments, and in the assessments themselves, try to express yourself as clearly as possible. You should strive to find the most accurate way to convey what you want to say to your reader and to use the simplest language you can to achieve this. Here are some ways you can do that.

2.3.1 Avoid nouns derived from verbs

Use the verb itself rather than a noun derived from it. This helps create a more immediate effect.

Avoid	Use instead
'make an admission'	admit
'give consideration to'	consider
'effect a termination'	terminate or end

2.3.2 Avoid legalese and jargon

Jargon is a broad term and may include the specialised language of a professional, occupational or other group which is often meaningless to outsiders. It may also include slang. While jargon can be a useful professional shorthand, it should never be used where it might obscure meaning.

⭐ *Example*

- Bilateral probital hematoma *medical terminology for a black eye*

- Ab initio *Latin/legal terminology for 'at the beginning'*

- HTH, web cookie *computer/Internet jargon for 'Hope this Helps', and the name for a small text file that is sent to your computer via your web browser when you visit certain websites*

As ever, when you are considering whether to use technical language you should consider your audience. Your opponent in litigation will know the meaning of 'Part 36 offer' and 'Tomlin order', or the expression 'res ipsa loquitur' but your lay client will not.

2.3.3 Avoid unnecessary acronyms

Similarly, avoid using acronyms which might be unfamiliar or have several different meanings, e.g. CPR (Civil Procedure Rules, cardiopulmonary resuscitation, Canadian Pacific Railway, etc.), unless the meaning is obvious from the context.

If using legal or technical terms is unavoidable, consider providing a plain English translation. It is worth noting that in June 2006 the Coroner Reform Bill became the first Bill to feature a plain English explanation of every legal clause.

2.4 Written style

You will already have your own written style which you have developed throughout your studies and this will continue to evolve throughout your career as a lawyer. You can pick up useful style tips from your colleagues' work; from correspondence and documents received from other law firms and from reading judgments and legal articles.

In this context it is important to consider the purpose for which you are writing. Are you trying to reassure your client; put pressure on your opponent in litigation or set the law out clearly for the busy partner? While all these communications will have something in common you should also bear in mind the Legal Writing Assessment Criterion which requires you to 'use an acceptable style of communication for the situation and recipient'.

Here are some tips to help you achieve a suitable style in your written communication.

2.4.1 Keep it short

In long sentences, the verb, subject and object may be separated by too many sub-clauses. This places a strain on the reader's memory and understanding. Always try to keep the sentence core together.

 Example

> *The evidence, including evidence from independent surveys as well as that gathered personally by the writers of this report and the results of investigations formally commissioned by this department, suggests that the public, while acknowledging an overall increase in the actual level of government spending on health, by which is meant on health care both at the doctor–patient level and in hospitals, still views the problems and defects in the National Health Service and in particular in National Health hospitals as the result of a general lack of funding.*

The sub-clauses break up the main thought of the paragraph so that it is difficult to follow. The paragraph would be better rewritten in separate sentences with the main thought first, even though this may increase its length. Brackets may be used for subsidiary points where appropriate. For example:

> *The evidence suggests that the public still views the problems and defects in the National Health Service and in particular in National Health hospitals as the result of a general lack of funding. This is so even though the public acknowledges an overall increase in the actual level of government spending on health care both at the doctor–patient level and in hospitals. (Evidence on this issue includes evidence from independent surveys, that gathered personally by the writers of this report and the results of investigations formally commissioned by this department.)*

2.4.2 Avoid unnecessary words

Tautology, or saying the same thing twice using different words, should be avoided. For example:

- 'unfilled vacancy'
- 'true facts'
- 'now current'

Similarly, avoid excessive use of adjectives which do not make the meaning more precise. For example:

- 'grave and fatal error'
- 'careful and detailed consideration'.

Avoid wordy expressions and see if you can say the same thing more simply.

Avoid	Use instead
'in accordance with'	under/by
'by reason of'	by/through
'with reference to'	about
'in order to'	to

2.4.3 Use the active voice

Use the active and not the passive voice (or tense) where possible.

In a sentence where the verb is in the active voice, the subject of the sentence acts upon the object of the sentence. Where the verb is in the passive voice, the object of the sentence is acted upon by the subject. Compare:

'The defendant struck the claimant.' [Active voice]

'The claimant was struck by the defendant.' [Passive voice]

Problems with the passive

Over-use of the passive voice lengthens a sentence and can make it sound weak. In the worst cases, it obscures meaning. For example:

'It is hoped that resources will be relocated so that changes may be made in the methods by which the system is administered.'

Where the verb is in the passive, you may accidentally omit the phrase which indicates who or what is doing the acting. For example:

'The claimant was struck.'

In a legal context, the effect of this omission may be important. For example:

'Notice will be served.' [By whom?]

Exercise 3

Try rewriting the following using the active tense (answers in the appendix):

(i)   A final warning letter is to be written by the line manager.

(ii) The matter will be considered by the committee at the next meeting.

(iii) Notice was given by the solicitor.

Some uses for the passive

The passive can sound more objective and detached, and therefore more appropriate in certain legal contexts. For example:

> 'The allegations are denied.'

sounds better than:

> 'Our client denies the allegations.' [This introduces a personal note.]

It is correct to use the passive where the subject of the legal action is irrelevant. For example:

> 'The common seal of X Co was affixed ...' [It does not matter who affixed it.]

The passive may also be used in a legal context to cover the possibility of action by a number of different persons, some of whom are unknown. For example:

> 'If the goods are damaged, we will refund the cost.' [This could cover damage by the supplier, the carrier, or any third party.]

2.5   Inclusive language

The Statement of Solicitor Competence, at A1, requires solicitors to act honestly and with integrity, in accordance with legal and regulatory requirements and the SRA Standards and Regulations, including (at A1.e) 'respecting diversity and acting fairly and inclusively'.

You should always strive to use language that is inclusive and respectful. This is an ethical obligation as well as good practice. Inclusive language avoids use of words, expressions or assumptions that would stereotype, demean or exclude people. Choice of language can be a sensitive area, and preferences are not necessarily universal. There are some forms of language which are generally unacceptable, and examples of these are set out below. Best practice and terminology have changed and will continue to evolve. You should not assume that etiquette regarding inclusive language is international, and what is acceptable will vary according to location and culture.

If you have concerns or questions about the most appropriate form of language in legal practice, you should, if possible, ask those you are dealing with what their preferences are. Engage in open discussion where necessary about the choice and use of language, particularly in some of the areas set out below.

2.5.1   Forms of address

Always use the preferred form of address etc. when known. If addressing a woman when their preference is not known, you should use Ms rather than Mrs if you wish to use a courtesy title. Ms is more inclusive and can refer to any woman regardless of marital status. As an alternative, some writers use the addressee's full name, e.g. 'Dear Olivia Willis'.

When you do not yet know which pronouns someone goes by, it is generally a good idea to use 'they/them' where necessary. The use of 'they/them' is gender-neutral and has been commonly used for a long time. Many organisations encourage employees to include their pronouns on ID badges and email signatures to make preferences easier for others to adopt. The use of pronouns is discussed further below.

Be consistent in how you address people, for example if you refer to one person by their name, last name, courtesy title or profession then others should be referred to in the same way.

 Example

'Professor Rajesh Singh and Hester will both be attending the settlement meeting.' While the man has been given his first name, surname and professional title, the woman has been referred to by first name only.

'Professor Rajesh Singh and Dr Hester Rowe will both be attending the settlement meeting.' In this example both people attending are consistently referred to using the same forms of address.

2.5.2 Gender-neutral language

As part of ensuring that you use inclusive language, you should aim to use gender-neutral language where possible. Avoid gender-biased words and expressions which may reinforce gender stereotypes.

Examples:

- chairman, statesman etc.
- mankind
- manmade
- manpower.

The use of some gendered nouns referring to job title or position such as 'actress' or 'manageress' is outdated, and words such as actor, manager etc. should be used regardless of sex or gender.

There are many techniques that may be used to achieve gender-neutral language, and the choice you make should be determined by identifying the most effective, clear and concise in each circumstance. If redrafting documents to ensure they are gender-neutral, take particular care that meaning and clarity are not compromised. Here are some suggestions.

2.5.2.1 Repeat the noun

One of the simplest options is to repeat the noun rather than using a pronoun. This can work well but tends to add length and detract from fluency. You can also use a defined term.

 Example

Annual salary, in relation to a person, means sums payable to him in connection with his employment over the course of a calendar year.

Annual salary, in relation to a person, means sums payable to a person in connection with the person's employment over the course of a calendar year.

2.5.2.2 Pairing

Pairing is the use of both male and female pronouns ('she/he', 'her/his'). It is the best choice when you want to explicitly include both women and men or draw attention to the inclusion of both. It is not a generally recommended practice as it adds length and is distracting to the reader, particularly in texts where narrative is important. It may also risk creating inconsistencies and inaccuracies.

Some writers alternate placement of male and female pronouns in order to avoid giving precedence to either male or female. Again, while this may be a useful technique in some circumstances, it also risks confusing or distracting. Another disadvantage of pairing is that it is not fully inclusive.

 Example

> *When an apprentice accepts an offer of employment, he or she must be able to provide proof of address and identity. To qualify for overtime payments, she or he must provide written authorisation from a manager.*

2.5.2.3 Change the pronoun

There are several ways in which you may change the pronoun used. The most common is to use 'they/them'. Care needs to be taken that using the plural form does not change the meaning or lead to ambiguity.

 Examples

> *It is an offence for a person to carry a prohibited article into the building unless he can prove that he has a valid reason as set out in* **5.3** *below.*

> *It is an offence for a person to carry a prohibited article into the building unless they can prove that they have a valid reason as set out in* **5.3** *below.*

> *A judge is required to familiarise himself with the rules on equality and diversity.*

> *A judge is required to familiarise themselves with the rules on equality and diversity.*

2.5.2.4 Use the pronoun 'one'

 Example

> *A member of staff located outside London earns less than he would in London.*

> *A member of staff located outside London earns less than one would in London.*

2.5.2.5 Use the relative pronoun 'who'

 Example

> *A person commits a breach of the terms of the agreement if he does not comply with the provisions of paragraph 5.2 of this agreement.*

> *A person who does not comply with the provisions of paragraph 5.2 commits a breach of this agreement.*

2.5.2.6 Omit the gendered word

 Example

> *An officeholder may be removed from office if he is convicted of a criminal offence.*

> *An officeholder may be removed from office if convicted of a criminal offence.*

2.5.2.7 Use the passive voice

While using the passive voice has disadvantages and can lead to a lack of clarity (see **2.4.3**), it is another way in which you can avoid including gendered language. When using the passive voice, make sure that it is clear who has to do what.

⭐ *Example*

A complainant must supply written evidence of the situation he is complaining about.

A complainant must supply written evidence of the situation complained about.

Exercise 4

Rewrite the following using gender-neutral language. There may be more than one correct answer. One or two suggested answers can be found in the Appendix.

(i) Before he is formally appointed, the candidate must have written approval from the Chairman.

(ii) A person must be a permanent employee at the firm for 20 years before he may apply for a long-term service benefit.

(iii) In the event of an absence, mothers should contact the receptionist before 09:00 and give her details of the child's cause of absence.

(iv) The Managing Partner may remove a Committee Member from office if he has failed to attend a meeting for a period of six months or more. The Managing Partner may, at his discretion, appoint a replacement Committee Member for the remainder of the calendar year.

2.6 Presentation

Having made sure that the style and content of your work is appropriate, do not allow the presentation to let you down. In legal practice and in the SQE2 assessments you should use the layout and presentation of your document to enhance its readability and usefulness. You will probably have found that it is very difficult to focus on a text which is very dense and not broken up and far easier to follow one which is separated by paragraphs and headings.

The detailed requirements for the layout and presentation of legal documents and letters are set out in **Chapters 5–8** on Legal Writing and Legal Drafting. What follow are therefore some basic guidelines on presenting your work.

2.6.1 Check the legal requirements

For many court documents there are very detailed requirements as to how you should present your document. Check that you have followed any relevant rules or guidelines. For example, the Civil Procedure Rules set out detailed requirements for the presentation of court documents. These are considered in **Chapter 7**.

2.6.2 Use paragraphs

Using paragraphs makes prose more readable and helps to avoid cumbersome clauses and sub-clauses. If you are drafting a legal document, always number your paragraphs if possible as this aids navigation and will help anyone using the document as specific clauses can be identified.

Paragraph numbering can change as the draft develops so make sure that cross references to paragraphs are correct when you proofread the final draft.

2.6.3 Use bullet points where appropriate

Where a letter or email includes a list, it can be helpful to use bullet points to break up the text. However, bullet points are rarely appropriate when you are drafting a legal document and numbered paragraphs rather than bullet points should be used in statements of case so that your opponent can respond precisely to each point.

2.6.4 Use sub-headings

Using sub-headings helps to make your writing clearer. For example, if you are writing to a client about three separate points (a Part 36 offer; amendment to the particulars of claim and preparation of witness statements) it is very helpful to flag these topics by using sub-headings. This prevents the client from being overwhelmed by information, particularly if the letter is long and enables them to find the topic they are looking for quickly.

2.6.5 Numbering

Where a series of points is being made, numbering may improve clarity and aid later cross-referencing. Legal documents are likely to involve sub-paragraphs and so a very simple system of numbering will rarely be useful.

Examples of numbering systems include:

4.5.1 The system adopted in this book and known as the decimal system.

4(5)(a)(i) A system based on the legislative approach and known as the alphanumeric system.

4.5(a)(i) A combination system using elements of both decimal and alphanumeric systems.

2.6.6 Tabulation

To tabulate information means to organise it by using columns or a table. This aids clarity and can help to avoid ambiguity. Consider the sentence:

Any trainee solicitor is entitled to paid leave to attend a conference, lecture, or seminar *provided by The Law Society*.

How much of the sentence is the phrase in italics intended to qualify? Does it apply only to 'seminar', or to 'conference' and 'lecture' as well? The sentence is unclear.

Compare:

Any trainee solicitor is entitled to paid leave to attend:

(a) a conference; or

(b) a lecture; or

(c) a seminar,

provided by The Law Society.

Care should be taken, however, not to indent the final phrase 'provided by The Law Society' to the same margin as 'a seminar' or the ambiguity would remain.

A useful basic rule is that any sentence longer than three lines is a good candidate for tabulation, if it includes a compound or series.

2.7 Checking your work

Always check your work. It may be easy to overlook this step if you are working under time or costs pressure in legal practice or if you are running out of time in the SQE2 assessments but try to build in time for this step if you possibly can.

Here are some tips for proofreading a piece of writing in the SQE2 assessments:

- Always confirm that the names of the parties have been spelt correctly and that dates and figures are accurate. In particular, clients will always notice if their names have been misspelt.

- Check all cross references in a legal document to other clauses or to schedules.

- Above all, check that what you have written reflects your instructions, whether these are from a client or a partner. Have you covered all the points you have been asked to address?

Here are some tips that you can use in legal practice:

- If possible leave the piece of writing for a while and then come back to it.

- Ideally get someone else to check it.

- Reading your written work aloud can be a good way of identifying mistakes or poorly drafted material.

- Print out your work and read from hard copy rather than trying to check it on screen.

- Do not always read from the beginning. Try starting from the middle or towards the end. The later parts of long pieces of writing tend to be less familiar and less well checked.

- Do not rely on automated spelling or grammar checks.

You can test your proofreading skills by doing the exercise below (answers in the appendix).

Exercise 5

(a) Identify the errors in the following paragraph.

(b) Then try rewriting the paragraph using the rules and recommendations set out in this chapter.

I am writing with reference to your enquiry concerning the use of the entrance area and hallway at the gallery for the purpose of displaying informational materials and presenting visual displays on the subject of recycling. In the circumstances the central question will be whether the internal content origins and visual qualities of the material hereinbefore mentioned are to be felt to be appropriate after due consideration has be given by the Gallery Board, such permissions are at the sole dicretion of the board. The Boards decision concerning any such request will be made after it has met in session on the first Thursday of each calendar month and notification will be sent within 14 days of the said meeting.

APPENDIX TO CHAPTER 2

Answers to Exercises

EXERCISE 1. Spelling

Answers

  (i)   accommodation

  (ii) unnecessary

  (iii) privilege

  (iv) embarrass

  (v)   professor

EXERCISE 2. Punctuation

Apostrophes

  (i)   Who's likely to be delayed by a few minutes of rain?

  (ii) We've always valued both the local Gardening Institutes' lectures.

  (iii) I'm sure he said it's a ten o'clock train we need to catch.

  (iv) The children's enjoyment of the fair was greater than ours.

  (v)   The girls' football shirts hung on pegs in the cloakroom's main aisle.

Other punctuation

  (i)   MARY DAVENPORT WRITES WELL. HOWEVER, LUCIEN GRANT HATES WRITING.

  (ii) MY PRINCIPAL AREA OF SPECIALITY IS TAX. MY SECOND SPECIALITY IS FINANCE.

  (iii) The trainee was quite clear that he needed to work harder if he wanted to get taken on. It was quite possible for the firm to hire all the trainees that year. His friend had already been given an indication that he would be offered a job and he had been working really long hours.

  (iv) Edward O'Grady, however, always wanted to surf the Internet rather than do his work.

  (v)   The solicitor walked up to her office, opened the door, took off her coat and slumped into her chair.

  (vi) For business meetings, the firm offered tea, coffee, water, fruit juices, biscuits and sandwiches.

  (vii) I read the Legal Times before work every day; it keeps me on top of changes in the law.

  (viii) The employer wrote to the employee to complain about his time keeping; workers ought to know that starting work on time is essential.

EXERCISE 3. Active and passive

  (i)   The line manager will write a final warning letter.

  (ii) The committee will consider the matter at the next meeting.

  (iii) The solicitor gave notice.

EXERCISE 4. Gender-neutral language

  (i)   Before being formally appointed, the candidate must have written approval from the Chair.

  (ii) A person must be a permanent employee at the firm for 20 years before applying for a long-term service benefit.

        or

        A person must be a permanent employee at the firm for 20 years before they may apply for a long-term service benefit.

  (iii) In the event of an absence, parents/guardians should contact the receptionist before 09:00 and give details of the child's cause of absence.

  (iv) The Managing Partner may remove a Committee Member from office if he/she has failed to attend a meeting for a period of six months or more. The Managing Partner has discretion to appoint a replacement Committee Member for the remainder of the calendar year.

EXERCISE 5. Proofreading and rewriting

  (a) Errors

  • The structure of the paragraph is confusing and illogical, e.g. we are told the criteria for decisions before we are told who has authority to make them.
  • The provision relating to time is ambiguous.
  • Sentences are too long, use archaic terminology and unnecessarily complicated words and phrases, e.g. 'informational materials', 'hereinbefore mentioned'.
  • There are numerous padding words and phrases and compound prepositions, e.g. 'with reference to'.
  • There are spelling and grammatical errors.
  • The paragraph uses archaic terminology.
  • The paragraph uses the passive tense.

The overall effect of these errors is to make the paragraph difficult to understand and pompous in tone.

  (b) Set out below is an example of how the paragraph might be rewritten.

        I am writing about your request to use the entrance area and hallway at the Gallery for a display about recycling. Permission to mount a display is given by the Gallery Board ('the Board') which meets on the first Thursday of each month. The Board will decide whether the quality and content of the material is appropriate. The Board will let you know its decision within 2 weeks of and including the date of the meeting.

The original paragraph was 120 words. The paragraph above which contains the same information is only 76 words. It is also easier to read and understand.

RESOURCES AND FURTHER READING

BBC Teach, *English for adults*. This is a free website with a lot of helpful resources.

Grammar and punctuation

J Butterfield, *Fowler's Concise Dictionary of Modern English Usage* (3rd edn, 2016)

RL Trask, *The Penguin Guide to Punctuation* (Penguin, 1997)

L Truss, *Eats, Shoots and Leaves* (Fourth Estate, 2009)

Plain English

M Adler, *Clarity for Lawyers* (3rd edn, 2017)

E Gowers, *The Complete Plain Words* (1987)

Gender-neutral language

Gov.uk, *Guide to Gender-Neutral Drafting* (2019)

3 Negotiation

SQE2 syllabus

This chapter will help you to identify appropriate solutions for a client's matter and to achieve the SQE2 Assessment Criterion of providing 'client-focused advice'.

Learning outcomes

By the end of this chapter you should be able to:

- explain the purpose and benefits of negotiation;
- undertake core preparation for a negotiation;
- explain how to formulate options for settlement; and
- understand how to conduct a negotiation.

3.1   Introduction

Negotiation is a process by which two or more parties attempt to come to an agreement which meets their respective needs. Skilled negotiators are aware that negotiation is a subtle art. It is not a simple battle of wills where one side must succeed at the expense of the other. Using principled interest-based negotiating techniques, it is often possible for both sides to achieve a solution which satisfies their needs and delivers much of what they want, i.e. a genuine solution acceptable to all the parties.

Solicitors frequently undertake negotiations on behalf of their clients. In transactional matters the solicitor will often be required to broker an agreement, not just in respect of the headline points, such as the purchase price, but also the fine detail of the terms of the contract. In dispute resolution cases, at some point the solicitor will almost invariably have to engage in the process of attempting to settle the matter short of a final court hearing. It is essential that solicitors add value in negotiation if they are to serve their clients well. Adding value requires an understanding of the principles of good negotiation and regular practice in implementing the techniques and tools involved. The ability to negotiate successfully is therefore a key skill for legal practice.

This chapter looks at:

- negotiation and SQE2;
- the forum for negotiation;
- the ethics of negotiation;
- objectives, interests and priorities;
- formulating options/proposals;
- presenting the case;
- finding a compromise; and
- closing negotiations.

3.2   Negotiation and SQE2

There is no separate assessment for negotiation skills in SQE2. Instead, negotiation skills will be assessed as part of:

- Legal Writing; and/or
- Case and Matter Analysis; and/or
- Interviewing and Completion of Attendance Note/Legal Analysis.

In each delivery of SQE2 there will be *at least* one assessment which involves negotiation. You can read more about the SQE2 assessments in **Chapter 1**. In the appendix to that chapter, you can see how the Statement of Solicitor Competence applies to negotiation.

The nature of the SQE2 assessments is such that you will not have to conduct a face-to-face negotiation. However, you may, for example, be required to advise a client on a negotiation strategy or the terms of a reasonable compromise; write a letter putting forward or responding to a proposal for settlement; identify and explain negotiation as a process option. Even though you will not be conducting a face-to-face negotiation it is still important to understand the principles. For example, you might want to encourage the client to think about their BATNA (see **3.6.2**) when they are considering a proposal from the other side.

The fact that an individual SQE2 assessment is one which incorporates negotiation could be stated in the instructions/facts. However, there is no guarantee that this will be the case, so it is important to read the instructions/facts carefully. Wording which, for example, asks you to advise on the client's options or to analyse the risks/benefits of a particular course of action or to devise a strategy for achieving the client's objectives may indicate that negotiation forms part of the assessment. By the same token, it is important not to completely ignore negotiation just because it is not a formal part of the assessment. In the SQE2 Legal Research assessments (see **Chapter 11**), for example, it may be appropriate to incorporate a recommendation for negotiation as part of the advice for the client.

3.3   The forum for negotiation

In legal practice the forum for negotiation could be correspondence, telephone, a meeting (face-to-face or virtual) or any combination of the three. In contentious cases negotiation may also take place as part of a formal dispute resolution process such as mediation or, indeed, at the doors of the court.

It is usually a matter of the solicitor choosing the best medium for the client's case, and then being prepared to change if it later ceases to be appropriate or circumstances change. For example, in many cases negotiations might start through correspondence, but that could later become unnecessarily rigid and time-consuming. It may be wise to suggest a meeting when the solicitor has developed a strong enough case to be able to take advantage of face-to-face contact.

Negotiation by correspondence is capable of being orderly and reasoned; there is time to think and reflect and so avoid over hasty decisions. It is often the preferred method at the outset of complex cases or when negotiating contractual terms. However, formulating and sending correspondence takes time and there is a risk of points being overlooked or misinterpreted in the exchange. The inevitable time lag makes it difficult to 'bargain' and trade concessions. A key disadvantage to negotiation by correspondence is that there is no opportunity to observe body language and even tone can be difficult to convey or interpret in writing.

Negotiation conducted by telephone has the advantage of speed which makes it particularly useful for resolving individual points. There is no body language, but tone of voice is more noticeable. Silences are even more powerful on the telephone than in meetings. There is, however, the risk that either of the parties could subsequently 're-interpret' what was said.

Face-to-face meetings are the most common method of conducting negotiations. Meetings are immediate. They give greater commitment to explore the case thoroughly and/or to settle. Body language and silences are readily apparent and capable of use. The discussion is more fluid and gives greater possibilities of fine movements, nuances, and the trading of concessions. The main disadvantage of meetings is the logistical one (and its associated costs implications) of gathering everyone together in one place at one time. It is also the case that some people find face-to-face meetings intimidating. A good deal of planning needs to go into a face-to-face meeting. Elements such as attendees (should clients be present?), venue (one party's solicitor's office or a neutral venue?) and even seating arrangements (sitting at an angle is less confrontational than sitting directly opposite the other party) can all influence the tone and process of the negotiations.

Virtual meetings are a relatively recent development. They are straightforward to arrange and can replicate a face-to-face meeting in many respects. However, body language is often difficult to read, and the subtleties of the discussion can be lost. There is also a risk of the technology 'getting in the way' of the negotiation if signal problems, time delays or inexpert use of the 'mute button' interrupt the flow of the discussion.

3.4 The ethics of negotiation

When a solicitor takes on the role of negotiator they are, of course, subject to the same rules of professional conduct and standards of ethical behaviour which underpin the rest of their legal practice. The requirements to act with independence (Principle 3), with integrity (Principle 5) and not taking unfair advantage of others (Paragraph 1.2 SRA Code of Conduct for Solicitors, RELs and RFLs) are but a few examples of rules which are particularly engaged when conducting negotiations. To practise effectively, it is essential not only to understand the professional and ethical rules which apply but to uphold them.

Negotiation involves arguing the strengths of the client's case and highlighting the weaknesses in the other side's case. However, care must be taken not to overstep the mark and misrepresent the position. Making misrepresentations will be a matter of professional misconduct. Added to which, an agreement entered into on the basis of misrepresentations is capable of being rescinded.

A solicitor must not misrepresent the position, but equally a solicitor is not under a duty to volunteer information which is adverse to their client's position. If asked a direct question on such a point a solicitor cannot lie, but can refuse to answer, offer no comment or attempt to deflect the question (e.g. by offering a partial answer or by parrying with a counter-question). However, it is likely in such circumstances that the other solicitor will guess what the true position is, and it may have been tactically wiser to have made an admission.

Where negotiations are reaching their conclusion and an agreement is close it can be tempting to concede a further point or to offer to pay a little more in order to secure the deal. However, a solicitor must not exceed the client's instructions even though the solicitor believes that doing so would be in the client's best interests. The appropriate course of action in such a situation would be to adjourn the negotiations for the purpose of seeking further instructions.

A solicitor must be an ethical negotiator, not simply because they are bound by a code of conduct, but also because any failure to uphold the highest ethical standards will diminish the solicitor's effectiveness as a negotiator. The solicitor will lose the trust of the client and of the other side if they breach ethical standards. Negotiation is based on establishing trust between the parties. Once lost it is extremely hard to rebuild.

3.5 Objectives, interests and priorities

The successful negotiator possesses many skills; these include the abilities to communicate, listen, persuade, analyse and create. These talents must, however, be supported by a bedrock of knowledge of the facts, the law and the procedure relevant to a particular case. Without that knowledge, the negotiator loses any chance of controlling the negotiating process. In the SQE2 assessments you will need to read and analyse the facts in order to establish what information is key to the negotiation.

There is much to be gained by finding a solution through negotiation. A desire to achieve these benefits will often be common ground between the parties from the outset. In litigation cases a successful negotiation may save costs, save time, minimise acrimony, avoid the uncertainties of trial, reduce stress and, perhaps, avoid adverse publicity. In transactional matters a successful negotiation will 'seal the deal' but may also save costs, save time, preserve a business relationship and/or maintain reputations.

It is essential at the outset for the solicitor to clearly establish the client's objectives in entering into the negotiation. What 'end point' does the client envisage? What is the minimum they are prepared to accept? Have they reached this position with the benefit of all available information? If they are proceeding under certain misconceptions, it is part of the solicitor's role to correct them.

Clients will often be forthcoming with their negotiating position: they want compensation, a fixed-term contract, or the removal of a tenant. However, it is important to look behind their stated position and try to identify their underlying interests, i.e. not just what the client's stance is, but why the client has adopted that particular position. In the SQE2 assessments the facts are likely to give an indication of the client's thoughts, feelings and motivations surrounding the issues. For example, the client might be 'due' compensation, but it may be clear from the facts that their actual interest is to preserve their good reputation.

It is also necessary to anticipate the other side's interests. Only by factoring the other side's interests into the equation will the solicitor be able to formulate proposals which are realistic and likely to lead to compromise. Identifying the other side's underlining interests and understanding their needs and wants often allows common ground to be identified and a wider range of bargaining points to be developed. In the SQE2 assessments the 'other side' might be, for example, an investor in a company, the seller in a property purchase or the opponent in litigation. So, as well as noting the facts you should look out for information about such matters as deadlines or commercial pressures which are impacting on the other side.

 Example

In negotiating a lease of the major unit in a new shopping centre, the landlord might demand from their major 'anchor' tenant absolute bars on assignment, sub-letting or change of use. The tenant might demand absolute freedom on all three. This presents an apparent impasse. However, the landlord's underlying interest might be to use the anchor tenant to attract 'satellite' tenants to the other, smaller units, while the tenant's interest might be the long-term freedom to move elsewhere. A compromise which might satisfy both parties' underlying interests would be to have a short-term restriction rather than one which lasted for the whole duration of the lease.

Looking for underlying interests is particularly important in transaction-based negotiations or multi-issue claims. It is less likely to be productive in debt collection, personal injury or other single issue, 'money only' claims. However, it should always be investigated. For example, in debt collection it may be that the creditor has an underlying interest in the survival of the debtor's business.

Some negotiations require just a single point to be settled: the purchase price, for example. However, many negotiations involve the resolution of several issues. It is advisable in such cases to isolate each issue. This helps to ensure that all relevant matters are covered in the negotiation.

 Example

The client is a retailer who has a contract with a manufacturer for the supply of an exclusive range of golfing accessories. The client has suffered losses owing to the manufacturer failing to meet agreed supply dates. The client wants compensation but is aware that the stocking of the contract goods generates a great deal of their custom.

The issues are:

- *the claim for compensation*

- *the continuation of a profitable relationship*

Having identified the issues, it is necessary to assess the relative importance to the client of each one, so as to establish the client's priorities. In the above example, the client would almost certainly be of the view that the claim for compensation should not be pressed too hard if it would put at risk the continuation of the relationship.

3.6   Formulating options/proposals

The purpose of any negotiation is to arrive at a solution which is acceptable to both parties. A necessary part of the process is to identify what that solution could look like and 'pitch' it to the other side for discussion. This must be based on a careful analysis of the client's case.

3.6.1   Strengths and weaknesses

The first step in formulating any options for resolving the matter or a proposal for settlement is to assess the factors which support and those which undermine the client's case, i.e. what are the chances of the client getting what they want? This will involve a combination of legal factors (e.g. the client's case is supported by strong legal precedent) as well as practical considerations (e.g. the client is in financial difficulties which makes it essential for them to reach an early agreement).

It is also vital to identify the strengths and weaknesses in the other side's position. For example, will they risk court action if their main concern is to avoid bad publicity? Having identified the strengths, it may be possible to take steps to counter them, for example by obtaining other evidence or reinterpreting existing evidence.

3.6.2   BATNA

One of the best known books on negotiation is Fisher and Ury's *Getting to Yes*. Their acronym, BATNA, stands for Best Alternative To a Negotiated Agreement. In other words, *if the negotiations were to break down and you failed to settle*, what would you be left with? What would be the true cost or value of that alternative? In transaction cases, the BATNA could be to do a deal with a third party rather than with the other side, or not to do a deal at all. In dispute resolution cases, the BATNA will often be litigation. It is important to ensure that the perceived BATNA is a realistic alternative and not just a vague possibility.

According to Fisher and Ury, the recommended approach is to identify, evaluate and develop the client's BATNA and also try to identify the other side's BATNA. If the client appears to have an attractive alternative available, this strengthens their negotiating position. Developing the client's BATNA might involve, for example, pressing ahead with litigation procedures simultaneously with trying to negotiate an out-of-court settlement.

The aim of the BATNA approach is to help to gauge where to pitch an offer and provide a yardstick against which to assess the value of any offer made by the other side in the negotiation. Identifying the client's BATNA helps to decide on the 'resistance point' in the negotiation (see **3.6.3**). It can therefore offer protection from being too generous (i.e. agreeing to give the other side more than the value of the client's BATNA) or being too obstinate (i.e. rejecting a final offer which is in fact better than the client's BATNA).

In some instances, the client may have more than one alternative course of action available. If so, it is important to assess the feasibility of each alternative and consider whether it is worthwhile trying to develop each alternative or to concentrate on just one.

3.6.3   Opening bids and resistance points

On each issue, it is necessary to make an assessment of the most favourable result that the client would hope to achieve and the least favourable result that they would be prepared to accept. The discussion that follows is based on negotiating a figure because the principles are easier to understand in that context. However, the principles are equally applicable in other contexts. For example, an exclusion clause in a contract can provide the client with a range of protection from liability; it is a matter of deciding at which point along that spectrum to offer/settle.

3.6.3.1 The most favourable result

The most favourable result that the client would hope to expect should be or inform the client's 'opening bid'.

To begin by making demands which are wildly optimistic, and which bear no relation to the parties' positions will result in both solicitor and client losing credibility. The solicitor is bound to look foolish if they are unable to give sound reasons to justify their position.

The opening bid should be the highest justifiable outcome, after taking into account the law and facts which support the client's case, i.e. try to predict the settlement that would be obtained if all the factors which support the client's case were accepted without any counter-arguments being put forward by the other side.

⭐ *Example*

> *A buyer orders goods from a seller for £80,000 to be paid for on delivery. Delivery is to be on 1 June. The seller tries to deliver the goods on 1 June, but the buyer refuses to accept the goods. The seller is able to sell the goods elsewhere, but, for a quick sale, the seller accepts a price of £25,000.*
>
> *The most favourable result for the seller would be to obtain damages of £55,000 (the difference between the amount actually received and the amount which the seller would have received if the contract had been properly performed). It is a bid which can be justified on contractual grounds. Any arguments which the buyer might put forward about the seller's duty to mitigate their loss is ignored at this stage.*

If valid counter-arguments are raised, one of the benefits of 'aiming high' at the outset is that it allows the solicitor to 'come down' and offer concessions. This can be an important way of showing the other side that they have been listened to and understood and that the client is prepared to compromise. Any compromise requires 'give and take'. It allows people to save face; honour is satisfied. If, however, the solicitor refuses to move from the opening figure, the other side may perceive both solicitor and client as obstinate and unreasonable, and therefore may refuse to settle even when the opening bid is in fact realistic.

Generally speaking, the opening bid should only be the client's final figure if:

(a) it is the tradition or culture in that particular field of law; or

(b) the client has a case or bargaining position that is obviously strong.

In either case, it is good practice to explain clearly to the other side that it really is a case of 'take it or leave it'.

3.6.3.2 The least favourable result

The solicitor should also identify the poorest deal the client should accept, i.e. what settlement the solicitor would expect to negotiate if the other side put forward all the relevant counter-arguments to the client's case. This is the client's 'resistance point'.

The resistance point is not an absolute 'bottom line'; it should not be rigidly adhered to if further information which affects the client's position comes to light in the negotiation. The solicitor must be flexible enough to take on board the significance of any new information and adapt their expectations and those of the client accordingly.

Deciding on the resistance point is complicated by two other factors. First, in cases where the client has an acceptable alternative course of action, the resistance point is the point below which the client is likely to receive less from the negotiation than might be obtained by pursuing the BATNA. For example, the solicitor might decide that (even after taking into account the extra costs) the client would receive more than is currently being offered by allowing the court to decide on the level of compensation.

Secondly, the client may have given the solicitor instructions not to settle below a certain figure. If the solicitor thinks the client is being unrealistic, they should try to persuade the client to adopt a more sensible position. However, if the client will not be moved, the solicitor must comply with their instructions.

With multi-issue negotiations, the position becomes even more complicated. The client might be prepared to go below the resistance point on one issue if it means they would obtain a favourable result on another. It is important to keep the whole package in mind.

The client's priorities are the key to the decisions made in this area. Items which are of no great significance to the client could be conceded altogether in exchange for concessions which are of more importance to them.

3.6.4 Settlement zones

The solicitor should have identified a spectrum from the best justifiable settlement that the client could achieve to the poorest outcome that the client should accept. The other side will have undertaken the same exercise and identified their own parameters. The settlement zone lies where the two overlap. Before embarking on the actual negotiation, the solicitor must try to gauge where that settlement zone lies. The solution is somewhere within the settlement zone. The solicitor can then add value by getting the maximum possible within a settlement zone for their client or by minimising what is paid, depending on which side the solicitor is acting for.

 Example

Continuing the contract example above. The seller's maximum expectation is £55,000. Assume that the seller's solicitor has advised them that the least favourable result they should expect is a payment of £35,000 (taking into account the duty to mitigate loss). The buyer, on the other hand, has been advised that a payment of £30,000 is probably the best result they could hope to achieve, but it is prepared to pay up to £45,000 if necessary, to avoid any bad publicity. As illustrated by Figure 1, the possible settlement zone between the parties is £35,000 to £45,000.

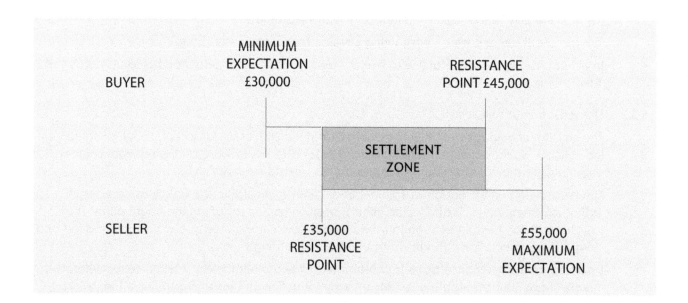

Where within the zone the solicitor is able to settle is a measure of how effective they have been as a negotiator. Negotiation is harder when the possible settlement zone is very narrow. By working to identify the settlement zone, the solicitor can help to speed the negotiation (saving time and costs). In some cases, it may be possible to identify that there is no settlement zone and that either something must change, or a negotiated settlement will not be possible.

3.6.5 Variables and unorthodox approaches

Another consideration in assessing the opening bid and resistance point will be the existence of 'variables'. Variables are those factors which allow for some give and take in the negotiation and which could therefore help to achieve a settlement. For example, the client might be prepared to pay a higher amount of compensation if they are allowed to pay by instalments rather than in one lump sum.

Other examples of variables which might be brought into play (depending on the subject matter of the negotiation) are inclusion/exclusion of costs, payment in a different currency, promises of future orders, quantity of goods (e.g. buy more, but at a lower price per unit), quality of goods (e.g. buy a lower grade at a lower price).

Sometimes, there may be other unconventional ways to resolve problems which have benefits for both sides. One of the great benefits of negotiation is that it enables points to be included in the settlement which could not be ordered by the court if the matter proceeded to trial, such as placing future orders for goods. It is important to be as creative as possible in seeking a solution.

✪ Example

A solicitor is acting for a company which runs a parcel delivery service. One of its business customers is threatening to take action against the company because of its failure to deliver a consignment of goods. The goods have disappeared, and the customer is asking for compensation. An orthodox settlement would involve a cash payment to the customer. A different approach would be to offer to make free deliveries for that customer over an agreed period. Such an offer could represent a good deal for the customer but could still be a cheaper solution for the company compared with a cash payment (the deliveries could probably be accommodated within its regular delivery service and so would not add greatly to overall costs). This approach also gives the company a chance to rebuild the customer's confidence in its service, making it less likely that the customer will go elsewhere in the future.

3.7 Presenting the case

3.7.1 Strategy

Negotiations, particularly those conducted face-to-face, are to an extent uncertain. It is not possible to predict exactly what the other side will say or precisely how they will respond. The solicitor will therefore need to be flexible. Nevertheless, a solicitor should not enter into negotiations without having an overall strategy in mind.

The strategy obviously encompasses the client's opening bid. Although the solicitor should have identified the best possible outcome for the client (see **3.6.3.1**) that does not mean that the opening bid must be at that level. A better strategy may be to start with a more reasonable offer which is more likely to be accepted by the other side if, for example, there are pressures on the client requiring an urgent settlement.

The strategy should also cover the conduct of the negotiations. What points are non-negotiable from the client's point of view? What concessions is the client prepared to make and in what order? Will the client's position change on one issue if concessions are made by the other side on another?

The strategy must also include the ending of the negotiation. At what point will the client 'walk away'? The solicitor should identify the point at which there is no further benefit to be gained for the client in continuing with the negotiations, and where it is better for the client, for example, to lose the deal or take their chances in litigation.

3.7.2 Framework

To ensure the best chance of success, any negotiation should be clearly structured. Negotiations should not commence until a clear process has been identified. Adopting a clear process helps to ensure that all parties feel that the negotiation is fair and assists in establishing an effective structure and tone. It is advisable to set the ground rules in terms of whether the negotiation is to be conducted through an exchange of correspondence or by way of a meeting and whether the discussions are to be conducted 'without prejudice' and/ or 'subject to contract'. It is also good practice to set a framework. For a meeting it is a matter of setting an agenda which incorporates a preliminary opening statement from each party, a structured discussion of each point and a time frame. In a negotiation by correspondence, it may be necessary to establish who is to 'make the first move', set a clear time frame etc.

3.7.3 Making the first move

Waiting to see if the other side will make the first move is not a strategy and should be avoided. By waiting to see the other side's approach, the solicitor risks losing the initiative. If both parties 'wait and see', it wastes time and valuable opportunities to build rapport by implementing a clear, interest-based approach to the negotiation. The negotiation should allow for flexibility in response to new information and the attitude of other parties.

In some fields of law, the issue of which person makes the first bid is determined partly by tradition. For example, in property transactions, the solicitor acting for the landlord or seller draws up the draft lease or contract. In litigation, if the claim is for a liquidated sum (e.g. a contractual debt), the opening bid belongs to the claimant. If the claim is for unliquidated damages, in certain cases (e.g. personal injury claims) there is an argument that the claimant should simply wait until the defendant makes an acceptable offer.

Where the position is not clear cut, the advantages of going first are that it allows the solicitor to exert an immediate and powerful influence and it shows confidence. The disadvantage is that, if the solicitor is underprepared, they risk misjudging the bid.

3.7.4 Opening statements

The opening phase of a negotiation is important for two reasons. First, it creates the climate for the negotiation. Patterns, styles and pecking order establish themselves early and are difficult then to change. Secondly, energy and concentration are high at the outset of the negotiations but later may deteriorate.

Negotiation meetings usually begin with the solicitor for each party making an opening statement setting out their expectations of the negotiation, explaining their client's positions and, usually, making an opening bid.

Proper, well prepared opening statements benefit most negotiation meetings. They:

- help to avoid unintentional false assumptions from hindering the communication process;
- help to reinforce the tone established at the outset of the meeting;
- provide structure and order;
- help everyone to 'settle down'; and
- remind everyone of the background, the areas of agreement, and the areas of dispute.

The substance of an oral opening statement is replicated in negotiations by correspondence. It would be unusual, for example, to send a letter putting forward a proposal for settlement without 'setting the scene' in terms of identifying the areas of dispute, setting out the client's position and explaining the reasoning behind the proposal.

In an opening statement a solicitor should present the client's case confidently and concisely and, usually, employ a collaborative tone and demeanour. The purpose is to highlight the merits of the client's position and convince the other side to move towards it. The opening statement should therefore be designed to be persuasive. There is no set way to present an opening statement, but some points to cover are as follows:

- the purpose of the negotiation;
- the client's position;
- the benefits for the other side in the client's solution;
- the rationale for the client's position; and
- why this is the best approach.

If the opening statement is to incorporate a bid, particularly if it is to be presented orally at a meeting, it may be appropriate to delay disclosing the actual bid until the end. This increases the chances of the other side paying proper attention to the reasoning, rather than just focusing on the terms of the proposal.

It may be appropriate to anticipate arguments that the other side may put forward. However, generally speaking it is usually not advisable to use an opening statement as an opportunity to express assumptions about the other side's interests and priorities, as this could annoy or antagonise them. It is better to allow the other side to make their own case in their opening statement.

3.7.5 Responding to an opening statement

It is important to pay proper attention to the other side's opening statement, whether presented at a meeting or through correspondence. It is obviously vital to note the terms of any proposal put forward. It may be necessary to seek clarification if there are any points of uncertainty. A key task is to assess what the opening statement reveals about the other side's underlying interests and priorities as this will be invaluable in identifying where compromise may be possible.

The other side will have gone through the same process in presenting their opening statement. So, a solicitor should expect the other side to have spotted the weaknesses in the client's case and to raise issues or ask questions which could expose those weaknesses. The solicitor should anticipate these questions and prepare carefully worded replies which, as far as possible, protect the client.

In considering the other side's opening statement, the solicitor should identify any questions that could be raised to exploit the client's strengths and which probe for weaknesses in the other side's position. The phrasing of such questions should be carefully considered to make it difficult for the other side to avoid giving a straight (and it is hoped revealing) answer.

To negotiate effectively the solicitor must be assertive in advancing the client's case and tenacious in seeking replies to their questions. However, this should be done within the constraints of a professional and detached approach. If the general tone of questioning (or answers) is aggressive, sarcastic or discourteous, it is likely to sour relationships and prevent productive discussions.

3.8 Finding a compromise

3.8.1 Discussion

Once each party has stated (and, if necessary, clarified) their position it is possible to move on to explore the possibility of reaching some middle ground. This forms the longest and most concentrated part of the negotiation. In a negotiation meeting there will be a verbal discussion, perhaps with each side breaking off from time to time to reconsider or for solicitor and client to confer. In negotiation by correspondence the 'discussion' will take place through an exchange of letters/emails and, in a transactional matter, perhaps incorporating drafts and redrafts of the contract.

It is not simply a matter of exchanging a series of offers and counter-offers. The solicitor will need to present the client's case persuasively. It is also necessary to challenge and probe the other side's case, for example by questioning the criteria or evidence used to justify their bid, their underlying interests or their interpretation of the law or of the facts, as well as exploring other ways of accommodating their needs. In other words, this stage requires the solicitor to employ all their skills in order to 'move' the other side towards the best outcome for the client.

It is at this stage that negotiating styles come to the fore. An individual's negotiating style largely derives from their own personality and as such is unique. However, for most solicitors their style will be a combination of cooperation and assertiveness in varying degrees. It is important for a solicitor to identify their own predominant negotiating style but be prepared to vary it according to the needs of a particular negotiation. Effective negotiators are highly flexible and will vary their style according to the merits of the case they are pursuing, and the style adopted by the other negotiator.

Neither end of the spectrum results in effective negotiation. Being excessively cooperative is likely to result in capitulation in the face of a proposal which is not favourable to the client. Assertiveness can tip into aggression, which is likely to create mistrust, distort communication, increase tension and provoke retaliation with the result that negotiations break down. In practice a balance is needed. A solicitor should aim to be sufficiently assertive to press their own client's case and to avoid being trampled on by an aggressive opponent; at the same time, the solicitor should be sufficiently co-operative to search for any possibility of a mutually beneficial solution. This is particularly important where there will be (or the parties would like there to be) a continuing business or personal relationship after the present dispute has been resolved.

3.8.2 Bargaining

Generally speaking, parties do not embark on a negotiation unless they are prepared to compromise, i.e. to bargain. Bargaining involves the trading of concessions. Compromise is achieved by both parties moving from their original positions. Without the capacity to compromise, deals would never be made, and disputes would never be settled.

There are a number of factors beyond the legal merits of the case which frequently motivate compromise. These include avoiding:

- the uncertainties of trial (on liability or quantum);
- the possible publicity arising out of litigation;
- the delay involved in going to trial;
- the emotional stress that continued litigation could involve;
- the legal costs of going any further (even if the client wins in court, they are unlikely to recover all their legal costs from the other side);
- the further loss of management time for a commercial client;
- the transaction falling through; and
- souring an ongoing relationship between two commercial parties or between members of a family.

Compromise is not to be equated to simply 'splitting the difference' between the two sides' positions. There may occasionally be good reasons for securing a deal in this way, but in practice a compromise must be based on the objective merits of the respective parties' positions. It is always necessary to take a step back and carry out an evaluation using relevant criteria to calculate the basis on which the client should offer or accept compromise.

Bargaining will usually be in relation to the entirety of the case. However, it may be appropriate to bargain item by item or clause by clause in multi-issue cases, but it is still important to keep the whole package in mind. It might be sensible not to finalise an agreement on any particular issue until the shape of the whole agreement is clear (including, for example, costs).

3.9   Closing negotiations

In an ideal world the negotiation comes to a close because an agreement has been reached. It is still necessary to carry out some further important and immediate tasks, such as:

- confirming what has been agreed;

- preparing an immediate agreed written summary (sometimes referred to as 'heads of agreement');

- ensuring that details are clarified in order to avoid later disputes; and

- preparing a list of actions to be taken (if appropriate) by both sides.

However, it may be necessary to bring negotiations to a close because an agreement looks unlikely. If the gap between the parties is small, it is a good idea to check the BATNA to see whether it is possible to move further or try to induce the other side to do so. Alternatively, the solicitor should seek to find criteria or principles upon which the parties could agree to divide or accommodate the difference. If there is one outstanding point, it might be possible to agree that the point be adjudicated by an agreed independent third party.

The timing of the close of a negotiation will depend on a cost–benefit analysis. It will be necessary to assess how much more can be achieved and balance this against the cost to the client in terms of time, money and stress. The manner of closing the negotiations will depend on the circumstances. It may simply be a matter of stating that the client has reached their final position. Otherwise, it can be sensible to 'telegraph' the close in the hope of producing some movement from the other side: for example, delivering a deadline or ultimatum or making a concession and expressing it as a final gesture.

Bringing negotiations to an end should not mean closing the door for good. It may be appropriate to put the negotiations on hold for a while to give both sides the opportunity to reconsider their positions. Or it may be advisable to pursue negotiations by other means, for example through alternative dispute resolution.

4 Case and Matter Analysis

SQE2 syllabus

This chapter will help you to achieve the SQE2 Assessment Objective of demonstrating that you are able to produce a written report to a partner giving a legal analysis of the case and client-focused advice.

Learning outcomes

By the end of this chapter you should be able to

- understand what Case and Matter Analysis is and why it is important in legal practice;

- use the IRAC model; and

- produce a written report which has the appropriate tone and content.

4.1   Introduction

What is case and matter analysis? It is a key skill for solicitors which involves analysing the facts, setting these in the context of their legal knowledge and experience and devising a strategy which meets the client's needs. Skilful case and matter analysis will enable the client to make an informed, well advised decision on how to proceed. It is one of the reasons why people seek, and value, advice from solicitors.

Although it is assessed as a separate topic, case and matter analysis is a skill which runs through all the SQE2 assessments. For candidates, it can present a challenge in the transition from the academic study of law to legal practice. Simply reciting the law will be of no help to your clients. What is required, in legal practice and the SQE2 assessments, is an analysis of the law as it relates to the client's particular project (e.g. forming a company) or problem (e.g. challenging a will). It should take into account the client's circumstances and objectives and produce some workable solutions. The analysis should explain the pros and cons of the options open to the client, so that they can select most appropriate one. It should also reflect the needs and objectives of the other parties, as far as you can discern these.

'Case analysis' refers to contentious work and 'matter analysis' to non-contentious work, but the approach you can adopt is the same for both.

This chapter looks at:

- the assessments and practical considerations for SQE2;
- the IRAC model;
- case analysis in the context of Dispute Resolution;
- negotiation;
- ethics and professional conduct issues; and
- the written report.

It can be read in conjunction with **Chapter 2**, which looks at the basics of written communication, and **Chapter 3**, which considers negotiation.

4.2   The SQE2 assessments

4.2.1   Form

In the SQE2 Case and Matter Analysis assessments candidates will be required to produce a written report to a partner giving a legal analysis of the case and providing client-focused advice. This may, but will not necessarily, include options and strategies for negotiation.

Candidates will sit a total of three Case and Matter Analysis assessments in the practice areas below. Questions in these practice areas may draw on underlying black letter law in the Functioning Legal Knowledge (FLK) shown in brackets next to each one:

- one in the context of either Dispute Resolution *(Contract Law and Tort)* or Criminal Litigation *(Criminal Liability)*;
- one in the context of either Property Practice *(Land Law)* or Wills and Intestacy, Probate Administration and Practice *(Trusts)*; and
- one in the context of Business Organisations, Rules and Procedures (including Money Laundering and Financial Services) *(Contract Law)*.

Remember that questions on ethics and professional conduct will be pervasive throughout SQE2.

(See the SRA website for the full syllabus.)

Your instructions, in the form of a case study with documents, will be provided electronically. You will have 60 minutes in which to complete your answer.

4.2.2 Criteria

In the SQE2 Case and Matter Analysis assessments candidates will be assessed against the following Assessment Criteria:

Skills

(1) Identify relevant facts.

(2) Provide client-focused advice (i.e. advice which demonstrates an understanding of the problem from the client's point of view and what the client wants to achieve, not just from a legal perspective).

(3) Use clear, precise, concise and acceptable language.

Application of law

(1) Apply the law correctly to the client's situation.

(2) Apply the law comprehensively to the client's situation, identifying any ethical and professional conduct issues and exercising judgment to resolve them honestly and with integrity.

You can read more about the SQE2 assessments in **Chapter 1**. In the appendix to that chapter you can see how the Statement of Solicitor Competence (SoSC) applies to the skill of Case and Matter Analysis. This includes, at B3, developing and advising on relevant options, strategies and solutions, including:

(a) Understanding and assessing a client's commercial and personal circumstances, their needs, objectives, priorities and constraints.

(b) Ensuring that advice is informed by appropriate legal and factual analysis and identifies the consequences of different options.

4.3 Practical considerations

In the SQE2 assessments you will be asked to produce a written report to a partner which must give a legal analysis of the case and client-focused advice. What is the best way of going about this in the 60 minutes available?

4.3.1 Time management

It is important that you allow yourself enough time to read and consider the documents provided, however great the temptation to start writing straightaway. One approach is to decide in advance how you are going to organise your time. For example, you might allocate 20 minutes to reading and planning, 30 minutes to drafting and 10 minutes to checking your work. You can practise these timings until you find a system which works for you and you can adjust them in the assessment itself to reflect the amount of information provided. But do not abandon your timetable altogether and do not be afraid to stick to it, even if you can see other candidates typing all around you.

4.3.2 Initial read through

You should, of course, start by reading through the case study provided. You may need to do this more than once. You will be looking for the subject matter (considering a will or a letter of offer, for example) and the background story. You will then need to identify the issues which the client and the partner want you to address in your analysis.

It is important to check whether your instructions identify any issues which you do *not* need to consider, such as taxation or client care matters. You might be presented with a Part 36 offer but told that you do not need to consider whether the offer complies with the Part 36 regime. It may sound obvious, but you should not waste any time on such matters. In the assessments you will not gain any marks for doing so (and in legal practice you would also be wasting costs). Nonetheless, candidates frequently fail to follow clear instructions in assessments and waste time and marks as a result. Focus on what you have been asked to advise upon, and the specific issues which arise from your instructions.

4.3.3 Planning

It is important to allow for planning in your timetable. You should allocate time in the assessments to mapping out the contents of your written report, before you begin to draft it. Having pinpointed the issues, you might then use bullet points next to each one to pick out the relevant facts from your instructions and then set out your analysis (for example: 'Shareholding: will have 70% of issued shares/ can pass ordinary resolution/ not special resolution'). This plan need not be elaborate, but you can use it to jot down ideas as they occur to you and to build up a structure for your written report. When you are checking your report, you can use your plan as a tick list, to make sure that you have covered everything.

4.3.4 Providing analysis and advice

Your written report to the partner must contain both analysis and advice. Giving legal analysis without advice will make your answer too academic but giving advice without analysis will not assist the partner, nor will it be reassuring to the client.

For example, simply recommending that the client should try to negotiate settlement up to £75,000 without further explanation is not sufficient. You will need to 'show your working' so that it is clear to the partner why you have reached the conclusion you have. As with a mathematical problem, this approach allows the partner to check that they agree with the reasoning which has led to your recommendation and identify any errors or points of disagreement. A more helpful combination of analysis and advice would be:

> *The client should be willing to negotiate settlement up to £75,000. This represents 65% of the value of her claim and takes into account a possible reduction for contributory negligence and other risks of litigation. Correspondence from the other side suggests that they are willing to increase their offer from £60,000 so settlement should be available at this level.*

4.3.5 Using a model

There is no single correct way of carrying out your analysis or of drafting the written report. Over time, you will develop your own approach. Until you have that experience, you may find it helpful to adopt a model. As explained elsewhere, a 'model' is merely a predetermined structure, under which your analysis is divided into a logical sequence of stages. This chapter suggests using the IRAC model, which is explained below, but this is not the only way to proceed. You should use the approach that works best for you, provided that you address all the issues in your instructions and, in doing so, give a legal analysis of the case and provide client-focused advice.

4.4 The IRAC model

The IRAC model is widely used in legal practice and in legal education as a strategy for analysing cases and individual issues. The four stages are:

Issue

Rule

Application

Conclusion

The IRAC model can be used for case analysis (contentious cases) and matter analysis (uncontentious). This chapter also considers a slightly different approach which can be taken to case analysis in the context of Dispute Resolution (see **4.5**).

4.4.1 Issue (instructions)

Put simply, the issue is the question which arises from your instructions and the case study, and which you have been asked to address: 'Can Mary sell the property to Peter as she proposes?', 'Is there a better way of structuring the deal which will achieve the client's objectives?'

In the SQE2 assessments the issues may well be flagged for you in the documents. They may be framed quite precisely ('Please set out your advice and analysis on the following') ('Is the company in time to bring a claim against D Plc?') or more generally ('Are there any other issues of which the company should be aware?'). The latter reflects the position in legal practice, where you may need to spot issues of which the client will be unaware, such as limitation difficulties in a civil claim or taxation issues when you are drafting a will.

As in legal practice, you may have to sift through the information provided to establish what is relevant to the issues which you have been asked to advise upon and discard anything irrelevant. What if there are gaps in the information provided? This is very likely to occur in legal practice. You will find that as you review your instructions you will start to list what is missing and needs to be requested from the client. Where possible it is much more efficient, for you, and for the client, to deal with all such requests in one go and not piecemeal.

In the SQE2 assessments you will not, of course, be able to ask the client questions. What if the information which you are given is incomplete, and you would need instructions from the client to advise fully on a particular point? You should flag this in your written report ('To advise fully I will need to know the date upon which the breach of contract occurred'). In your analysis and conclusion sections you can then consider alternative scenarios ('If the breach of contract occurred more than six years ago then x, if not then y...').

You can use the IRAC model to deal with each issue individually or to combine them as appropriate.

4.4.2 Rule

This refers to the legal principles which will be used to determine the issue(s). These may be derived from statute, case law or a practitioner work (such as *Chitty on Contracts*).

For example, if one of the issues in a claim for breach of contract is limitation, the rule you would apply is that the limitation period in contract is six years from the date of breach. In legal practice you would usually set out the source of the rule and identify that the six-year limitation period is derived from s 5 of the Limitation Act 1980, which reads:

Time limit for actions founded on simple contract.

> An action founded on simple contract shall not be brought after the expiration of six years from the date on which the cause of action accrued.

However, in the SQE2 assessments the position is different: you will not be expected to know or address detail that a Day One solicitor would look up. For SQE1 purposes, the SRA provided that,

> *On occasion in legal practice a case name or statutory provision, for example, is the term normally used to describe a legal principle or an area of law, or a rule or procedural step (e.g. Rylands v Fletcher, CPR Part 36, Section 25 notice). In such circumstances, candidates are required to know and be able to use such case names, statutory provisions etc. In all other circumstances candidates are not required to recall specific case names, or cite statutory or regulatory authorities.*

The same provision arguably applies by analogy to SQE2.

Of course, if the materials provided to you in the SQE2 assessments do include legal detail, in the form of a case or legislation, or an excerpt from a practitioner text, then you would be expected to refer to this.

4.4.3 Application

Having identified the relevant issues and legal principles, the next stage of the model is application (or analysis). This is the section of the process which candidates can find most difficult, but it is the aspect of your work which will be the most valuable to your client in legal practice and it is important for the SQE2 assessments. Avoid the temptation to jump straight from the facts to the conclusion: instead focus your attention on how the legal principles you have identified apply to the facts of the case study. In simple terms, carrying out your analysis means asking yourself: what does this mean for the client? If you find yourself getting stuck come back to this question.

4.4.3.1 The facts

You will recall that the SQE2 Assessment Criteria require you to 'identify the relevant facts'. Do not be afraid to mention specific facts in your written report: candidates often skate over or summarise these, but you need to be precise about the facts so that you can apply the law to them accurately.

4.4.3.2 Applying the law to the facts

The SQE2 Assessment Criteria also require you to apply the law correctly and comprehensively to the client's situation. For an answer to be legally comprehensive, it must go further than identify the issues (which may be apparent from the instructions) and provide a legally comprehensive analysis of those issues. For the purposes of the SQE2 assessments, this includes approaching the issues from different angles: from the client's point of view and the other side's point of view and considering the advantages and disadvantages of a particular course of action.

If you are analysing an offer of settlement from the other side, you might want to consider these questions. You will see that they involve law, fact or a mixture of the two:

- What is the amount offered as a percentage of the amount sought in the particulars of claim? (fact)

- What are the risks of litigation: is it possible or likely that the client will lose the case? (law)

- If the client wins, how likely are they to achieve the sum sought? Are there factors such as contributory negligence which might reduce the award of damages? (law)

- What are the costs consequences of rejecting the offer? (law)

- Should the client put forward a counter-offer? (law and fact)

- What do we know about the client's attitude? Risk averse? Anxious about the trial? Willing to give evidence? (fact)

The final bullet point reminds you to consider the client's commercial and personal circumstances and their needs, objectives, priorities and constraints, as required by the SoSC at B3.a.

In the SQE2 assessments and in legal practice, addressing these issues may sometimes require you to look outside the brief and to consider the bigger picture. As noted above, part of the solicitor's role is to identify risks which the client has not considered. In legal practice, your ability to do this will flow from your experience of dealing with other transactions and will develop as your career progresses. It may also benefit your client if you can set their case or matter in a wider context. Again, your capacity to do this will develop during your career and will come from your appreciation of developments in the client's own industry: for example, if new legislation is about to be introduced which will affect them. You can also draw on your understanding of current affairs and how these may impact on the client's position. This is sometimes referred to as a PESTLE analysis, to refer to the political (P), economic (E), social (S), technological (T), legal (L) and environmental (E) changes that can affect commercial organisations.

4.4.4 Conclusion

Having analysed the law and the facts, you need to pull the threads together and bring your analysis to a conclusion. A common mistake is to set out an analysis but fail to round this off with clear recommendations.

The client is looking for is a solution, or a choice of solutions, tailored to their individual circumstances. It will rarely be the case, in legal practice or in the SQE2 assessments, that there is one clear and obvious solution or course of action. Do not let this put you off. Your job is to identify the realistic options available to the client and to set out the consequences of each. You may also want to suggest which of these is most appropriate for the client.

What if you are missing a key piece of information? In that situation you can advise on different hypotheses. You could recommend that the missing information be obtained (as a matter of urgency if appropriate) and state 'If the breach occurred more than six years ago, then the client could do x, if not then the client could do y'.

There is a case study with an example of the IRAC model at the end of this chapter.

4.5 Case analysis in Dispute Resolution

You will recall from your study of Dispute Resolution for SQE1 that it is important to analyse the evidence which is available at the outset of a case so that you can give the client some preliminary advice on liability and quantum and identify further lines of enquiry. You will need to identify:

- The cause of action: breach of contract? negligence?
- The breach: what did the other party do wrong?
- The consequences of breach: what happened as a result of the breach?
- The financial consequences for the client: what loss have they suffered?

This structured approach is helpful as it reflects the order in which the issues will be pleaded in the particulars of claim in due course.

You can find a case study for a case analysis in a breach of contract claim in The University of Law SQE1 manual *Dispute Resolution*. You will note that where the cause of action is breach of contract you will need to find out the type of contract (oral or written) and whether there is any dispute about whether a contract was formed at all. You will also need to look at the terms of the contract. Are there are any relevant express terms? Are there any further terms which are implied by statute (such as the implied term to carry out a service with reasonable care and skill, under the Supply of Goods and Services Act 1982)?

As a final stage of your analysis, you should try to anticipate any arguments which the proposed defendant might raise. For example, might they argue that your client failed to mitigate their loss? Or that some of the losses which they seek to recover are too remote? You can then set about obtaining instructions and further evidence to counter such arguments.

The example of case analysis at the end of this chapter uses the IRAC model, but you could also use the approach above to arrive at the same conclusion.

4.6 Negotiation

The written report which you will be asked to provide may, but will not necessarily, include options and strategies for negotiation. You should therefore be prepared to provide, as part of your written report, suggestions and recommendations to the partner as to how they, or the client, might negotiate a favourable outcome.

The skill of negotiation includes identifying all parties' interests, objectives and limits; developing and formulating best options for meeting parties' objectives and presenting options for compromise persuasively.

As well as highlighting your client's interests and objectives, your instructions might also indicate the position of the other party. They could be a potential investor in a company, the other side in a property deal or the opponent in litigation. Is it clear from your instructions that there is a deadline, an ambition or a commercial pressure which is important to them? Remember to factor this into your analysis, so that the proposals you make are realistic and likely to lead to compromise. It is no help to your client to suggest a solution which would work well for them but will clearly be unacceptable to the other side.

You can read more about the topic of negotiation in **Chapter 3**. The example of the IRAC model at the end of this chapter also deals with possible negotiation.

4.7 Ethics and professional conduct issues

Ethics and professional conduct issues will not arise in every SQE2 assessment scenario. Your task is to identify when they do and to exercise judgment to resolve them honestly and with integrity. They will not be flagged. This reflects the position in legal practice where you should always be alert to such issues. In particular, at the outset of a case you should consider the risk of a conflict of interest. This may arise between two clients who both want to instruct the firm on a business venture but whose interests might diverge. The interests of a potential client might conflict with those of an existing one. In the course of a case, a client might ask you to withhold information from their opponent or the court in a way which amounts to a breach of the SRA Code of Conduct for Solicitors, RELs and RFLs.

If ethical or conduct issues arise in the SQE2 assessments, you will need to address them in your written report, unless your instructions make it clear that this is not required. Having identified the issue, you should go on to recommend how this could be resolved. In the example above you might say that the client must be told that the firm cannot continue to act if they insist upon the information being withheld. The IRAC method can be used here to identify the ethical or conduct issue; what the Codes say about it; what it means for the firm and the client; and how it can be resolved.

You can refresh your knowledge of the SRA's Principles and Codes by referring to The University of Law SQE1 manual *Ethics and Professional Conduct*.

4.8 The written report

Having carried out your analysis you must prepare a written report to a partner giving a legal analysis of the case and providing client-focused advice. How should you go about this?

4.8.1 Presentation

You may not be provided with a template for your report in the SQE2 assessments. In legal practice there is no fixed format for a report, although your firm may have a preferred format. It is usual for a report sent within a firm to say who it is from (you) and to (the partner). It should have a heading: which can be the subject line of an email.

You will probably find it helpful to divide up the text using sub-headings and numbered paragraphs, which correspond with the issues you have been asked to address. Whatever layout you choose, it should immediately be clear to the reader that you have addressed all the issues. It is perfectly acceptable to use the questions you have been asked as sub-headings, for example:

1. What are the risks to the client?

4.8.2 Style

The tone and language which you use should be appropriate to a report addressed to a partner. Remember that this is not an academic essay, but a practical analysis of the client's situation. You can assume that the partner is aware of the law, and that you do not need to explain terms like 'Part 36 offer' or 'Licence to Assign' to them. You do not need to spell out basic legal principles (such as how a Part 36 offer works) unless you are asked to do so. It may be that the client has specifically asked for advice on a particular point (will they have enough votes to pass a resolution on a particular issue?) and if so you should set out your answer in a clear way which the partner could, if necessary, cut and paste into a letter of advice to the client.

As you are writing to a partner your tone can be more informal than it would need to be if you were writing to a client or opponent, but it should still be professional.

4.8.3 Content and structure

As you are writing an internal report to a partner you can assume that they are familiar with the case or matter. Therefore, *unless you are asked to do so*, you should not spend time in the assessments summarising the facts. However, it can be useful to have an introductory paragraph which sets out any key propositions which arise from the facts: such as the time limits for serving a Notice to Complete or the date when the relevant period for accepting a Part 36 offer will expire.

Using the IRAC (or other) model you can then deal the with the issues, individually or together. Make sure that you consider each aspect of a question. If, for example, you are asked to consider the advantages and disadvantages of a particular course of action from the point of view of both parties you should end up with a minimum of four points to make.

Having set out the options, you will often conclude a report by identifying which of these appears most appropriate for the client and briefly giving the reasons why.

4.9 Example IRAC model

Set out below is an example for using the IRAC model.

Case study

Your client, B Limited, has recently refurbished its office. It has come to you with a complaint about the bathrooms which have recently been installed by Y & Sons, a company which specialises in plumbing. It complains that the taps in the bathroom sinks do not close properly; that water does not drain from the sinks quickly enough and that the bathrooms have begun to smell unpleasant, causing B Limited's clients and employees to complain. B Limited and Y & Sons entered into a basic written contract which set out the price of the work and the completion date but did not mention the standard to which the bathrooms should be installed.

B Limited will have to pay another plumber to replumb the sinks. In addition, the problems with the bathrooms mean that B Limited cannot host its annual conference in the office and will have to hold this elsewhere, at additional expense. The MD of B Limited can recall telling Y & Sons that the bathrooms had to be ready in time for the conference. In discussions, Y & Sons have denied this and refused to meet the cost of relocating the annual conference, although they would be willing to reimburse some of the cost of the replumbing.

B Limited would like advice on its legal position and what losses it can expect to recover from Y & Sons. It would like to know in general terms what it should do but does not want detailed advice or any legal documents drafted at this stage.

While B Limited is keen to recoup its losses, it is reluctant to get involved in litigation if this can be avoided. It is in merger talks with another company and concerned that litigation against Y & Sons would be a distraction for its management team, who are all very busy. Its impression is that Y & Sons may be willing to compromise as they are keen to maintain their reputation locally.

How would you use the IRAC model to approach and structure your analysis?

4.9.1 Issues

According to your instructions, B Limited would like advice on two issues:

- *What legal steps are open to it? (Issue 1)*
- *What losses can it seek to recover from Y & Sons? (Issue 2)*

As a solicitor, you may also have identified two further issues, which might not be apparent to B Limited:

- *Even if the contract is silent as to the standard of the work, can a term be implied which stipulates this? (Issue 3)*
- *Is the cost of holding the annual conference elsewhere a foreseeable loss? (Issue 4)*

At this stage, it is worth noting what you have *not* been asked to do. Your instructions state that B Limited does not want detailed advice or any legal documents drafted at this stage.

The case study clearly flags up the possibility of negotiation.

You should check that the instructions do not give rise to any ethical issues (none are apparent on these facts).

4.9.2 Rule, application and conclusion

The rules, application and conclusion which apply to these issues are set out in the table below. You will see that there is some overlap between them.

The rules which apply here are a mixture of procedural and black letter law.

Having identified the issues and the relevant legal rules, you should analyse the facts in the case study and apply the law to them. Remember that you are also looking for, and flagging up, any missing information which you would need to complete your analysis.

	Issue	Rule	Application	Conclusion	Additional information
1	What legal steps are open to B Limited?	A party which has suffered loss because of another party's breach of contract can issue proceedings in the civil courts to recover damages. Before doing so, however, they must follow any relevant pre-action protocol.	Y & Sons were in breach of contract. The sinks were not installed with reasonable care and skill. The evidence for this is that: - The taps on the sinks do not close properly. -The water does not drain away properly. - The bathrooms have begun to smell unpleasant. - Clients and employees have complained. B Limited has suffered losses as a result (see below).	B Limited should be able to bring a claim against Y & Sons to recover its losses. The exact form and venue for those proceedings will depend on the value of the claim.	Level of losses
2	What losses can B Limited seek to recover from Y & Sons?	The aim of damages in a contract claim is to place the claimant the position it would have been in, had the contract been performed.	B Limited has suffered two types of loss: the cost of replumbing and the cost of holding the annual conference elsewhere.	Subject to the argument about foreseeability (below) B Limited should be able to recover these losses from Y & Sons, to put it into the position it would have been in had the contract been properly performed. (It will not be able to recover what it paid to Y & Sons for the installation of the bathrooms as it would always have had to pay this amount).	

(continued)

Table (*continued*)

	Issue	Rule	Application	Conclusion	Additional information
3	Even if the contract is silent as to the standard of the work, can a term be implied which stipulates this?	Where a contract for services is entered into between two businesses, a term will be implied into the contract that the services are to be carried out with reasonable care and skill [By way of information this is by virtue of s.13 of the Supply of Goods and Services Act 1982].	B Limited and Y & Sons both entered into the contract in the course of their businesses: B Limited is a company and work was carried out to their offices. Y & Sons are a company specialising in plumbing.	As both companies entered into the contract in the course of their businesses, a term should be implied into the contract that the installation of the bathrooms should have been carried out with reasonable care and skill.	The contract.
4	Is the cost of holding the annual conference elsewhere a foreseeable loss?	Whether a party can recover consequential damages for a breach of contract from the party in breach of contract will depend upon whether the party in breach could have foreseen the losses on the information available to them [By way of information this is by virtue of *Hadley v Baxendale (1854)*]	B Limited will also incur a loss in paying to hold the annual conference elsewhere. Y & Sons are refusing to meet the cost of this. B Limited can recall telling Y & Sons that the bathrooms would need to be completed before the annual conference. Y & Sons deny this.	There is a conflict of evidence on this point. B Limited should succeed if it can establish that it told Y & Sons about the need for the bathrooms to be completed before the conference. Additional information is required.	Details of precontract discussions between B Limited and Y & Sons about the need for the plumbing of the bathrooms to be completed before the annual conference.

4.9.3   Negotiation

Negotiation would make sense on these facts. B Limited does not want the demands of litigation to distract the management team from the merger talks. If a settlement could be negotiated with Y & Sons at an early stage this would be an advantage for B Limited as this would be less time consuming and allow it to concentrate on its commercial priorities.

As with any settlement, a possible consequence of negotiation and compromise might be that B Limited will have to accept a proportion of its losses and not the full amount. More information is required, but B Limited's losses in relation to the costs of the conference may be more difficult to prove so this might be an area for compromise.

Looking at the situation from Y & Sons' point of view, they seem willing to compromise. They are keen to protect their reputation locally. This suggests that they might be willing to negotiate a settlement (which could be kept confidential), rather than run the risk of adverse publicity from litigation. Y & Sons have indicated that they are willing to reimburse some of the cost of replumbing, but not of holding the conference elsewhere. This is an area where more evidence (of the pre-contract discussions) should be obtained so that B Limited can press Y & Sons in negotiation.

A negotiated settlement should therefore be in the interests of both parties.

5 Legal Writing

SQE2 syllabus

This chapter will help you to achieve the SQE2 Assessment Objective of demonstrating that you are able to produce a letter or an email as the solicitor acting in a matter.

Learning outcomes

By the end of this chapter you should be able to:

- write using clear, correct and concise language;
- apply a logical, consistent and appropriate structure to written communications; and
- write in a style and tone appropriate for the recipient and the purpose of the communication.

5.1 Introduction

Solicitors use various means to communicate with others using the written word: letters, reports, memos, marketing materials, texts, social media posts etc. Some methods are better suited to a particular purpose than others. In legal practice it is usually a matter of selecting the right method for the circumstances. This chapter focuses on the writing of letters and emails although many of the points made are equally applicable to other forms of written communication.

General written communication skills were considered in **Chapter 2**. This chapter considers the specific requirements of the SQE2 Legal Writing assessments.

This chapter looks at:

- the assessments;
- letters;
- emails;
- purpose;
- the recipient;
- language;
- structure;
- layout;
- tone;
- legal content; and
- ethics and professional conduct issues.

5.2 The SQE2 Assessments

5.2.1 Form

In the SQE2 assessments candidates will be required to produce a letter or an email as the solicitor acting in the matter, which clearly and correctly applies the law to the client's concerns and is appropriate for the recipient.

Candidates will sit a total of three Legal Writing assessments in the practice areas below. Questions in these practice areas may draw on underlying black letter law in the Functioning Legal Knowledge shown in brackets next to each one:

- one in the context of either Dispute Resolution (*Contract Law and Tort*) or Criminal Litigation (*Criminal Liability*);
- one in the context of either Property Practice (*Land Law*) or Wills and Intestacy, Probate Administration and Practice (*Trusts*); and
- one in the context of Business Organisations, Rules and Procedures (including Money Laundering and Financial Services) (*Contract Law*).

One or more of the assessments may involve negotiation (see **Chapter 3**). Remember that questions on ethics and professional conduct will be pervasive throughout SQE2.

(See the SRA website for the full syllabus.)

Candidates will receive their instructions for each assessment in the form of an email from a partner. The email will set out the relevant facts, explain what the candidate is required to do and stipulate whether the answer is to take the form of a letter or an email. The email from the partner may be accompanied by a document or documents.

The email/instructions will be provided electronically. Candidates will have 30 minutes in which to complete their answer.

5.2.2 Criteria

In the SQE2 assessments candidates will be assessed against the following Assessment Criteria:

Skills

(1) Include relevant facts.

(2) Use a logical structure.

(3) Advice/content is client and recipient focused.

(4) Use clear, precise, concise and acceptable language which is appropriate to the recipient.

Application of law

(1) Apply the law correctly to the client's situation.

(2) Apply the law comprehensively to the client's situation, identifying any ethical and professional conduct issues and exercising judgment to resolve them honestly and with integrity.

You can read more about the SQE2 assessments in **Chapter 1**. In the appendix to that chapter, you can see how the Statement of Solicitor Competence applies to the skill of Legal Writing.

5.3 Letters

5.3.1 Overview

Whilst letters have given way to various electronic forms of communication in many aspects of life, they remain a common way for solicitors to communicate with their clients and others.

In the SQE2 assessments candidates may be provided with a 'template' for a letter. However, this is likely to be little more than a firm's letterhead perhaps with the recipient's contact details completed. You will therefore need to set out the letter in an appropriate way.

There is no set format for a letter. Therefore, there is discretion as to how a letter is presented, although this is constrained by some conventions which must be followed when writing letters in a professional or business context. In legal practice, firms tend to have their own house style. The letter template suggested here is simply intended to follow a logical structure to aid the recipient's understanding of the contents. An explanation of the elements of the template follows.

5.3.2   Template

Firm's headed notepaper
Name of firm
Address

Recipient
Name
Address

Reference
Date

Dear Recipient

Main heading

Introductory paragraph

Sub-heading

[Facts – if appropriate]

Sub-heading

First key point/issue

Sub-heading

Second key point/issue

Sub-heading

[Summary – if appropriate]

Sub-heading

[Next steps/action points – if appropriate]

Closing

Yours sincerely/faithfully

Name
Status
Enc:
cc:

5.3.3 Explanation

Recipient's name and address.

The recipient's name (including the surname) and postal address should appear at the top of a letter. In legal practice the words 'private and confidential' may also appear above the name. The name and address may have already been inserted into the 'template' in the SQE2 assessments.

Date

A letter must be dated. This enables the sequence of correspondence to be readily seen. It is also important if, for example, the letter sets a time limit for a response such as '14 days from the date of this letter'.

The date may have already been inserted into the 'template' in the SQE2 assessments.

Reference

Firms usually assign a unique reference number to a client's matter as a means of identifying that particular file. A firm will have its own method of referencing which will usually take the form of a combination of initials and numbers. By convention the reference appears at the top of the letter. In a letter to another firm of solicitors it is usual to include that firm's reference as well.

You should use any reference provided in the SQE2 assessments.

Salutation

The salutation appears as the first part of the body of letter and addresses the recipient. In a professional/business context by convention this is done by using the word 'Dear' followed by the recipient's title and surname. A comma may also be added. For example:

- Dear Mr Brown
- Dear Professor Singh
- Dear Dr Solomon,

If the identity of the recipient is unknown, 'Dear Sir or Madam' or 'Dear Sir/Madam' are used.

When writing to a woman who does not have, for example, a professional title, 'Miss', 'Mrs' or 'Ms' are all possibilities. If you are unsure which title the recipient prefers, 'Ms' should be used as the more inclusive option.

Even in a professional/business context it is acceptable to use a first name where the recipient is well known to the writer and has given permission: 'Dear Julie'. You may be asked to write a letter in the name of someone else in the firm in which case you should check whether that person usually addresses the recipient using their first name. It is better to err on the side of formality if you are unsure.

Traditionally one firm of solicitors writing to another would use the salutation 'Dear Sirs'. Whilst this is still seen in practice it is gradually being abandoned in favour of the more neutral 'Dear Sir/Madam' or 'Dear [name of the firm]'.

Main Heading

Immediately below the salutation it is usual to include a heading identifying the matter. This is often written in bold font or underlined so that the recipient can immediately see at a glance what the letter is about.

The wording will vary depending on the circumstances. The heading should be succinct and sufficiently precise to enable the recipient to readily identify the matter. For example, the heading 'The company' may be too vague, whereas 'Purchase of shares in ABC Ltd' clearly identifies the particular transaction. Sensitivity must also be exercised. For example, in a letter to a recently bereaved client the heading 'Your father's estate' is to be preferred over 'Frederick Green (Deceased)'.

In legal practice many firms use the prefix 'Re' (meaning 'in the matter of'). For example, 'Re: Purchase of 8, Church Street, Bristol'. However, others consider 'Re' to be unnecessary as it adds nothing of substance to the heading.

Main Content

There may be one or more elements to the main content depending on the nature of the case and the purpose of the letter.

- **Introductory paragraph**

It is usual to start the main body of the letter with a short introductory paragraph to explain the purpose of the letter. For example:

> 'Further to our meeting yesterday, I am writing to confirm the points that we discussed about....'

> 'We act for Jessica Williams in respect of her proposed purchase of 5, Station Road, Blackpool. We have reviewed the draft contract and have set out our comments below for your consideration.'

As part of the introductory paragraph, it may be necessary to acknowledge the recipient's last communication or, if it is the first contact with the recipient, explain the solicitor's involvement.

- **Facts**

In some cases, it will be appropriate to present a summary of the facts. For example, a letter of claim should include the facts which give rise to the claim (see The University of Law SQE1 manual *Dispute Resolution*). Similarly, in a letter to a new client immediately following a first interview it is helpful to include a brief summary of the facts so that the client can be certain that the solicitor has correctly understood all the relevant information. However, a summary is usually unnecessary where the matter is established, and the relevant facts can be woven into the remainder of the letter.

- **Key points**

This is the substance of the letter. It comprises one or more paragraphs addressing the key points or issues.

- **Summary**

In a long and/or complex letter it may be helpful to summarise the key points. Similarly, where a client has to consider a number of options, it is helpful to summarise them towards the end of the letter so that the client can refer to them easily.

- **Next steps/action points**

If the letter requires next steps to be followed or further action to be taken it is usually logical to set these out at the end of the letter. It should be clear exactly what needs to be done and by whom.

- **Closing**

It is usual to conclude a letter with a short closing paragraph. This ensures that the letter concludes in a professional manner rather than slowly petering out or coming to an abrupt end. Depending on the context the closing paragraph might comprise words of reassurance, invite further contact or set expectations:

> 'Please do not hesitate to contact me if you have any queries about the contents of this letter. Otherwise, I look forward to receiving your further instructions....'

> 'If you do not provide a full reply within 14 days of the date of this letter, we are instructed to begin legal proceedings without further reference to you.

> We suggest that you consult a solicitor before responding to this letter.'

Sign-off

In a letter that begins 'Dear Sir/Madam' the sign-off is 'Yours faithfully'. In a letter that begins 'Dear [name]' the sign-off is 'Yours sincerely'. A comma should be added if used in the salutation.

The letter will be signed by the individual solicitor or in the name of the firm as appropriate. It is usual to print the name of the firm or the individual and, in the case of an individual, their status within the firm.

Enclosures

In some cases, documents may be enclosed with the letter. Any such documents should be listed at the end of the letter. The list should be prefaced with 'Enc:'.

Copies

It is sometimes necessary to copy a letter to a third person. That person's name and address should appear at the end prefaced by 'cc:'.

5.4 Emails

5.4.1 Overview

Emails have long been used by firms as a quick and convenient method of internal communication. They are now also a common method of communicating with those outside the firm, including clients. In legal practice caution needs to be exercised in the use of emails. It is all too easy, for example, to 'reply to all' by mistake or press 'send' before properly proof-reading the content.

There is no set template for an email, and, unlike letter writing, there are no established conventions to follow. This creates the risk that emails are viewed as more informal so less care is taken in their presentation with the result that they lose their professional tone and appearance. In reality the same care and skill needs to be applied in the writing of an email as a letter.

In the SQE2 assessments candidates may be provided with a 'template' for an email. However, this is likely to be little more than mock-up of a standard email heading.

5.4.2 Template

From:
To:
CC:
BC:
Date:
Subject:

Dear Recipient

Sub-heading

Sub-heading

Your sincerely

Name
Firm
Firm's address
Telephone number
Website

5.4.3 Explanation

In legal practice firms often have their own house style for emails. Otherwise, it is sensible to follow the same format as for a letter, but with some necessary adjustments. Obviously, the usual first section of a letter containing name, address, date and reference is not necessary as such information as is required will appear in the email heading. Any documents will appear as attachments. If the email is to a colleague a less formal sign-off, such as 'kind regards', is acceptable. In practice the writer's details at the end are often added by auto-signature.

The equivalent heading for a letter would appear in the subject line for an email. The subject line is particularly important for emails as its wording will influence when and if the recipient opens it. It may therefore be necessary to adjust the wording to incorporate more of the purpose of the email, for example 'Update on purchase of shares. Action required'. In legal practice great care needs to be taken with the subject line as it will be visible whenever the inbox is opened and so there is a potential confidentiality issue.

5.5 Purpose

Before embarking on any piece of legal writing it is important to establish the purpose of the communication. Letters/emails can have a variety of purposes:

- to seek or to confirm instructions
- to record documents received
- to give advice

- to set an agenda

- to propose or to persuade

- to request action

The purpose, coupled with the identity of the recipient (see **5.6**), will not only determine the contents of the letter/email, but also influence the language, structure, tone etc. For example, a letter sent to another firm of solicitors for the purpose of demanding action is likely to have a different tone than one sent for the purpose of negotiating a settlement. In other words, the purpose of the letter/email dictates, not just what to say, but how to say it.

5.6 The recipient

Written communications must be suitable for the intended recipient. In the SQE2 assessments there is a range of possible recipients for the letter/email including a client, a third party, the other side (in a case or a transaction) and a partner within your own organisation.

5.6.1 The client

The purpose of a letter/email to a client is usually to give advice. Almost invariably on receiving instructions at the start of a matter a solicitor will write a follow-up letter confirming the instructions, setting out the client's legal position and the next steps in the case. The solicitor will usually continue to correspond with the client at various points as the case or transaction proceeds, for example to report a development in the matter, advise on the legal consequences and seek further instructions.

Writing letters/emails to clients can be challenging. They need to strike the right balance of friendliness with professionalism. Usually, a client will have little or no legal knowledge. This means that not only must the correct advice be given, but it must be communicated in a way that a lay person can understand. Complex legal concepts may need to be carefully explained. A solicitor may be taking all the correct legal steps, but if they are unable to communicate this it may result in client dissatisfaction. Miscommunication is a frequent cause of client complaints about solicitors.

5.6.2 The other side

Solicitors frequently send letters/emails to the solicitors representing the other side in the case or transaction, or to an unrepresented opponent personally. Such letters/emails are usually written in the name of the firm rather than the individual solicitor dealing with the matter and as such take on a more formal air.

Letters/emails to the other side can have one of several purposes and this will be reflected in the tone and style. The letter/email may be a straightforward neutral request for information. If the purpose of the letter/email is to set out the allegations which form the substance of the client's claim, it will be more forceful in tone. If the letter contains a proposal for settlement it is likely to be more conciliatory and will often be marked 'without prejudice save as to costs' (see **5.15**).

5.6.3 Third parties

There are many third parties that a solicitor may have cause to correspond with during the conduct of a client's matter. In a personal injury case, for example, it may be necessary to write to an expert instructing them to carry out a medical examination and prepare a report on the client's injuries. Or in a criminal matter the solicitor may need to write to a potential witness seeking permission to interview them about the incident. The tone of such letters/emails will reflect the fact that they are, in effect, asking for the recipient's help.

Other communications to third parties may be simply informative. For example, solicitors regularly correspond with the courts, His Majesty's Revenue and Customs, Companies House etc. This is usually just for the purpose of submitting documents and forms, although many of these interactions now take place online.

5.6.4 Colleagues

It would be unusual for a solicitor to send a letter to someone in their own firm. Such communication takes place via a memorandum or, more commonly, email. Colleagues usually send emails to each other where they are working collaboratively on a client matter. So, for example, the purpose of the email might be to update the recipient on a development in the case, or to report on some legal research. Even though the email is to a colleague, it is still important to adopt a professional tone and style.

5.7 Language

Clarity of expression is key. The language used in Legal Writing must be pitched at the right level and be simple enough to be easily read and understood by the recipient. Simple is not the same as simplistic. It is possible to explain even the most complex legal concepts without appearing patronising or condescending to the recipient.

Some solicitors have a tendency to overcomplicate their language in letters/emails. For example, choosing longer words over shorter ones, or introducing words which would never be used in everyday speech such as 'aforementioned' and 'herewith'. In fact, the opposite is required. Complicated, legalistic language only serves to impact on clarity. Instead, language must be clear and straightforward. These days most firms encourage the use of plain English in all forms of written communication.

In legal practice it is always necessary for a solicitor to adapt their writing style to ensure that the language meets the needs of and/or is appropriate to the particular recipient. The language must cater for the recipient's level of knowledge and understanding. A lay client, for example, will usually have little or no knowledge of the law and so jargon and technical terms (sometimes referred to as legalese) should not be used as a general rule, and should never be used without explanation. In contrast when writing to another lawyer using technical language is more acceptable. For example, it would be appropriate to use the term 'tenants in common' when writing to a lawyer, but if it was necessary to use it in a letter to a client an explanation would need to be added.

Effective Legal Writing demands a concise style. Long or complex sentences can confuse the reader and risk the meaning being lost altogether. Shorter sentences are usually easier to understand. Measures such as removing superfluous words, avoiding repetition and using the active voice (see **Chapter 2**) will help to keep sentences short. However, short sentences can sometimes appear to the reader as abrupt or discourteous. It is a matter of striking the right balance.

Acronyms and abbreviations can also help to keep sentences short. They can be useful, for example, where a phrase or name of an organisation needs to be repeated throughout the letter/email. However, they should only be used if they will be familiar to the recipient or they are explained. For example, 'His Majesty's Revenue and Customs (HMRC)' or 'Marchant Engineering UK Ltd (Marchant)'.

Some communications are in the name of the individual solicitor, in which case they must be written in the first person singular: 'I am writing...'. Others, for example letters/emails to the other side, are written on behalf of the firm, and therefore the first person plural must be used: 'We expect to hear from you by'. The use of 'I' and 'we' must be consistent throughout the letter/email.

Correct spelling, grammar and punctuation are essential in any piece of Legal Writing. The use of incorrect words or misplaced punctuation may alter the meaning of a sentence resulting in a misunderstanding between writer and recipient. Errors in spelling, grammar and punctuation detract from the content. For example, a proposal for settlement is unlikely to be convincing if it is riddled with spelling mistakes. Such errors also reflect poorly on the writer.

In preparation for the SQE2 assessments you should make sure that you are confident in your language skills (see **Chapter 2**). Remember that in the SQE2 assessments you may not have access to functions such as spellcheck and grammar-check.

5.8 Structure

There are no set rules about how to structure a piece of Legal Writing save that it must be logical. The content of letters/emails should be broken down into a series of paragraphs, each one dealing with a separate topic. Presenting the content in manageable sections in this way makes it easier for the recipient to follow and understand. Detailed paragraphs addressing a range of different issues make it hard for the recipient to identify the key points in the content. There is no specific requirement as to the length of a paragraph. At one end of the spectrum, it will rarely be appropriate for a paragraph to consist of a single sentence. At the other end of the spectrum, a lengthy paragraph is difficult to follow.

With only 30 minutes in which to complete the SQE2 assessment it is important to plan for and have a structure in mind. Following the templates at **5.3.2** and **5.4.2** will give an overall logical structure to your letters and emails and ensure that you include the required elements. However, it is important to be flexible. It may be necessary to remove certain elements or add further structure depending on the circumstances. The main content, for example, will always require careful consideration. It will usually be sensible to assign each key point or issue a separate paragraph. How those paragraphs are arranged will depend on the purpose and subject matter of the letter/email. It may be more logical to deal with the most important point first and then go on to secondary points. Conversely it may be more sensible to build up to the main issue by establishing preliminary points first. In other cases, a chronological approach may be more appropriate. The aim is always to make the content easier to follow.

5.9 Layout

The layout of any piece of Legal Writing should be such as to create a professional appearance. A good layout will help the reader to navigate the content and make it easier for the reader to understand what has been written. To use a colloquial expression, the layout should make the communication 'easy on the eye'.

Legal Writing usually benefits from the use of sub-headings, although they may not be necessary in, say, a very short email. A sub-heading should be short, ideally no more than two or three words. Writing the sub-heading in bold text will make it stand out. On a first reading a sub-heading forewarns the reader of the content of the paragraph or paragraphs that follow and then enables the reader to go back and easily find the content that they wish to consider further. Where there are several key points or issues to be dealt with in a letter/email, for example, it is sensible to deal with each point/issue in a separate paragraph with its own sub-heading.

Incorporating bullet points in letters and emails can be useful. They can be employed to highlight or summarise key elements, for example where there are a number of options or action points. They also help to keep the letter/email concise. However, they should be used with caution. If used to excess bullet points can confuse the eye and their brevity can result in the meaning being lost. Bullet points can also give a letter/email a 'clinical' appearance which may be a consideration if the content is of a sensitive nature. The key question to ask in each case is whether bullet points help to make the content clearer and easier to follow.

In contrast to many legal documents, it is not usual to number the paragraphs in a letter/email. However, it might be considered if the letter/email is lengthy, especially where the recipient is required to reply to or comment on the contents in detail.

5.10 Tone

The appropriate tone to adopt in a letter/email can be described as courteous, professional and business-like. More formality is required than in, say, everyday speech. So, for example, contractions (e.g. 'can't', 'shouldn't', 'he'll'), slang and colloquial language are all to be avoided. This should not result in a letter/email which is brusque or clinical. It is possible, for example, to appear friendly or express empathy whilst maintaining professionalism. By the same token it is not necessary to introduce the same level of formality as is required in the drafting of a legal document. For example, it is not usually necessary to use defined terms (see **6.4.1**) in a letter/email.

The style of writing in a professional letter/email should be restrained. It will rarely be appropriate, for example, to express surprise, amazement, outrage or use exclamation marks. Unnecessary adverbs create an overemphasis and so should be avoided (e.g. 'totally unhappy', 'completely inaccurate'). Jokes and witticisms are not acceptable.

Emails to colleagues need particular care. It can feel artificial to adopt a formal tone when, day to day, you are on friendly terms with the recipient. However, an email sent in a professional context should be written in a professional manner. It is important to remember that if the email concerns a client's matter, it is a document of record about that matter. It will be kept on a client file in exactly the same way as a letter or report would be. It may be necessary at some point in the future, for example, to forward the email to the client or for it to be read out in court.

5.11 Legal content

Perhaps unsurprisingly the SQE2 Assessment Criteria stipulate that the law must be applied correctly. The legal content must therefore be accurate and unambiguous.

It may be necessary to set out the law, for example, in an email to a colleague where the purpose is to report on legal research or case analysis. However, in letters/emails it is usually a matter of using or explaining the law rather than setting out the detail. For example, a letter of advice to a client should explain how the relevant law applies to the facts of the client's case.

Precision is important. For example, rather than writing in generic terms about 'tax consequences', if there is sufficient information available calculating how much tax will be payable and including that figure in the letter/email will be more helpful for the recipient.

Letters/emails do not usually require the use of case names or statutory references. They are almost invariably inappropriate where the recipient is a lay person as they will simply not be understood. They will usually be unnecessary if the recipient is a lawyer. This can be a difficult habit to break as so often during their legal education students/trainees are expected to cite the authority for any proposition they put forward. Examples of their use being acceptable is when writing to a lawyer and the case name or statutory reference is a common form of legal shorthand (e.g. 'Part 36 offer' and 'the test in *Banks v Goodfellow*') or, as above, where the purpose of an email is to convey the results of a piece of legal research or case analysis.

The SQE2 Assessment Criteria also stipulate that the law must be applied comprehensively. Matter analysis (see **Chapter 4**) is crucial to effective Legal Writing to ensure the letter/email is complete. You must therefore analyse the facts carefully to identify all the issues and ensure that each one is addressed in your letter/email. It is also necessary to think about the case in the round. For example, it may be necessary to take account of the client's commercial considerations, or that one course of action may be more tax efficient than another.

5.12 Ethics and professional conduct issues

Ethics and professional conduct issues will not arise in every SQE2 assessment scenario. Your task is to identify when they do and to 'exercise judgment to resolve them honestly and with integrity'.

Ethics and professional conduct issues can arise in a Legal Writing context in a variety of ways. A solicitor may be asked by an opponent or a client to give an undertaking in circumstances where it would be inappropriate to do so, for example because the subject matter is beyond the solicitor's control. Or a solicitor may be asked by a client to advise someone else involved in the case or transaction in circumstances where there would be a conflict of interest. Although a solicitor has a duty to act in a client's best interests, that does not mean that you must do everything the client says. In such circumstances it is a matter of explaining why, as a matter of professional conduct, you cannot do what the client asks.

The content of a letter/email should not be such as to place the writer in breach of the rules of professional conduct or to act in an unethical manner. For example, a letter/email should not contain statements which are untrue. Care needs to be taken in a negotiation where it is usual to argue the strengths of the client's case and not to highlight the weaknesses. It is important not to overstep the mark and, in effect, lie or misrepresent the position.

The tone of a letter/email must be considered carefully from an ethics/professional conduct perspective. In its Warning Notice on offensive communications the SRA states that whilst 'robust' communication with opponents is permissible, solicitors 'should ensure such communications do not cross the line by using inflammatory language or being gratuitously offensive, either to the other side or about their client'.

There are a number of client care matters (such as costs) which must be dealt with at the outset of a client's case as a matter of professional conduct (as well as money laundering checks etc) (see The University of Law manual *Oral Skills for Lawyers*, Chapters 3 and 4). Whether you will be required to deal with all or any of them in the SQE2 assessments will depend in the first instance on the scenario. It might be necessary to do so if, for example, you are asked to write a letter to a client following a first meeting. However, you must check your instructions carefully as there may be a specific direction to the effect that such matters do not need to be addressed.

5.13 Example letter

The example letter that follows is based on the following scenario:

The client, Mr Frost, bought his present property five years ago for £350,000. He obtained a home buyer's report from a firm of surveyors, Pelman & Partners. The report stated that there was no evidence of subsidence in the property and that it was not situated in an area where properties had historically been affected by subsidence.

Mr Frost is now trying to sell the property and the firm is acting for him on the sale. He accepted an offer from cash buyer. However, the buyer has just withdrawn her offer. The buyer said that her reason for pulling out of the purchase is that the home buyer's report she commissioned reported that there were cracks in the property indicating subsidence which was consistent with other known cases of subsidence in the area.

Mr Frost believes that Pelman & Partners were negligent in preparing their report five years ago. He thinks that the property may now be unsellable or sellable only at a reduced price and wants to know what action he could take against Pelman & Partners.

[Firm's headed notepaper
Not produced here]

Mr Neil Frost
14, West Lane
Cambridge
CM22 6AD

Ref:21/5678/FRO
24 November 20[XX]

Dear Mr Frost

Claim against Pelman & Partners

Thank you for coming in to see me yesterday. I am writing to advise you further on your claim in relation to the purchase of your house.

Basis for the claim

As a professional firm of surveyors Pelman & Partners owed you a legal duty to carry out the survey to the standard to be expected of a reasonably competent surveyor. You also entered into a contract with them that they would carry out the survey, and this contract contains an implied term that they would carry out the survey with reasonable skill and care. Provided we can demonstrate that a reasonably competent surveyor would have spotted both actual subsidence and a history of subsidence in the area, you will be able to prove that the surveyor was negligent and in breach of contract.

Damages recoverable

In cases where a buyer acquires a property which is defective in some way, the court will typically award the amount by which the buyer 'overpaid' plus interest from the purchase date. To work out the overpayment for your house we will need to find out what the value would have been had the subsidence been known about and subtract this figure from the £350,000 which you actually paid.

Further steps

We need to investigate whether a reasonably competent surveyor would have spotted actual subsidence in your house and a history of subsidence in the area and, if so, what the price for your house would have been taking these issues into account. To do this it will be necessary to instruct a local surveyor to address these two questions, with a view to providing an expert report to the court in due course should proceedings be issued against Pelman & Partners.

Once I have the surveyor's views, I will be able to advise you further on how likely it is your claim will succeed and the amount of damages you are likely to recover.

Please confirm that you are happy for me to instruct a local surveyor as proposed. If so, I will contact some local firms to find out about the likely cost, then contact you to confirm that this is acceptable to you before proceeding.

Please do not hesitate to telephone me if you would like to discuss the contents of this letter.

Yours sincerely

David Brown

Solicitor

5.14 Example email

The example email that follows is based on the following scenario:

Paxton Engineering Ltd is an existing client of the firm. The company wants to allot £1 ordinary shares for cash consideration to its three directors, two of whom are existing shareholders.

A partner, Amy Wiseman, asks a member of her department to review the file and provide her with information which she can use as the basis of a letter to the client on the need for shareholder involvement in relation to:

- amending the company's constitution;
- obtaining authority for the board to allot the shares; and
- disapplying the existing shareholders' right of pre-emption.

The file contains documents relating to the company and its constitution which are not reproduced here.

From: Sanjeev Khan
To: Amy Wiseman
CC:
BC:
Date: 5 October 20[XX]
Subject: Paxton Engineering Ltd – Proposed allotment

Dear Amy

As requested, I have reviewed the Paxton Engineering Ltd (Paxton) file and set out my findings below.

Altering Paxton's constitution

It will not be necessary to alter Paxton's constitution. As it was incorporated on or after 1 Oct 2009, the company is deemed to have unlimited shares to allot, unless the articles of association impose a limit. I have checked Paxton's articles and they do not include any such restriction.

Board's authority to allot shares

It will not be necessary for the shareholders to grant authority to the board to allot the shares. The Companies Act 2006 gives the board this authority, because:

- Paxton is a private limited company
- all of Paxton's existing shareholders have the same class of shares, i.e. ordinary shares
- the proposed allotment will only involve the same class of shares, i.e. ordinary shares
- Paxton's articles of association do not prohibit the proposed allotment.

Existing shareholders' right of pre-emption

It would be sensible to ask the shareholders to pass a special resolution under s 569 Companies Act 2006, authorising the board to allot the shares without giving the existing shareholders their statutory right of first refusal.

Without this special resolution, the board will have to offer each current shareholder a right of pre-emption over the new shares in proportion to their existing shareholding. This would be a convoluted process and an unnecessary one if, as seems to be the case, the existing shareholders are in agreement with the allotment proceeding in accordance with the current plan.

I hope this provides the information you need to send a letter of advice to the client. Please let me know if I can be of further assistance.

Kind regards

Sanjeev

5.15 Example Part 36 letter

It will be evident from the content of this chapter that in order to be effective Legal Writing must be clear, concise and correct. However, in some instances there is the additional requirement that a piece of writing must comply with certain formalities if it is to have its intended legal effect, for example a letter of claim intended to comply with the pre-action protocols (see The University of Law SQE1 manual *Dispute Resolution*).

A common example of a piece of writing needing to comply with legal formalities is a letter making an offer of settlement under Part 36 of the Civil Procedure Rules. You will recall the requirements for a Part 36 offer from SQE1 (see The University of Law SQE1 manual *Dispute Resolution*).

A Part 36 offer is treated as 'without prejudice save as to costs' and it is usual to head the letter in this way. The effect of this is that the trial judge will not be made aware of the offer until the case has been decided, both on liability and quantum. Only when the issue of costs falls to be dealt with will any relevant offer be produced to the judge.

The rules of deemed service apply to a Part 36 offer and therefore it is usual to include in the letter a calculation of the date upon which service will be deemed to have occurred.

The example letter that follows is based on the following scenario:

The claim arises from an accident which took place on the claimant's driveway. The defendant crashed his car into the claimant's house, partially destroying an extension. The claimant has brought proceedings against the defendant alleging negligence and seeking damages of £185,000 plus interest. The defendant is defending the claim alleging that the claimant was responsible for the accident and is counterclaiming for the cost of repairing his car.

The claimant has made a Part 36 offer.

[Firm's headed notepaper
Not produced here]

Maybreth & Co
30 Bridge Street
Plymouth
Devon
PL2X 5PP

Our reference: 1234/PO
Your Ref: CF/GIT/13
12 November 20XX

Dear Sir/Madam

Simpson v Templar
PART 36 OFFER: WITHOUT PREJUDICE SAVE AS TO COSTS

We refer to previous correspondence in this matter.

Our clients are confident that should this matter proceed to trial they will be successful in establishing liability and recovering the full amount claimed from your client. However, in a final attempt to settle the matter we have our clients' instructions to make your client an offer of settlement. For the purposes of CPR, Rule 36.5(1)(b) we confirm that it is our intention that this offer is made pursuant to and should have the consequences set out in Part 36.

In accordance with CPR, Rule 36.5(1)(d) and (e), the offer on the part of our clients is to accept the sum of £175,000 in relation to the whole of their claim for damages, after taking into account your client's counterclaim. For clarity we would confirm that the offer is inclusive of interest.

In accordance with CPR, Rule 36.5(1)(c) the relevant period is 21 days from the date of service. As we are sending this to you today by first-class post we calculate that the offer will be deemed to be served on 15 November 20XX. Please acknowledge and confirm.

Yours faithfully

6 Legal Drafting: Principles

SQE2 syllabus

This chapter will help you to achieve the SQE2 Assessment Objective of demonstrating that you are able to draft a legal document or parts of a legal document for a client.

Learning outcomes

This chapter covers the principles of good drafting and considers the steps which you will need to take when approaching a piece of drafting in legal practice. **Chapter 7** looks in more detail at the specific requirements of the SQE2 Legal Drafting assessments and provides some more specific guidance on the types of legal document which you may be asked to draft. **Chapter 8** contains some examples of completed legal documents.

These chapters should be read in conjunction with **Chapter 2**, which covers the basics of written communication.

By the end of this chapter you should be able to:

- recognise the elements of a common document structure;
- understand different ways to order clauses within a legal document;
- identify different ways of structuring a clause;
- understand how to use precedents;
- use definitions in a legal document correctly; and
- avoid some pitfalls which can make your drafting ambiguous.

6.1 Introduction

Drafting is a core part of a solicitor's work, whatever their area of practice. While there is an overlap between writing and drafting, drafting is the expression used to refer to the task of creating a legal document. This can include preparing such a document from scratch; following a template or precedent; or completing a form.

Good drafting requires a four-stage process:

(1) **Preparation and research:** take full instructions, undertake any further enquiries which are needed, identify the objective(s)/purpose of the legal document, research the law.

(2) **Planning:** decide on the best structure and necessary content.

(3) **Drafting:** clearly and concisely set out the information/points following your plan.

(4) **Checking:** cross-check your document to ensure that it is correct, unambiguous and meets the objectives you identified.

The different stages of this process are considered below. It is recommended in **Chapter 7** as the approach which you follow in the SQE2 assessments.

6.2 Preparation and research

6.2.1 Taking instructions

The first step will always be to take instructions from your client. You must have a clear understanding of what your client wishes to achieve and of all the relevant facts. They may well have reached agreement in principle with another party. Part of your role as a solicitor is to ensure that you identify everything you need to know at this initial stage. You will also be able to identify the potential pitfalls for your client (what happens if an obligation is not fulfilled, for example?) and to address these in your drafting.

⭐ *Example*

Your client instructs you to impose an obligation on a buyer of part of his land to put up a 2.5 metre fence along what will become the common boundary. You must identify the need for further information as to:

(a) what type of fence is required;

(b) the time limit to be imposed;

(c) who will be required to maintain the fence; and

(d) who will obtain planning permission and what happens if planning permission is not granted.

6.2.2 Researching the law

Before you can decide how best to advise your client and/or how to draft any necessary documentation, you must research the relevant law. At the most basic level, you will need to check that the client is permitted by law to do the thing which is the subject of the agreement. For example, a client who runs a paintball company might ask you to draft an agreement for their customers to sign, excluding liability for personal injury and death resulting from negligence in the event of an accident. You would need to advise the client of the Consumer Rights Act 2015, which prevents such exclusions. Otherwise, the client will be left with a document which may be impeccably drafted, but which they cannot enforce.

6.3 Planning

Once you have full instructions and have mastered the current legal position, you can begin to plan your draft. You will now need to select the most appropriate structure.

In some cases, the structure of the legal document will be dictated for you. For example, if you are drafting particulars of claim the form and content which must be followed are set out in the Civil Procedure Rules (CPR). Similarly, if you are drafting a will there are certain clauses which must be included. In neither case would it be appropriate, or to your client's benefit, to draft the document from scratch. You will be using a precedent or template to provide a structure to assist with the drafting, as discussed further below.

On the other hand, you may be asked to draft a legal document to cover a unique situation. In this case, where there may not be a precedent or template which exactly fits the client's objectives, you will still need to have a structure in mind so that you do not omit any important protections for your client.

This chapter sets out a common structure for a legal document in a non-contentious matter. The structures and requirements for some specific legal documents are discussed in **Chapter 7**.

6.3.1 Common document structure

Many legal documents will contain the following elements:

- commencement;
- date;
- parties;
- recitals;
- operative part;
- testimonium;
- schedules; and
- execution and attestation.

As you will see from the commentary below, not all these clauses are essential and you will want to consider whether to incorporate them into your own drafting. However, they have been included for completeness and so that you recognise them when you come across them in a legal document.

6.3.1.1 Commencement, date and parties

A legal document will normally begin with a commencement which describes the nature of the document, for example 'This Agreement', 'This Conveyance'. Alternatively, the document's title can simply be set out as a heading, as in the example below. Deeds may also use the word 'deed' in the title, for example 'This deed of conveyance'.

A space should be left for insertion of the date when the document is completed.

The full names and addresses of the parties should be inserted. (In the case of a company, the address of its registered office should be inserted.)

Example

SERVICE AGREEMENT

DATE:

PARTIES: (1)   *Weyford Products Limited whose registered office is at 32 Bridge House, Wharf Road, Milton, Berefordshire.*

(2)   *Joan Alice Bennet of 8 High Street, Milton, Berefordshire.*

A long and complicated legal document can benefit from an index or table of clauses (preferably at the front).

6.3.1.2   Recitals

Recitals clauses ('Whereas ...') are not essential and you should consider carefully whether or not to include them. You can use them to set out the background facts leading up to the creation of the document and so make it more self-explanatory. For example, in a conveyance of land by a personal representative, the date of the deceased's death and the date on which a grant of representation was obtained could be recited.

Recitals are also sometimes used to introduce and summarise the contents of the operative part of the document but, except in complicated documents, this is generally not necessary and increases the risk of introducing ambiguities.

6.3.1.3   Operative part

The operative part of a legal document is the section which creates the legal rights and obligations.

The contents of the operative part will depend on the nature of the document. For example, a commercial agreement will generally contain:

(a)   conditions precedent (conditions which have to be satisfied before the agreement comes into force);

(b)   agreements (the rights and obligations of the parties);

(c)   representations and warranties (i.e. statements about factual and legal matters which one of the parties requires to be made to them in a legally binding way);

(d)   'boiler-plate' clauses (i.e. standard clauses inserted into all agreements of such a type and dealing with, for example, the service of notices under the agreement, or the jurisdiction for action where the agreement has an international element).

6.3.1.4   Testimonium

A testimonium clause is not essential but, if used, it introduces the signatures of the parties and may describe a particular method of executing where, for example, a company is using its seal as part of its execution.

6.3.1.5   Schedules

Schedules are used, where appropriate, to avoid breaking the continuity of a document with too much detail. The operative part of the document then refers to the schedule, and the schedule contains the detail.

 Example

TENANT'S COVENANTS

The Tenant covenants with the Landlord to observe and perform the covenants set out in Schedule 1.

SCHEDULE 1

1.   To pay the rent ... etc.

Note that the obligation or right is created in the operative part of the document. Only the detail of the obligation or right is put in the schedule.

6.3.1.6   Execution and attestation

A legal document will end with an execution clause. This will refer to the signatures of the parties and any other formalities necessary to give the document legal effect. The wording of this clause will vary depending on the nature of the party executing it, whether the document is executed as a deed, and whether the party's signature is witnessed (or 'attested').

For a legal document executed by an individual and not intended to take effect as a deed, the clause could read:

Signed by ALAN JONES)   (Alan Jones signs here)

in the presence of:)

(Witness signs here)

If the legal document is intended to take effect as a deed the clause could read:

Executed as a deed   )   (Alan Jones signs here)

by ALAN JONES   )

in the presence of:)

(Witness signs here)

Chapter 7 considers the execution of some specific legal documents in more detail.

6.3.2   Order of clauses in the operative part

It is difficult to lay down rules as to the order of clauses. It will vary according to the nature of the legal document, but it is often a matter of common sense and logic.

Deciding on the best structure to adopt when drafting the operative clauses of a legal document is the most important stage in planning your document. Some possibilities are considered below.

6.3.2.1   Chronological order

One possibility is to list topics in chronological order. This is often particularly suitable for a legal document that deals with one simple transaction.

Imagine a contract for the hire of a car. The order of topics could be:

*   parties
*   definitions
*   agreement by Owner to hire out car to Hirer on the terms set out in the agreement
*   payment
*   insurance
*   promises by Owner as to the state of the car at the start of the hire
*   duration of hire
*   what the car can be used for

- who may drive
- Hirer's promises as to the return of the car
- remedies for breach of the agreement.

For a contract such as this, a chronological structure will produce a simpler and less repetitious document than dividing the topics into Owner's Obligations and Hirer's Obligations.

6.3.2.2 Categorical order

A categorical structure sets out the duties and responsibilities in categories. An example of this is a lease.

The structure of a typical lease is:

- parties
- definitions
- the grant of the term by Landlord to Tenant
- Tenant's covenants
- Landlord's covenants
- provisos, e.g. the Landlord's power to forfeit the lease.

Here, the division into landlord's obligations and tenant's obligations is essential. The obligations must be performed throughout the entire term of the lease. There is no chronological order to them.

6.3.2.3 Order of importance

This could be the order used in a simple contract, where the obligations are not to be carried out in any chronological order. An example could be an agreement between employer and employee on severance of employment.

6.3.2.4 Combinations

A legal document may use a combination of the above structures. A contract with a firm of furniture removers could list the firm's obligations in chronological order, for example:

- to pack the contents of the house
- to transport to storage
- to store
- to transport to new house
- to unpack

and then list the owner's obligations.

In a lease, a combination of structure is used: all the tenant's covenants will be put together but will appear in order of importance.

6.3.3 Structuring a clause

When you are structuring clauses and sub-clauses within the operative part:

- use a separate clause for each separate matter
- use sub-paragraphs to avoid long, cumbersome clauses and provisos
- number each clause and sub-clause
- give each clause or group of clauses a heading that correctly defines the subject matter of the clauses, e.g. 'Tenant's Covenants'.

Look at the following two examples and decide which you think is easier to understand.

 Example 1

> *The Licensee shall purchase exclusively from the Grantor all materials used in making the Invention provided that the licensee shall be entitled to relieve itself of its liability to observe this obligation upon giving the Grantor three months' notice in writing.*

 Example 2

> 1. *Subject to Clause 2, the Licensee must purchase exclusively from the Grantor all materials used in making the Invention.*
>
> 2. *The Licensee may end the obligation contained in Clause 1 by giving the Grantor three months' notice in writing.*

Both examples contain the same provisions, but the second is easier to understand because it uses separate numbered clauses for each point.

6.3.3.1   Structuring a clause according to Coode

Read the following clause and think about the structure. Do you think the structure adopted helps to make the meaning clear?

Clause X

The Company shall reimburse the Replacement Value of lost or damaged goods provided that the value of the claim does not exceed £1,000 and the Policyholder notifies the loss within 7 days from (but excluding) the date of its occurrence PROVIDED ALWAYS THAT the above shall not apply to claims made under Clause 10 of this Policy.

This clause starts with a statement of a legal obligation which at first sight appears absolute. The conditions and exceptions attaching to the obligation are not stated until afterwards, so that it is necessary to reconsider the obligation in the light of them. This kind of clause construction is very common in legal drafting, but it is not the most logical way to structure a clause and it makes it more difficult to understand.

In 1843, George Coode wrote a treatise on 'Legislative Expression'; or 'The Language of The Written Law'. His general principle is that a clause should be structured in the following order:

*   circumstances/exceptions (i.e. circumstances where the right or obligation does or does not exist);

*   conditions (i.e. conditions on which the right or obligation depends);

*   obligation or right (i.e. who must do what or who may do what).

Words suitable for introducing circumstances are:

'where ...'

'if ... then'

'when ...' or 'on ...'

Words suitable for introducing an exception are:

'except where ...'

'save where ...'

Words suitable for introducing conditions are:

'if ...'

'provided that ...'

These are two examples of Coode in legislation:

Section 2(1) of the Land Registration and Land Charges Act 1971

If any question arises as to whether a person is entitled to an indemnity under any provision of the Land Registration Act 1925 [circumstance] [...] he [person] may apply to the court to have that question determined [the right].

Section 23(1) of the Matrimonial Causes Act 1973

On granting a decree of divorce ... [circumstance] the court [person] may make any one or more of the following orders ... [right].

This is an example of Coode in a legal document:

15. Compensation on termination of contract

Except where otherwise provided [exception], if before 1 December 2020 this contract is terminated by the Buyer [circumstance], then provided the Seller is not in breach of any of his obligations under this contract [condition] the Buyer must pay the Seller the sum of £5000 [obligation].

The rule produces a logical and, to lawyers, a familiar structure, but it does not have to be followed invariably.

Imagine that an owner of land has employed consultants to design and build an amusement park. The consultants want to control the use of their name in any advertising material issued by the landowner. Their name is to be used only if certain conditions are met.

If the clause were drafted using Coode's rule, it would read:

Only where

(a) the Landowner has given the Consultants advance details of any advertising material it plans to use; and

(b) the Consultants have given their express written approval; and

(c) the Consultants have not ended this Agreement under sub-clause 11(1)

may the Landowner use the Consultants' name in advertising material.

The clause could make the point in a stronger and more natural manner if Coode were ignored and it were drafted to read:

The Landowner may only use the Consultants' name in advertising material where:

(a) the Landowner has given the Consultants advance details of any advertising materials it plans to use; and

(b) the Consultants have given their express written approval; and

(c) the Consultants have not ended this Agreement under sub-clause 11(1).

In other words, the right is set out first, followed by the circumstances in which it may be exercised.

⭐ *Example*

*Coode's structure can be a useful tool in preparing legal documents. The clause set out at the beginning of **6.3.3.1** has been redrafted below using Coode's structure and other techniques to improve its clarity.*

Clause X Claims for lost or damaged goods

Where:

(a) a claim does not exceed £1,000; and

(b) the Policyholder notifies the loss within 7 days from (but excluding) the date of its occurrence; and

(c) the claim is not one made under Clause 10 of this Policy

the Company shall reimburse the Replacement Value.

6.3.4 Precedents, templates and forms

When you are presented a piece of drafting in legal practice, such as an application for an extension of time for service of a defence, your first instinct will probably be to look for a precedent or template. Using these can save much time and effort by avoiding reinventing the wheel although, for the reasons given below, they should not be used uncritically.

In this manual, the term 'precedent' is used to mean an existing legal document whose structure and content can be followed or adapted to the facts of another case or matter. A 'template' provides a pattern for a particular type of document without reference to particular facts. You can find examples of precedents and templates in **Chapters 7** and **8**.

6.3.4.1 Precedents and know-how in legal practice

Many firms hold their own banks of know-how and precedents for their staff to use in similar transactions. These will often be accessible via the firm's intranet. This allows good practice and know-how to be passed on within the firm and a house style to be maintained.

A variety of commercial publications also reproduce versions of prescribed or common legal documents. Some are limited in scope and aim to assist the specialist practitioner, such as *Parker's Will Precedents*. Others are more general in scope, such as *Kelly's Draftsman* which gathers into one book the most frequently needed precedents in general practice (and is also available online via *Kelly's Legal Precedents* on *Lexis+ Legal Research*).

Two complementary publications give comprehensive coverage: *Atkin's Court Forms* and the *Encyclopedia of Forms and Precedents*. Both of these substantial encyclopedias are published by LexisNexis and are available online via *LexisLibrary*. The online texts may be accessed individually or searched in combination (via the Forms and Precedents search form).

In recent years, a variety of online publishers have developed clusters of precedents, templates and other know-how that may be accessed upon payment of a subscription. Prominent in this field are *Practical Law* and *Lexis+ Legal Research*.

6.3.4.2 How to use precedents

Using a precedent can help in the planning of your legal document by giving an example of:

- suitable structure;
- provisions that you have not thought of and that will benefit your client;
- suitable wording; and/or
- legal problems you had not considered.

However, precedents should be used with caution and for this reason they are often described as a 'good servant, but a bad master'. Blindly following a precedent can result in a document which might look good but fails to reflect the client's instructions or has unintended consequences. Here are some guidelines to ensure that the precedent works for you:

- look for a precedent only after you have researched and planned your legal document
- always check that the precedent is up to date and legally correct, particularly if you have borrowed it from another transaction
- adapt the precedent to your transaction, not your transaction to the precedent
- do not copy words from a precedent unless you are sure of their legal effect
- do not change words in a precedent unless you are sure that the change will not have an unexpected legal effect. This is particularly true of precedents for wills
- never assume a precedent cannot be improved
- do not copy clauses that are irrelevant or, worse, are to the disadvantage of your client
- do not adopt inappropriate or archaic wording.

6.3.4.3 Forms

Rather than creating a legal document, the drafting which you carry out in legal practice or in the SQE2 assessments may require you to complete a form, such as a TR1 which is the HM Land Registry form used to transfer the whole of a property where the title is registered. Again, you can use precedents to assist you. Although to a certain extent the form will provide the structure for the drafting you will still need to construct your response to the individual sections carefully, following the guidance on the form. **Chapter 7** looks at some forms which you may come across.

6.4 Drafting

Having carefully prepared and planned the content and structure of your legal document, you can put pen to paper with confidence. Your document should be as easy as possible to read and understand. It is essential that everything you draft is precise, unambiguous and expresses exactly your client's objectives.

You should try to be as concise as possible. Concise legal documents are easier and quicker to read. Your document should, of course, be free from errors of grammar, punctuation and spelling. At best these will undermine the reader's confidence in the document and at worst they may cause ambiguity. **Chapter 2** looks at some of the basic rules of written communication and how to avoid some of the common pitfalls.

Some guidelines to make your drafting clear, professional and effective are set out below. Remember that, in legal practice and in the SQE2 assessments, you may be reviewing draft legal documents prepared by other parties as well as drafting your own documents. You must always check that the draft which you are reviewing accurately reflects your client's instructions. You can use the guidelines below to help you identify any ambiguity and uncertainty which you can correct by amending the document. In legal practice you will often need to take instructions from your client on whether the draft accurately reflects their understanding of what was agreed and their intentions.

6.4.1 Use definitions

A definition can do two things.

First, it can create a 'tag' or 'nickname'. This avoids repetition of lengthy names or phrases. This use is often seen in the description of parties to a legal document.

⭐ *Example*

This agreement is made between

(1) Everett Kingdom Finance plc ('Everett')

(2) Samuel Luke Stowe ('SLS')

In the rest of the document it is only necessary to refer to Everett and SLS.

⭐ *Example*

In this agreement

1. 'the Period of Hire' means from 9am on 1 November 2020 until noon on 23 November 2020.

A subsequent clause might then say something such as 'if the Hirer does not return the Car at or before the end of the Period of Hire ...'.

Secondly, a definition can also create a private dictionary for the document by giving a word something other than its ordinary meaning, or by giving a word an unusually extended or restricted meaning.

⭐ *Example*

In this agreement

'Boat' includes a sailboard.

⭐ *Example*

'Notified' means notice is given in writing by the insured, or its insurance agent, to the insurer.

Where to put the definitions

Definitions that are to apply throughout the document should be put in alphabetical order in a definitions clause at the start of the operative part of the document.

⭐ *Example*

Definitions

In this Agreement

(1) 'Arbitration' means ...

(2) 'Balance Sheet' means ... etc.

If a definition will be used only in one part of a document or in one clause, you can put the definition at the start of the relevant part or clause.

⭐ *Example*

4.1 In this clause, 'Promotional Material' means ...

4.2 The Landowner must ensure that all Promotional Material is ...

In a simple document, a 'tag' may be given to a name or phrase the first time that it is used, and the tag may then be used throughout the rest of the document. For example, in a contract for the sale of land, a clause may say:

The Seller, for the benefit of his adjoining property, 10 Smith Avenue, Morton, N. Yorks ('the Retained Land') reserves a right of way on foot ...

Later clauses can then refer to the Retained Land.

This method should be used only for simple short documents. In a long document, it wastes time to have to search through the clauses to find the one in which the tag was first adopted.

Finally, here are some guidelines for using definitions:

- It is usual to give the definition a capital letter and to use it with the capital letter throughout the document (for example, the Period of Hire). This alerts anybody reading it to the fact that a particular word or expression has been given a particular meaning by the document.

- A definition should only define. It should not be used to create a substantive right or obligation. The right or obligation should be created in the clause that uses the definition.

- Having defined a term remember to use the definition consistently throughout the document.

- When you use a defined term in a clause, check that it makes sense within the clause.

- Do not define by reference to other, undefined terms. So do not define the Retained Land as 'the neighbour's garden', as the reader does not know who the neighbour is, and the extent of the garden may be unclear.

6.4.2 Attach a plan

Legal documents frequently refer to areas of land. It will often be much clearer to define these by reference to a plan than to describe them in words. For example, an agreement which refers to the use of parking bays might attach a plan in which the parking bays are outlined in different colours. It will often make sense to have 'Plan' as a defined term, as you can then refer, for example, to 'the area edged red on the Plan'. Unless the plan is intended to define the extent of the land, you should make it clear that the plan is for illustration purposes only.

6.4.3 Take care with word order

Words or phrases in the wrong place may create ambiguity. Consider the sentence:

We undertake to repair or replace goods shown to be defective <u>within six months of the date of purchase.</u>

It is not clear whether the underlined phrase governs the repair/replacement or the notification of defect. It could be rewritten as:

Where, within six months of the date of purchase, goods are shown to be defective, we will repair or replace them.

(assuming this was the intended meaning).

6.4.4 Do you mean 'and' or 'or'?

Consider:

The Seller may serve notice of termination, recover goods already delivered and retain all instalments already paid.

The use of 'and' in this sentence suggests that the list is conjunctive, i.e. that the seller may do *all* of the things in it. But can they choose to do only some of them?

Compare:

The Seller may serve notice of termination, recover goods already delivered or retain all instalments already paid.

The use of 'or' here suggests that the list is disjunctive, i.e. that the seller may do only one of the things in the list. But it could also mean that they might both serve notice and either recover goods or retain instalments.

To avoid such ambiguity, consider (depending on the meaning required) using phrases such as:

The Seller may do all or any of the following:

or

The Seller may exercise one only of the following rights:

As should be clear from the above, when you are drafting or considering a draft prepared by another party and identify some ambiguity you will need to seek your client's instructions on what they intend.

6.4.5 Avoid the 'undistributed middle'

Take care with provisions 'before/after' a particular date or 'over/under' a particular weight or measure. Consider the following examples:

Where the company delivers the goods before 1 January ... /Where the company delivers the goods after 1 January ...

What happens if it delivers them *on* 1 January?

Goods over 20kg must be sent by rail ... /Goods under 20kg may be sent by air

What about goods weighing exactly 20kg?

This is what is meant by the 'undistributed middle'. Make sure that you address this in your drafting so that no uncertainty arises.

6.4.6 Make deadlines clear

Documents which you draft will often impose deadlines. These need to be expressed as clearly as possible to help the parties and avoid arguments at a later date. Take care to avoid ambiguity.

Consider:

The Buyer must pay a deposit within 7 days of today's date.

Does the 7 days include or exclude today? The answer is unclear which could clearly cause uncertainty for the parties.

For legal and practical reasons, avoid expressing periods of time in the following ways which are similarly unclear:

*   from [a date];
*   by [a date];
*   within [so many days of] or from [a date];
*   until [a date].

It is safer to be clear by using one of the following expressions:

*   from but excluding/not including;
*   from and including;
*   on or after;
*   on or before;
*   within a period of 7 days commencing with;
*   until but excluding/not including;
*   until and including.

So, assuming that today's date was intended to be included in the calculation, the obligation above could be redrafted to say:

The Buyer must pay a deposit within a period of 7 days, beginning with the date of this agreement.

Alternatively, it could simply specify the date and time by which payment must be made:

The Buyer must pay a deposit by 5pm on 14 May 2020.

It is better to specify a precise time than to use an expression such as 'during business hours' since this concept is ambiguous. A good way to test the drafting in these examples would be to ask yourself whether it is clear to the Buyer when payment must be made and to the Seller when to expect payment. If it is not, the clause requires amendment.

6.4.7 Be clear about who must do what

As well as being precise about when a thing must be done, you should also be precise about who does it and avoid ambiguous pronouns.

Consider:

Where the Supplier fails to deliver the Goods to the Customer in accordance with Clause 9 or the Goods delivered do not correspond with the sample, they may terminate this Agreement.

Who may terminate the agreement: the Supplier or the Customer?

Where it is not clear to which noun a pronoun refers, the noun should be repeated. So the clause should be redrafted to read:

Where the Supplier fails to deliver the Goods to the Customer in accordance with Clause 9 or the Goods delivered do not correspond with the sample the Customer may terminate this Agreement.

6.4.8 Be clear whether you are creating an obligation or a discretion.

It is important to distinguish between these two concepts.

An obligation is created by the phrase:

The Customer shall pay a deposit on signing this Agreement. [In other words, the customer has no choice.]

A discretion is created by the phrase:

The Company may retain the deposit if the Customer does not collect the goods on or before 30 June. [In this situation the company has a choice.]

Take care when using 'shall'. It is grammatically correct to use it in the third person to indicate an obligation ('the Tenant shall pay the Rent'), but it is also used in the first person to indicate simple future ('I shall go to London'). Alternatively, you could use 'must' to create an obligation. You can read more about the use of 'shall' and 'will' in **Chapter 2**.

6.4.9 Avoid words of similar sounds or appearance

Words of similar sound or appearance are easily confused and may also confuse a lay client. Examples are mortgagee and mortgagor and lessor and lessee. While these are familiar terms to lawyers, and to commercial clients, consider whether they could be replaced with clearer terms for certain clients:

Avoid	Use instead
'mortgagee/mortgagor'	'lender/borrower'
'lessor/lessee'	'landlord/tenant'

6.4.10 Take care with lists: the ejusdem generis rule

Ejusdem generis is a Latin expression meaning 'of the same kind'.

Consider:

> *In consequence of war, disturbance or any other cause.*

Unless a contrary intention appears, 'any other cause' the ejusdem generis rule means that this will be construed as meaning only causes in the same category as those previously listed. This may not be what the client intended.

To avoid ambiguity, add (as appropriate):

> *whether of the same kind as [the causes] previously listed or not*

> or

> *or any other [cause] provided it is of the same kind as the [causes] previously listed.*

6.5 Checking

The final stage of the four-stage process is to check your work. You should always do this. In **Chapter 2** (at **2.7**), you can find some tips on checking and proofreading your draft legal document. Above all, you must always make sure that your document reflects your client's objectives and their instructions to you.

6.6 Practical considerations

Once your legal document has been drafted what happens next? In legal practice, in non-contentious work, once your draft has been approved by the client it will be submitted to the other side for approval or comment. Depending on the size and complexity of the transaction, the draft may go through many different versions before it is finalised. In the past this was a laborious process, involving different coloured inks and the retyping of many different versions. Usually, these days, drafts are sent and marked up electronically, which is quicker and reduces the risk of changes being missed. Nonetheless, there are some pitfalls to avoid. If you are acting for the party submitting the draft make sure that previous changes which you and your client may have made to the document (for example in track changes) are not visible to the other side unless you want them to be. If you are acting for the party reviewing the draft make sure that all the amendments which you have made are clearly identifiable when you return the draft.

If the legal document needs to be signed or executed a clean copy, known as a 'top copy' or 'engrossment', will be produced. Make sure that you give your client clear advice about any formalities which will need to be followed for the document to be legally effective. For example, if the client's signature must be witnessed, make sure they understand who can act as a witness and the steps they must take.

7 Legal Drafting: the SQE2 Assessments

SQE2 syllabus

This chapter will help you to achieve the SQE2 Assessment Objective of demonstrating that you are able to draft a legal document or parts of a legal document for a client.

Learning outcomes

By the end of this chapter you should be able to:

- approach a piece of drafting in a structured way (using the prepare, plan, draft and check process);

- draft legal documents which are legally accurate and give effect to the client's instructions; and

- understand some of the specific rules and formalities which apply to drafting legal documents in specific subject areas.

7.1 Introduction

The ability to draft legal documents which are precise, comprehensible and legally accurate is a key skill for solicitors. **Chapter 6** explored some general principles of drafting, including how to structure a legal document and how to structure an individual clause. It also suggested a process for drafting legal documents in the SQE2 assessments or in legal practice: prepare, plan, draft and check.

That process is followed in this chapter, which considers the specific requirements of the SQE2 Legal Drafting assessments.

The first part of this chapter looks at:

- the assessments;
- how to use the four-stage drafting process in the SQE2 assessments;
- different forms of drafting which may be tested in the SQE2 assessments; and
- ethical and professional conduct issues.

The second part of this chapter looks at the five practice areas in which Legal Drafting will be assessed and at some specific considerations relating to each one.

Chapter 8 goes on to provide some examples of completed legal documents.

PART I   GENERAL

7.2 The SQE2 assessments

7.2.1 Form

In the SQE2 Legal Drafting assessments candidates will be required to draft a legal document or parts of a legal document. This may take the form of drafting from a precedent or amending a document already drafted but it may also involve drafting without either of these.

Candidates will sit a total of three Legal Drafting assessments in the practice areas below. Questions in these practice areas may draw on underlying black letter law in the Functioning Legal Knowledge (FLK) shown in brackets next to each one:

- one in the context of either Dispute Resolution *(Contract Law and Tort)* or Criminal Litigation *(Criminal Liability)*;
- one in the context of either Property Practice *(Land Law)* or Wills and Intestacy, Probate Administration and Practice *(Trusts)*; and
- one in the context of Business Organisations, Rules and Procedures (including Money Laundering and Financial Services) *(Contract Law)*.

Remember that questions on ethics and professional conduct will be pervasive throughout SQE2.

(See the SRA website for the full syllabus.)

Your instructions and any supporting documents will be provided electronically. You will have 45 minutes in which to complete your answer.

7.2.2 Criteria

In the SQE2 Legal Drafting assessments candidates will be assessed against the following Assessment Criteria:

Skills

(1) Use clear, precise, concise and acceptable language.

(2) Structure the document appropriately and logically.

Application of law

(1) Draft a document which is legally correct.

(2) Draft a document which is legally comprehensive, identifying any ethical and professional conduct issues and exercising judgment to resolve them honestly and with integrity.

You can read more about the SQE2 assessments in **Chapter 1**. In the appendix to that chapter you can see how the Statement of Solicitor Competence applies to the skill of Legal Drafting.

7.3 Overview of the drafting process

In the SQE2 assessments you will be asked to carry out some drafting in three of the practice areas identified above. Although you will not be able to predict the content of the assessments you can prepare for it by thinking about the types of legal document which you may be asked to draft for each practice area and the relevant structure and rules. Some suggestions are provided in the second part of this chapter. You will see that this chapter cross refers to The University of Law SQE1 manuals for the various practice areas. This should reassure you that the SQE2 assessments will not require you to master any new law, but rather that you are being asked to apply the law which you already know in a different and more practical way: to prepare legal documents rather than to answer SBAQs.

The information which you receive in the SQE2 assessments should make it clear whether you are being asked to draft a whole document or part of one, or to amend an existing draft. Whatever the type of question you will find it helpful to adopt the four-stage process suggested in **Chapter 6**: prepare, plan, draft and check. This structured approach will help you to draft a legal document which is legally correct and comprehensive, as required by the Assessment Criteria.

7.3.1 Prepare

In the SQE2 assessments, you may be feeling under time pressure and be tempted to jump straight in and begin drafting right away. However, it is important that you take the time to organise your thoughts and plan the structure and content of your legal document. You might decide in advance that you are going to allocate a certain amount of the 45 minutes allowed, say 10 minutes, to preparation and planning. Allow yourself this time for reflection at the beginning of the assessments and do not be put off if you can see other candidates typing all around you.

There are certain things which you can look out for as you read through the materials provided in the SQE2 assessments. In particular, you may be given instructions on specific aspects of the document you are to draft, such as the basis and calculation of interest in particulars of claim. The materials may specify certain assumptions which you can make, for example that a calculation is correct or that a piece of legislation does not apply. They may also stipulate that you do not need to deal with certain matters (such as costs). It sounds obvious, but make sure that you take these instructions on board and do not waste valuable time in the assessments on unnecessary work.

Make sure that during the preparation stage, you pay attention to any instructions you have received from the client. These may take the form of correspondence, a note of a meeting with the client or a statement. They may be contained in an email from a partner. Remember that the client's instructions should be the starting point for any piece of drafting (see **Chapter 6**). Although you will not, of course, be able to take instructions during the assessments, the information you need should be provided. Focus on what is important to the client and what they want to achieve. For example, in a contract for the sale of goods, could a delay in receiving the goods have a knock-on effect on the client's business? If so, should the contract have a clause addressing this?

Remember that in the SQE2 assessments, as in legal practice, the client's instructions to you may be out of order, repetitive, even garbled if the client is in distress (for example if the client has given a statement at the police station). You should not assume that the legal document which you are drafting has to include all the information which has been provided to you. Avoid simply copying across large chunks of the assessment materials into your draft. Instead, you will need to sift through these to identify what is relevant. For example, you will remember that when you are drafting particulars of claim, you do not need to include evidence. Therefore, if the client has provided you with a proof of evidence, you will need to distinguish between the allegations which make up the client's case (which should be included) and evidence (which will appear later in the witness statements but is not needed for the particulars of claim). Having decided what information is relevant, your role is to convert this into a legal document which is concisely drafted; achieves the client's intentions; and is legally correct and comprehensive.

7.3.2 Plan

You will probably find it helpful to set out a structure before you begin to draft, using bullet points to remind you of the points you need to cover in each area. This will help you to ensure that the contents of the legal document are correct. Remember that one skills criterion against which you will be assessed is to 'structure the legal document appropriately and logically'. In some cases, this will involve creating an appropriate structure, and in others it will involve following a predetermined one.

Chapter 6 considered a common structure for a non-contentious document and the usual order of clauses. In this chapter and **Chapter 8** you will find some templates and examples for common types of legal document.

One type of drafting which you may be asked to carry out is to complete a form. For example, you may be asked to complete part of all of an application for legal aid in criminal proceedings (form CRM 14). Although part of this exercise may simply involve completing boxes you will also need to plan the contents of the more detailed parts of the form, such as the answers to question 29 ('Why do you want legal aid?'), to ensure that nothing is overlooked.

7.3.3 Draft

Once you have a clear structure mapped out you can begin to draft. In this context, you should be thinking of the layout and language of your legal document. The layout may be a standard one (such as for a will). It may be dictated by rules: for example the CPR in Dispute Resolution. It may be provided, or partly provided, by a precedent supplied in the SQE2 assessment. However, there are some common rules which apply to all the drafting which you will carry out, in the SQE2 assessments or in legal practice.

Layout

Focus on making the legal document as easy to navigate and understand as possible, by using numbered paragraphs and sub-headings (for more detail on these, see **Chapter 6**).

Language

The SQE2 Assessment Criteria require candidates to use 'clear, precise and acceptable language'. Focus, in the time available, on making your draft as easy to read as possible (see **Chapter 2** for some tips on this).

Definitions

Almost every legal document which you draft will include some defined terms. These are discussed in detail in **Chapter 6**. Think about which terms require definition ('The Playground', 'The First Deadline' and so on). If you are amending or continuing an existing draft you should usually adopt the existing definitions, unless there is a good reason not to.

Remember that defined terms are usually capitalised, for example, 'The Retained Land'. This makes them easy to spot quickly in the legal document, and readily identifiable as defined terms.

Having defined the terms, remember to use them all the way though the legal document: forgetting to do so is a common error.

Formalities

You will need to consider how to ensure that the legal document you are drafting is valid and effective, and to incorporate or select the appropriate provisions to achieve this at the end of the document. For example, are there provisions as to execution which need to be included? In a statement of case have you included a statement of truth and completed this correctly? The rules specific to the practice areas are considered in the second part of this chapter.

7.3.4 Check

In legal practice, and in the SQE2 assessments, it is vital to proofread your legal document and you should allocate some of the 45 minutes allowed to this. Try to read the document through the client's eyes: does it make sense?

Here is a quick checklist:

- Has information from your instructions been carried over accurately? Are names and dates correct?
- Have you used any defined terms correctly and consistently?
- Does the numbering work?
- Do the cross references to other parts of the document work?
- Are there any errors of spelling or grammar?

7.4 Forms of drafting in the SQE2 assessments

You have seen that the SQE2 Assessment Specification gives a broad description of the types of drafting which you might be asked to carry out: 'Candidates will be required to draft a legal document or parts of a legal document. This may take the form of drafting from a precedent or amending a document already drafted but it may also involve drafting without either of these.' This section considers the approach you can take to these different forms of drafting, whilst still following the basic process of prepare, plan, draft and check.

In the SQE2 assessments you may be asked to continue drafting a legal document which is partially complete. You will obviously look to see what has already been done: for example, have some terms already been defined? If so, you should use these in the section you draft. If the legal document is a form, the areas for you to complete may be greyed out and/or there may be notes which give you guidance on what to include. Use these 'flags' to help you. You will want to note them on your initial read through and check that you have complied with them as you proofread your completed draft.

You may be presented with a list of specimen clauses, such as clauses in a will or different orders for directions. You may be asked to select the appropriate ones and to incorporate these into your draft, amending them as necessary. The process of selecting the best clause is similar to the technique you will have used for answering SBAQs in the SQE1 assessments. Focus on the facts of the case and the client's instructions to choose the best option.

You may be presented with an existing draft and asked to amend this. The instructions in the SQE2 assessments should make it clear whether you need to show your changes to the draft. A danger when reviewing an existing draft, in legal practice or in the SQE2 assessment, is that you are beguiled by what is already on the page, and do not stop to consider what the legal document or clause needs to contain. To avoid this, you should still use the four-stage process as set out below.

Prepare: check what the client's instructions are – do not assume that these will be reflected in the existing draft.

Plan: in the planning stage, you might find it helpful to step back from the existing draft: remind yourself what this type of legal document or clause should contain and check your list of points against the version that has been provided.

Draft: having assessed how much amendment is required, you can now decide whether to redraft the whole thing or simply to tweak it, changing a few aspects until the drafting works.

Check: make sure that any redrafted section makes sense and, importantly, that it works with the rest of the document. For example, are there any defined terms in the existing document which must be used in the redrafted section? Is this section consistent with other clauses or does it now contradict them?

Remember that these exercises may be combined, so you may be asked to amend the existing definitions clause in a contract and then to draft the obligations clause.

The SQE2 Assessment Criteria make it clear that you may be asked to draft a legal document without a precedent or an existing draft ('drafting from scratch'). You can still follow the four-stage process above. As ever, your starting point is your instructions, and you are aiming to produce a legal document which is legally correct and gives effect to the client's intentions.

You will of course need to identify the type of legal document you are being asked to draft, if this is not clear from your instructions. Check whether you are being asked to draft the whole document or only part of it. For example, if you have only been asked to draft the part of particulars of claim dealing with breach and causation do not waste time on the heading or introductory paragraphs.

Depending on the type of legal document you have been asked to prepare, you may have an existing structure in your mind. You should also apply any rules particular to that practice area (such as the rules relating to the layout and contents of court documents, contained in the CPR – see **7.6**).

If the legal document you have been asked to draft is of a type you have not come across before, do not panic. In legal practice, you may not have come across, or have a template for, every situation which presents itself and the SQE2 assessments are testing whether you will be able to respond to these challenges when they appear. Remind yourself of the common elements of most documents as well as the basics of defining terms and structuring clauses and use these as your guide. Details of these can be found in **Chapter 6**.

7.5 Ethical and professional conduct issues

Ethical and professional conduct issues will not arise in every SQE2 assessment scenario. Your task is to identify when they do and to, 'exercise judgment to resolve them honestly and with integrity'.

As you will recall, the SRA Principles require solicitors to act in a way that upholds public trust in the solicitors' profession (Principle 2); with honesty (Principle 4); and with integrity (Principle 5). The SRA Code of Conduct for Solicitors, RELs and RFLs provides (paragraph 1.2) that, as part of maintaining trust and acting fairly, solicitors do not abuse their position by taking advantage of clients or others and (paragraph 2.4) that they do not mislead their clients, the court or others, either by their own acts or omissions or by allowing or being complicit in the acts or omissions of others (including their clients).

How do these provisions come into play in the context of legal drafting? In the practice area of Dispute Resolution, a solicitor must only make assertions or put forward statements, representations or submissions to the court or others which are properly arguable. So, for example, a solicitor should not allege in a statement of case that the opponent has acted fraudulently, unless there is an evidential basis for this.

Ethical issues can sometimes arise when legal documents are being amended and negotiated between the parties. Solicitors must not attempt to mislead the other side by concealing amendments they have made to the draft, for example by writing a covering letter which draws attention to some amendments and not to others. Nor should they take advantage of a clear mistake made by the other side. So, for example if the seller's solicitor submits a draft contract which states that the purchase price is £100,000 when the agreed figure is £1,000,000, the buyer's solicitor should point this out. If the solicitor does not do so, the other side may subsequently be able to claim rectification of the document to incorporate an omitted provision or to allege that the agreement is a nullity, so enabling them to resist specific performance.

Ethical and professional conduct issues can also arise in the context of undertakings. If you are asked to draft an undertaking in the SQE2 assessments or in legal practice, remember that you should only give an undertaking if you have your client's express authority to do so. The subject matter of the undertaking must be within your control. For example, it is customary in a property transaction for the seller's solicitor to provide the buyer's solicitor with an undertaking to redeem any charges over the property. The solicitor should only undertake to redeem the charges once the completion monies have arrived and should only undertake to send the necessary documents to the buyer's solicitors when they are received. In this way, the seller's solicitor is not promising to do anything outside their control.

Under paragraph 6.1 of the Code, which deals with conflict of interests, a solicitor should not act where there is an own interest conflict or a significant risk of such a conflict. This provision might come into play when a solicitor is drafting a will and the client wishes to make a gift of significant value to the solicitor or someone connected with them, such as a member of their family. What should the solicitor do in those circumstances? They should satisfy themselves that the client has taken independent advice before proceeding.

A client may commonly wish to appoint their solicitor as executor under their will. Again, this can give rise to a potential own interest conflict as the solicitor will wish to charge for their services acting as executor. In that situation the solicitor must ensure that the client has made the decision to appoint them on a fully informed basis, having explained the options available to the client as to the choice of executor and recording the advice that has been given.

Finally, in the context of will drafting, you should, of course, take care that you are acting only on the instructions of the testator themselves and not from another purporting to give instructions on their behalf.

You can read more about ethical and professional conduct issues in The University of Law SQE1 manual *Ethics and Professional Conduct*.

PART II   THE PRACTICE AREAS

In the SQE2 assessments you will be required to carry out three pieces of legal drafting on three separate days. One of these will be from the practice area of Business Organisations, Rules and Procedures. One will be from either Dispute Resolution or Criminal Litigation; and one from either Property Practice or Wills and Intestacy, Probate Administration and Practice.

This section considers each of the practice areas in turn. It looks at some of the formalities which must be observed in relation to any legal documents which may be drafted in those practice areas to ensure that they have legal effect. It also provides some templates for common documents. For Dispute Resolution the rules of drafting set out in the CPR are also considered.

It is not possible to cover in this manual every type of document which you may be asked to draft in the SQE2 assessments. However, **Chapter 8** contains worked examples of some common legal documents from the different practice areas. A more detailed explanation of the underlying law in relation to these documents can be found in the relevant University of Law SQE1 manuals and reference to specific chapters of these is made below.

7.6   Dispute Resolution

The CPR are the starting point for drafting any legal document for use in the civil courts, in legal practice and the SQE2 assessments. They set out rules on the form of any document prepared by a party for filing or use at court. These include, unsurprisingly, the requirement that all documents should be fully legible and should normally be typed, but also that they should be on A4 paper of durable quality and be securely bound.

The CPR also set out specific requirements for the presentation and contents of statements of case (by way of information this is CPR Part 16). You will recall from SQE1 that the statements of case are the documents in which the parties set out their cases and that these are served between the parties and filed at court. The claimant begins by serving the claim form and particulars of claim. If the defendant contests the claim, they serve a defence. The claimant may then serve a reply. If the defendant wishes to make a claim against the claimant, they will serve a counterclaim. To contest this, the claimant must serve a defence to counterclaim.

In addition to statements of case, Dispute Resolution solicitors draft other court documents which must also comply with the relevant rules set out in the CPR. These include application notices, witness statements, orders and lists of documents.

This section considers the rules which apply to the drafting of statements of case generally. It looks at the specific rules which apply to the particulars of claim and the defence, to witness statements and to the wording of the statement of truth and the claim for interest. Examples of other court documents not covered here, such as a request for further information, can be found in The University of Law SQE1 manual *Dispute Resolution*.

7.6.1   The CPR: general rules for drafting statements of case

7.6.1.1   Content

A statement of case must:

- be as brief and concise as possible and confined to setting out the bald facts and not the evidence of them;

- contain no more than one allegation per paragraph or sub-paragraph, so far as possible;

- set out the facts and matters alleged in chronological order (as far as reasonably possible);

- deal with the claim on a point-by-point basis, to allow a point-by-point response; and
- state any matter which, if not stated, might take another party by surprise.

7.6.1.2 Form

A statement of case must:

- be set out in separate consecutively numbered paragraphs and sub-paragraphs;
- (where a party is required to give reasons,) state the allegation first and then list the reasons one by one in separate numbered sub-paragraphs;
- have all numbers, including dates, expressed as figures;
- use headings, abbreviations and definitions where they will assist;
- have the pages numbered consecutively; and
- be signed in the name of the firm that prepared it.

The rule about expressing numbers as figures can cause confusion when it comes to dates. The day should be expressed as a figure, but not the month, so for example you should write '14 May 2021' and not '14/5/21'.

7.6.2 The case heading

Unless you are completing a form, such as a claim form or an application notice, you will need to include the case heading, or title of the proceedings, on each court document which you draft.

For example:

IN THE HIGH COURT OF JUSTICE   20XX No 876

QUEEN'S BENCH DIVISION

READING DISTRICT REGISTRY

BETWEEN

INDUSTRIAL MANUFACTURING LIMITED

Claimant

and

HEATECHS LIMITED

Defendant

PARTICULARS OF CLAIM

Using the correct heading enables the court to file the document correctly once it is received. You will see that it identifies:

- whether the claim is in the High Court, the County Court Money Claims Centre (for money only claims) or the appropriate County Court;
- if the claim is in the High Court, which division;

- if it is in the High Court whether it is in the Central Office (London) or in a District Registry;

- the claim number: this will be allocated by the court when it issues the claim form;

- the full names of the parties: they are then referred to as the 'Claimant(s)' and the 'Defendant(s)' throughout;

- the type of document: this should be in capital letters. It can also be put between tramlines.

If you are asked to draft a case heading in the SQE2 assessments, make sure that you incorporate the necessary details, such as the claim number, the appropriate court and the correct names of the parties from the information provided.

7.6.3   The statement of truth

Various legal documents, including statements of case, must be verified by a statement of truth, which must be in the witness's own language, signed and dated. Failure to include a statement of truth means that the court may strike out the document and, even if not, the claimant is precluded from relying upon its contents. It is therefore very important that this is included and drafted correctly. The forms of the statement of truth for various documents and the rules as to who must sign them are set out in the CPR (by way of information this is CPR PD 22).

Template

STATEMENT OF TRUTH

[I believe] [The claimant/defendant believes] that the facts stated in this [name of the document] are true. I understand that proceedings for contempt of court may be brought against anyone who makes, or causes to be made, a false statement in a document verified by a statement of truth without an honest belief in its truth.

Signed: [Signature]

[PRINT NAME]

[Position: for example director of the claimant/defendant company OR partner in the firm of [name of firm]]

This statement of truth was signed on [date].

You can find a detailed explanation of how to complete the statement of truth in Chapter 3 of the SQE1 manual. If you are asked to complete a statement of truth in the SQE2 assessments check whether you have instructions on who will sign it and make sure that you complete the form appropriately, inserting the correct names and, for example, selecting the correct option from 'I believe/ the claimant believes/ the defendant believes'. This is easy to overlook. Unless specifically instructed otherwise you should leave the spaces for the signature and the date blank, although you can insert the signatory's name and the position held, if appropriate.

7.6.4   The claim form and particulars of claim

The claim form is the document which starts the proceedings. It is created by completing form N1. You can find a commentary on the content of the claim form in Chapter 3 of the SQE1 manual.

The particulars of claim can be included in the claim form but in more detailed claims are usually set out in a separate document.

All particulars of claim follow some basic rules, as set out in the template below.

7.6.4.1   Template

Heading

Name of court, claim number and title of the proceedings

The title: PARTICULARS OF CLAIM

Content

- Must include a concise statement of the facts on which the claimant relies
- Should be divided into numbered paragraphs
- So far as possible each paragraph or sub-paragraph should contain no more than one allegation
- The facts and other matters alleged should be set out as far as reasonably possible in chronological order
- Where particulars are given of an allegation (such as breach or loss and damage), the allegation should be stated first and followed by each particular listed in separate numbered sub-paragraphs
- Have all numbers, including dates, expressed as figures
- Where a claim is based upon a written agreement, a copy of the contract or documents constituting the agreement should be attached
- Where a claim is based upon an oral agreement, set out the contractual words used and state by whom, to whom, when and where they were spoken
- Must include a claim for interest if the claimant is seeking interest
- Should be dated

Ending

- Statements of case drafted by a legal representative as a member or an employee of a firm should be signed in the name of the firm not the individual
- Must be verified by a statement of truth, the form of which is as follows:

I believe/ the Claimant believes that the facts stated in these particulars of claim are true. I understand that proceedings for contempt of court may be brought against anyone who makes, or causes to be made, a false statement in a document verified by a statement of truth without an honest belief in its truth.

Signed: [Signature]

[PRINT NAME]

[Position: for example director of the claimant company OR partner in the firm of [name of firm]]

This statement of truth was signed on [date].

- Must include the claimant's address for service

7.6.4.2 Particulars of claim for different causes of action

The precise contents of the particulars of claim will depend upon the relevant cause of action. You may need to consider the materials provided in the SQE2 assessments to analyse what the cause of action is: whether this is negligence or breach of contract. If the claim is for breach of contract you will need to consider whether the claim is specified or unspecified. A specified claim is a debt claim, in which the precise compensation sought (including interest) can be calculated: **see 7.6.4.3**. An unspecified claim is a claim for damages in which the precise amount which the claimant seeks cannot yet be quantified.

You can find an explanation of what the particulars of claim for each cause of action should cover and see how the particulars of claim in a breach of contract claim could look in practice, in Chapter 5 of the SQE1 manual.

The particulars of claim in a specified (debt) claim will conform to the same basic pattern as particulars of claim in an unspecified claim, but in a slightly simplified form.

- It will set out the parties to the contract, their status, the formation of the contract and the existence of the relevant express and implied terms in the same way as for an unspecified claim.

- The claimant will assert that they performed their side of the contract, for example providing goods or services. If the defendant has paid part of the amount due under the contract (part performance) this should be stated as well. The claimant should set out when they submitted their invoice or invoices.

- The claimant should then set out the defendant's breach: their failure to pay. The claimant does not need to go on to set out particulars of breach, or consequences of breach or the claim for loss and damage. The claimant can simply state that it claims the sum due from the defendant.

Chapter 8 contains examples of particulars of claim in a negligence claim (**8.1**). Again, the pattern will be familiar to you, but rather than asserting a breach of contract the claimant will specify the duty which the defendant owed and then set out how that duty was breached. The claimant will go on to plead causation and loss and to seek interest.

7.6.4.3 Interest

The CPR provide that where the remedy sought by the claimant is either damages or the repayment of a debt, the court may award interest on the sum outstanding, but only if it is claimed. The particulars of claim must therefore contain a claim for interest and must specify the basis upon which interest is claimed.

The claim for interest, which comes at the end of the particulars of claim, is easy to overlook but must be included to ensure that the client is fully compensated. Pay attention to any information in your instructions which is relevant to the claim for interest. You will need to identify the basis upon which interest is claimed, as this must be stipulated in the particulars of claim. You should also identify whether the claim is for damages (unspecified) or a debt claim (specified) as this affects the way the claim for interest is drafted.

The particulars of claim in a specified claim must include an interest calculation. You can find an explanation on how interest is claimed in Chapter 5 of the SQE1 manual, together with an explanation of how interest can be calculated in a specified claim. While this may seem complicated, it enables a defendant who wishes to pay the debt which is the subject of the claim to calculate the precise amount due.

In an unspecified claim, the standard wording for the claim for interest is as follows. The section in brackets should be altered if, for example, the claimant is applying the contract rate of interest instead.

Template

In respect of damages awarded the Claimant is entitled to interest pursuant to [s.35A of the Senior Courts Act 1981/ s.69 of the County Courts Act 1984] at such rates and for such period as the Court thinks just.

7.6.5 The defence

The defence is the statement of case in which the defendant sets out their response to the case put forward by the claimant in the particulars of claim. Again, the CPR govern the content of the defence. In particular they prescribe three ways in which the defendant can respond to the allegations which the claimant has made in the particulars of claim. You will recall from SQE1 that every allegation must be dealt with and the defence must state, for each allegation, whether it is:

(a) denied;

(b) not admitted; or

(c) admitted.

Remember that when a defendant denies an allegation, they must state

• their reasons for doing so; and

• their own version of events if different from that given by the claimant.

A non-admission is made where the defendant has no knowledge of the particular matter alleged.

To avoid confusion the defence will usually adopt any definitions used in the particulars of claim (such as 'the Contract' or 'the First Amendment').

A template for a defence is set out below. You can find more detail on the purpose and content of the defence and see an example of one in Chapter 5 of the SQE1 manual.

Template

Heading

Name of court, claim number and the names of the parties

The title: DEFENCE

Content

- Must be as brief and concise as possible and confined to setting out the bald facts and not the evidence

- The facts and other matters alleged should be set out as far as reasonably possible in chronological order

- Where particulars of claim make allegations on a point-by-point basis, answer each and every point

- Where particulars of claim use definitions, continue with these

- Should be divided into numbered paragraphs

- Have all numbers, including dates, expressed as figures

- Must state (a) which of the allegations in the particulars of claim are denied; (b) which allegations are not admitted [because of lack of knowledge]; and (c) which allegations are admitted

- Must state for each allegation denied (a) the reasons for doing so; and (b) if putting forward a different version of events from that given by the claimant, must state that version

- Give details of the expiry of any relevant limitation period relied on

- Give details of any allegations of contributory negligence or failure by the claimant to mitigate its loss

Ending

- Should be signed in the name of the solicitors' firm

Must be verified by a statement of truth, the form of which is as follows:

STATEMENT OF TRUTH

I believe/ the Defendant believes that the facts stated in this Defence are true. I understand that proceedings for contempt of court may be brought against anyone who makes, or causes to be made, a false statement in a document verified by a statement of truth without an honest belief in its truth.

Signed:

[PRINT NAME]

[Position: for example director of the defendant company OR partner in the firm of [name of firm]]

This statement of truth was signed on [*date*].

7.6.6   The defence and counterclaim, reply and defence to counterclaim

The defendant will make a counterclaim where they wish not only to defend the claim, but also to make their own claim against the claimant. For example, a plumber who installed a bathroom sues their client for payment of their invoice. The client defends the claim and also counterclaims for damages for losses arising from the plumber's negligent installation of the bathroom. The roles can be reversed, so if the client sues the plumber first, the plumber can counterclaim for payment of their invoice.

The defendant's defence and counterclaim will be set out in one document (the defence and counterclaim). You can read about the structure of a defence and counterclaim in Chapter 5 of the SQE1 manual and you can find an example of a defence and counterclaim in a negligence claim in **Chapter 8 (8.1.2)**.

If the claimant wishes to defend the counterclaim they must serve a defence to counterclaim. This is often combined with a reply.

You will recall that a reply is the statement of case which the claimant may file to respond to the defence, but it is under no obligation to do so. You can read more about the reply and defence to counterclaim in Chapter 5 of the SQE1 manual and you can see an example of a reply and defence to counterclaim in **Chapter 8 (8.1.3)**.

7.6.7   Witness statements

You will recall that if a party wishes to call a witness to give evidence at trial, they must serve a witness statement on the other parties setting out the evidence which that witness intends to give. Although witness statements are not statements of case, some of the same rules as to their content and presentation apply. Witness statements are also used in support of most interim applications and the same rules for their drafting apply.

The CPR prescribe the contents of witness statements and these are set out in the template below.

Template

Top RH corner

On whose behalf made (Claimant / Defendant)

Initials and surname of witness

Number

Exhibit/s (these are usually defined by giving the witness's initials and then a number, such as 'AEB 1')

Date

Heading

- Name of court, claim number and the names of the parties

- The title: WITNESS STATEMENT

Opening paragraph

- Full name, address, occupation or description of witness and state if a party or an employee of a party

Content

- The statement must, if practicable, be in the witness's own words
- The statement should be expressed in the first person ('I')
- A statement is the equivalent of the oral evidence which that witness would, if called, give in evidence
- The statement must indicate which of the statements in it are made from the witness's own knowledge and which are based on information or belief, naming the source if appropriate
- The process by which the statement was prepared must be included, for example face to face or over the telephone with the party's solicitor
- The statement should normally follow the chronological sequence of events
- The statement should be divided into numbered paragraphs
- Numbers should be expressed as figures ('3 stages' not 'three stages')
- Any documents that are attached are formally exhibited (for example, 'AEB 1')

Ending

- The witness must verify their witness statement by providing a statement of truth, the format of which is as follows:

STATEMENT OF TRUTH

I believe that the facts stated in this witness statement are true. I understand that proceedings for contempt of court may be brought against anyone who makes, or causes to be made, a false statement in a document verified by a statement of truth without an honest belief in its truth.

Signed:

[PRINTED NAME OF WITNESS]

This statement of truth was signed on [date].

There are special provisions that apply when the statement cannot be given in English. In such cases, the statement should be drafted in the witness's own language with the date and the details of the translation being included in the statement.

You can find a description of the form and content of a witness statement and an illustration of one in Chapter 9 of the SQE1 manual.

7.7 Criminal Litigation

In the SQE2 assessments you may be asked to draft the whole or part of legal documents relating to various stages of the criminal litigation process. Rather than preparing formal statements of case, such drafting may well involve completing a form, such as a Bail Appeal Notice or an application for legal aid in criminal proceedings. While this may appear to be a simple form of drafting it in fact requires a condensed approach: as knowledge of the law and application to the facts are 'packed in' to the answers inserted into the form.

You can find an example of an application for legal aid in criminal proceedings in **Chapter 8** (**8.2.2**). (Note that while in practice you are very likely to apply for legal aid online, for ease of reference the hard copy form CRM14 has been used.) You can see that question 29, 'Why do you want legal aid?', requires a detailed response. The applicant can select one or more reasons from the list of possible reasons. The guidance on the form requires an explanation to be given for each reason selected and for any evidence in support to be mentioned. In order to address reason 1, 'It is likely that I will lose my liberty if any matter in the proceedings is decided against me', the solicitor must first analyse the likely sentence which will be imposed if the client is found guilty. This in turn requires an analysis of the sentencing guidelines for the particular offence.

This manual cannot cover every situation that may be required but **Chapter 8** provides examples of some common legal documents:

- application for legal aid (**8.2.2**)
- bail appeal notice (**8.2.4**)
- defence statement (**8.2.5**)
- application to exclude hearsay evidence following notice (**8.2.6**)
- application to exclude evidence of a defendant's bad character (**8.2.7**)

For illustration, these examples are complete documents, but in the time available in the SQE2 assessments you may only be asked to draft certain sections of a legal document.

The documents are based on the case study of Gary Dickson who has been charged with assault occasioning actual bodily harm. To give you the background you have also been provided with the following documents:

- police station attendance pro forma personal details (**8.2.1**)
- Gary's statement to his solicitor (**8.2.3**)
- prosecution notice to introduce hearsay evidence (**8.2.6**)
- prosecution notice to introduce evidence of a defendant's bad character (**8.2.7**)

Again, these may be more detailed than any background documents you may be asked to consider in the SQE2 assessments.

A more detailed explanation in relation to these documents can be found in The University of Law SQE1 manual *Criminal Practice*.

7.8 Wills and Intestacy, Probate Administration and Practice

In the SQE2 assessments you may be asked to draft or amend all or part of a will, or any of the documentation involved in the administration of estates and trusts. This manual cannot cover every situation that may be required, but some examples of common legal documents are set out in **Chapter 8**.

Chapter 8 includes a simple will (**8.3.1**). You can read more about will drafting, including the structure of a will and common provisions to be included, in The University of Law SQE1 manual *Wills and the Administration of Estates*, Chapter 5. It is very important that the provisions in the will are clear and accurately reflect the testator's intentions, since, as you will recall, the court has very limited powers to look at external evidence to interpret the will, or to rectify it. In the SQE2 assessments, as in legal practice, it is important to pay attention to the testator's instructions.

You will recall that there are three requirements for a valid will: a testator must have the necessary capacity and intention and must observe the formalities for execution of wills laid down by statute. You can read more about these requirements in Chapter 1 of the SQE1 manual.

The template for an attestation clause below reflects the required formalities: the testator signs the will or acknowledges their signature in the presence of two witnesses. The two witnesses must be present at the same time. Next, the witnesses must sign the will in the presence of the testator.

Template

Signed by me [insert name of testator] in our joint presence and then by us in [his/hers]

[PRINT NAME OF TESTATOR] —————

[PRINT NAME OF WITNESS 1] ————

[PRINT NAME OF WITNESS 2] ————

If there is doubt, after the testator's death, that the formalities of execution were carried out correctly then an affidavit of due execution will be required to satisfy the Probate Service that the will was duly executed. You can find an example of such an affidavit in **Chapter 8 (8.3.3)** and more information in Chapter 8 of the SQE1 manual.

If a testator wishes to add to or change a will in a minor way, they may execute a codicil. You can find an example of a codicil in **Chapter 8 (8.3.2)**. A codicil must be executed in the same way as a will. You can read more about the preparation and effect of codicils in Chapter 3 of the SQE1 manual.

Making a will gives the testator the opportunity to select executors to carry out the administration of the estate and to appoint trustees of any trust created by the will, for example to manage property until young beneficiaries reach a specified age. The will should contain provisions to deal with the powers of the executors and trustees and, where appropriate, to vary their statutory powers and duties. You can find a discussion of clauses appointing executors and trustees, and setting out their powers, in Chapter 5 of the SQE1 manual.

After a person has died, their beneficiaries may decide that they wish to rearrange the dispositions in the deceased's will, in order, for example, to save inheritance tax or to benefit another member of the family instead. In those circumstances a deed of variation can be prepared. You can find an example of such a deed in **Chapter 8 (8.3.4)** and read about the relevant considerations in Chapter 7 of the SQE1 manual.

Chapter 8 of the SQE1 manual also deals with the administration of the estate and obtaining the grant: including the completion of the IHT 400 and the application forms for the grant (PA1P and PA1A).

7.9 Property Practice

In the SQE2 assessments you may be asked to draft or amend documents for a residential or commercial property transaction. The title may be leasehold or freehold.

You will recall from your study of Property Practice for SQE1 that the two milestones of a conveyancing transaction are exchange of contracts and completion. You may be asked to draft the legal documents to effect each one: the contract and the transfer.

The contract for sale is usually prepared by the seller's solicitor. It must be in writing, contain all agreed terms and be signed by all parties. It will normally comprise the particulars of sale, standard conditions of sale and the special conditions of sale. **Chapter 8** (**8.4.1**) includes an example of a contract and commentary on the way it has been completed. You can read more about preparation for and exchange of contracts in Chapter 4 of The University of Law SQE1 manual *Property Practice*.

The transfer deed is traditionally prepared by the buyer's solicitor (unless the transfer deed is to be annexed to the contract which is normal in a transfer of part when the transfer deed is then normally prepared by the seller's solicitor). It must be a deed and where the land is registered it must comply with Land Registry requirements. For the transfer of the whole of a registered freehold title Land Registry Form TR1 is used (TP1 is used for transfers of part). It must reflect the terms of the contract and the title deeds. You can find an example transfer, and a commentary on the drafting, in **Chapter 8** (**8.4.2**) and read more in Chapter 5 of the SQE1 manual.

You will recall that to be valid in law a deed must make it clear that it is a deed; be signed by the parties; and be delivered. The rules which apply to execution will depend upon whether the deed is to be executed by an individual or by a company.

An individual executes a deed by signing it and having their signature witnessed by an independent witness, who also signs the deed to signify that they were present when the deed was signed. You can see this in the example transfer deed in **Chapter 8** (**8.4.2**). A company may execute a deed in one of the three ways set out in the templates below.

Templates

1. ***By affixing a company seal***

   Executed as a deed by affixing the common seal of *(insert name of company)* in the presence of:

Common seal of company

   _____

   Signature of director

   _____

   Signature of [director][secretary]

2. ***By being signed by a director and the secretary, or by two directors of the company: provided that the document is expressed to be executed by the company***

   Executed as a deed by *(insert name of company)* acting by [a director and its secretary] [two directors]

Signature	
	director
Signature	
	[secretary][director]

3. ***By being signed by a single director in the presence of a witness who then attests that signature***

Executed as a deed by *(insert name of company)* acting by a director

In the presence of

Signature of witness

Signature
director

Name (in BLOCK CAPITALS)

Address

You can read more about the formalities of executing a deed in Chapter 5 of the SQE1 manual.

You may also be asked to draft a lease or specific clauses from one. Chapter 6 of the SQE1 manual sets out the usual structure of a lease and the types of covenant it will often contain. You will recall that if the tenant wishes to assign their interest in the lease, the landlord's consent will usually be required. Chapter 8 of the SQE1 manual considers licences to assign and the key provisions they should contain.

Undertakings are frequently provided in the course of a property transaction. The solicitor acting for a tenant will often provide an undertaking to meet the landlord's costs in connection with an alteration to a lease or a licence to assign. If you are asked to draft an undertaking, in the SQE2 assessments or in legal practice, you must first consider the ethical and professional conduct implications. Remember that failure to honour an undertaking amounts to professional misconduct. You must therefore ensure that you have your client's instructions, that whatever you undertake to do is within your control and that the undertaking is clearly and accurately drafted. You can find an example of an undertaking for costs in a leasehold transaction in **Chapter 8 (8.4.3)**.

7.10 Business Organisations, Rules and Procedures

In SQE1 you learnt about the different types of business and the features and advantages of each one. In the SQE2 assessments you may be asked to draft some of the legal documents which relate to these different business mediums.

You will recall that in order to incorporate a limited company the applicant must complete Companies House form IN01. You can find a commentary on the decisions which the individuals setting up the company will have to make and include in the form in Chapter 1 of The University of Law SQE1 manual *Business Law and Practice*.

Chapter 8 contains examples of some of the common types of legal document which are generated in connection with board meetings and general meetings: notice of a general meeting (**8.5.1**); agreement to short notice of a general meeting (**8.5.2**); written resolutions (**8.5.3**); minutes of a board meeting (**8.5.4**) and minutes of a general meeting (**8.5.5**). You can find out more about company decision making from Chapter 2 of the SQE1 manual. The key shareholders' resolutions are listed in appendix 1 to that manual.

In the context of partnerships, you will recall that it is desirable for the partnership to have a written partnership agreement. You can find out more about the clauses which a solicitor who is instructed to draft a partnership agreement should consider including in Chapter 6 of the SQE1 manual.

Finally, you will remember that it is important that companies use the correct execution clause when signing or executing a legal document or it may be invalid. There is a distinction between the formalities required for entering into a contract and executing a deed. Contracts can be entered into by the company using the company seal or on behalf of the company by a person acting on its authority, either express or implied. This will often be a director but could be another employee if entering into contracts is part of their role.

The formalities for a company executing a deed were considered above for property practice. Remember that the position with the company seal is more complicated if the company has the model articles, in which case the document must also be signed by at least one authorised person in the presence of a witness who attests the signature.

In the case of a partnership, contracts can be made by all the partners acting together or by just one of the partners. The question of the actual and apparent authority which a partner may have to bind the partnership is considered in Chapter 6 of the SQE1 manual.

8 Legal Drafting: Example Documents

Introduction

This chapter contains examples of some common legal documents from each of the five practice areas covered by the SQE2 Legal Drafting assessments. It should not be taken in any way as indicating or limiting the range of documents which you may be asked to draft in the assessments.

As discussed at **1.7**, for the SQE2 assessments, by analogy with SQE1, you will not usually be required to recall specific case names or cite statutory or regulatory authorities unless these are provided to you in the assessment. The case names and statutory references in these examples have therefore been included for illustrative purposes only.

To repeat the notice in the Preface, this manual is not intended to constitute legal advice. The publisher and writers are not responsible or liable for the results of any person acting (or omitting to act) on the basis of the information contained within this publication.

8.1   Dispute Resolution

The example statements of case that follow are based on the following scenario.

The claim arises from an accident which took place on the claimant's driveway. The defendant crashed his car into the claimant's house, partially destroying an extension. The claimant has brought proceedings against the defendant alleging negligence and seeking damages of £185,000 plus interest. The defendant is defending the claim, alleging that the claimant was responsible for the accident and is counterclaiming for the cost of repairing his car.

8.1.1   Example particulars of claim in a negligence claim

IN THE HIGH COURT OF JUSTICE   WF-22-1234
QUEEN'S BENCH DIVISION
WEYFORD DISTRICT REGISTRY

BETWEEN   MR WILLIAM ULYSSES SIMPSON (1)   Claimants
                              MRS RUPINDER SIMPSON (2)
                                        and
                              MR GEOFFREY IAN TEMPLAR   Defendant

---

PARTICULARS OF CLAIM

1. At all material times the Claimants owned the property known as 'Bliss Lodge', Steep Lane, Nowhere, Mythshire GU15 6AB ('the Property').

2. On 2 August 2021 at about 11.00 pm, the Defendant drove a Land Cruiser 4×4, 4.5 litre turbo model registration number GIT 13 ('the Car') down the driveway leading to the Property. In the circumstances, the Defendant was under a duty of care that he would exercise reasonable care and skill when using the driveway.

3. In breach of that duty and owing to the negligent driving of the Defendant, the Car left the driveway and collided with the Property, partially destroying a recently constructed two-storey extension.

PARTICULARS OF NEGLIGENCE

The Defendant drove negligently in that he:

(a) drove at excessive speed;

(b) lost control of the Car;

(c) swerved repeatedly on and off the driveway;

(d) failed to apply the Car's brakes sufficiently or at all;

(e) failed to steer, manage, control or stop the Car so as to avoid the collision.

4. Owing to the Defendant's negligence, the Claimants have suffered loss and damage.

PARTICULARS OF LOSS AND DAMAGE

	£
(a) Costs incurred rendering the extension safe following the collision:	
– Weather-proofing the extension	8,000.00
– Installation of temporary alarm system for parts of Bliss Lodge accessible from the extension	5,000.00
– Making safe electrical supply to and in the extension	1,000.00
– Sealing off plumbing supply to the extension	500.00
	14,500.00

(b) Particulars of the estimated costs that follow are given in the attached Schedule. Estimated costs to be incurred repairing damage to the extension:–

– demolishing and rebuilding the extension	96,000.00
– refitting custom-made kitchen	57,000.00
– refitting bedroom	10,000.00
– remedial and reinstatement works to garden and driveway	8,000.00
	171,000.00
TOTAL	185,500.00

5. In respect of damages awarded to them the Claimants claim interest under section 35A of the Senior Courts Act 1981 at such rate and for such period as the court thinks fit.

AND THE CLAIMANTS CLAIM:

(1) Damages as stated in paragraph 4 above;

(2) Interest as stated in paragraph 5 above.

Dated 4 March 2022   Signed: *ULaw LLP*
                                        ULAW LLP

STATEMENT OF TRUTH

I believe that the facts stated in these Particulars of Claim are true. I understand that proceedings for contempt of court may be brought against anyone who makes, or causes to be made, a false statement in a document verified by a statement of truth without an honest belief in its truth.

Signed: *William Ulysses Simpson*
....
WILLIAM ULYSSES SIMPSON
FIRST CLAIMANT

Dated: 4 March 2022

Signed: *Rupinder Simpson*
....
RUPINDER SIMPSON
SECOND CLAIMANT

Dated: 4 March 2022

The Claimants' solicitors are ULaw LLP of 2 Bunhill Row, Moorgate, London EC1Y 8HQ where they will accept service of proceedings on behalf of the Claimants.

To: the Defendant and the Court Manager

8.1.2   Example defence and counterclaim

IN THE HIGH COURT OF JUSTICE   WF-22-1234
QUEEN'S BENCH DIVISION
WEYFORD DISTRICT REGISTRY

BETWEEN   MR WILLIAM ULYSSES SIMPSON (1)   Claimants
                            MRS RUPINDER SIMPSON (2)
                                     and

                            MR GEOFFREY IAN TEMPLAR   Defendant

DEFENCE AND COUNTERCLAIM

DEFENCE

1. The Defendant admits paragraph 1 of the Particulars of Claim. The Claimants were the occupiers of the Property and the Defendant was a visitor within the meaning of the Occupiers' Liability Act 1957 ('the Act'). The Defendant visited the Property at the Claimants' invitation on 2 August 2021 to use accommodation in a converted stable block there under an agreement made on 18 July 2021.

2. The Defendant admits paragraph 2.

3. Save that the Defendant admits that he lost control of the Car and that it collided with the Property, the Defendant denies for the reasons that follow that he drove negligently as alleged in paragraph 3 or at all or that the matters complained of were caused as alleged or at all.

4. Further or alternatively, the collision was caused or contributed to by the breach of statutory duty of the Claimants.

PARTICULARS OF BREACH OF STATUTORY DUTY

The Claimants acted in breach of statutory duty in that they:

(a) unknown to the Defendant caused or allowed shards of broken glass to be present on the driveway of the Property which caused the front and rear offside tyres of the Car to suddenly burst, thus resulting in him losing control of the Car;

(b) failed by means of notices or otherwise to warn the Defendant of the presence and position of the glass referred to in (a);

(c) required or allowed the Defendant to use the driveway when it was unsafe;

(d) exposed the Defendant to danger and a foreseeable risk of damage to his property;

(e) failed to take proper care for the Defendant's safety.

5. As to paragraph 4, the Defendant admits that the Property was damaged by the collision but denies for the reasons set out above that he caused any damage. The Defendant otherwise makes no admissions as to the loss or damage alleged by the Claimants in paragraph 4 of the Particulars of Claim as he has no knowledge of such.

6. In the circumstances, the Defendant denies that the Claimants are entitled to the relief claimed in paragraph 4 or any relief.

COUNTERCLAIM

7. The Defendant repeats paragraphs 1 to 5 of the Defence.

8. Owing to the above matters, the Defendant has suffered loss and damage.

<u>PARTICULARS OF LOSS AND DAMAGE</u>

	£
(a) Value of Defendant's Car irreparably damaged	58,995.00
(b) Value of other items in the Car irreparably damaged:	
– Diasan PC notebook computer	6,500.00
– Mercuriam satellite mobile phone	2,000.00
(c) Towing charges paid to We-Haul in removing the Car	440.63
(d) Cost of storing the Car at We-Haul's premises for 9 weeks at £50.00 per week	450.00
(e) Alternative car hire charges for 13 weeks at £150.00 per week	1,950.00
(f) Additional cost of alternative accommodation in Nowhere	<u>1,825.00</u>
TOTAL	**72,160.63**

9. The Defendant therefore counterclaims from the Claimants damages in respect of the above.

10. The Defendant claims interest under section 35A of the Senior Courts Act 1981 on damages awarded to him at such rate and for such period as the court thinks fit.

AND THE DEFENDANT COUNTERCLAIMS:

(1) Damages as stated in paragraph 9 above;

(2) Interest as stated in paragraph 10 above.

Dated 18 March 2022

Signed: *Advocates &Co*
....
ADVOCATES & CO

STATEMENT OF TRUTH

I believe that the facts stated in this Defence and Counterclaim are true. I understand that proceedings for contempt of court may be brought against anyone who makes, or causes to be made, a false statement in a document verified by a statement of truth without an honest belief in its truth.

Signed: *GI Templar*
....
GEOFFREY IAN TEMPLAR
DEFENDANT

Dated: 18 March 2022

The Defendant's solicitors are Advocates & Co, 30 Cheapway, Nowhere, Mythshire, MB2X 5PP where they accept service of proceedings in behalf of the Defendant.

To: the Claimants

To: the Court Manager

8.1.3 Example reply and defence to counterclaim

IN THE HIGH COURT OF JUSTICE   WF-22-1234
QUEEN'S BENCH DIVISION
WEYFORD DISTRICT REGISTRY

BETWEEN   MR WILLIAM ULYSSES SIMPSON (1)   Claimants
                          MRS RUPINDER SIMPSON (2)
                                    and
                          MR GEOFFREY IAN TEMPLAR   Defendant

REPLY AND DEFENCE TO COUNTERCLAIM

REPLY

1. The Claimants admit paragraph 1 of the Defence.

2. The Claimants deny that they were in breach of statutory duty as alleged in paragraph 4 of the Defence or at all. The Claimants also deny that the collision was caused or contributed to by their breach of statutory duty. The Claimants contend that:

   (a) There was no broken glass and/or debris on the driveway. Alternatively, if there was broken glass and/or debris on the driveway, it was placed there by the actions of the Defendant, referred to in paragraph (b) below, whereby the Defendant swerved onto broken glass and/or debris on the grass and thereby caused it to scatter;

   (b) There was a small amount of builders' debris on the grass bordering the right hand side of the driveway. The debris was well away from the normal passage of any vehicle and did not constitute a hazard. It was solely due to the Defendant's excessive speed that he lost control of the Car, veered off the driveway onto the grass and drove onto the debris;

   (c) If the Defendant had been driving at an appropriate speed, he should have been able to control the Car, after the front and rear offside tyres burst, so as to avoid colliding with the Property.

3. Except where the Defendant has made admissions and except as appears in this statement of case, the Claimants join issue with the Defendant upon his Defence.

DEFENCE TO COUNTERCLAIM

4. The Claimants repeat paragraphs 1, 2 and 3 above.

5. As to paragraph 8 of the Counterclaim, the Claimants admit that the Defendant's Car suffered damage but deny for the reasons given above that they caused such loss and damage. The Claimants otherwise do not admit the loss and damage alleged in paragraph 8 of the Counterclaim as they have no knowledge of such.

6. In the circumstances the Claimants deny that the Defendant is entitled to any damages whatsoever.

Dated: 4 April 2022.

Signed: *ULaw LLP*

        ULAW LLP

STATEMENT OF TRUTH

I believe that the facts stated in this Reply and Defence to Counterclaim are true.
I understand that proceedings for contempt of court may be brought against anyone who makes, or causes to be made, a false statement in a document verified by a statement of truth without an honest belief in its truth.

Signed: *William Ulysses Simpson*
....
WILLIAM ULYSSES SIMPSON
FIRST CLAIMANT

Signed: *Rupinder Simpson*
....
RUPINDER SIMPSON
SECOND CLAIMANT

Dated: 4 April 2022

The Claimants' solicitors are ULaw LLP of 2 Bunhill Row, London EC1Y 8HQ where they will accept service of proceedings on behalf of the Claimants.

To: the Defendant and the Court Manager

Note that the expression 'joins issue' which is used in paragraph 3 means to disagree or to contest.

8.2 Criminal Litigation

The examples below are based on the following scenario.

Gary Dickson has been charged with assault occasioning actual bodily harm on Vincent Lamb in the early hours of the morning of 15 December 202_ outside Connelly's night club. [By way of information, assault occasioning actual bodily harm is contrary to Section 47 of the Offences Against the Person Act 1861.] Vincent Lamb is the DJ at the night club.

Gary's solicitor attended the police station and completed the Police Station attendance pro forma below. They draft an application for legal aid in criminal proceedings.

8.2.1 Police station attendance pro forma personal details

(Note that, in practice, this form would also contain the attending solicitors' details and reference numbers which have not been included for these purposes.)

PERSONAL DETAILS

Name:	*Gary Paul Dickson*
Date of birth:	*28/10/9_ (28 years)*
Address:	*17 Marsh Street* *Chester* *CH3 7LW*
Telephone number:	*01244 431809*
National Insurance Number:	*NS 61 52 43 D*
Employer:	*Self-employed scaffolder/steeplejack* *Also works part time as bouncer at* *Connelly's Night club*
Health Problems: If yes, details:	YES/NO
Outstanding criminal cases/on bail: If yes details:	YES/NO
Previous Convictions: If yes, details:	YES/NO *Common Assault (6 years ago)* *Theft (4 years ago)* *Threatening behaviour x 2 (2 years* *and 1 year ago)* *ABH (1 year ago)* *Failure to surrender (1 year ago)*

INFORMATION FROM CUSTODY RECORD

Date and time of arrest:	*15/12/2_ - 11.40*
Date and time of arrival at police station:	*15/12/2_ - 12.00*
Date and time detention authorised:	*15/12/2_ - 12.30*
Offence:	*ABH outside Connelly's night club*
Grounds for Detention:	*To obtain evidence by questioning*
Rights given:	YES/NO
Searches carried out If yes, details:	YES/NO *Search after detention authorised -* *various items retained by police*

Injuries/Police Surgeon required: If yes, details:	YES/NO
Samples taken: If yes, details:	YES/NO
Appropriate Adult required: If yes, details:	YES/NO

INFORMATION FROM INVESTIGATING OFFICER

Name and rank:	PC Chambers
Details of disclosure:	Handed disclosure statement by PC Chambers. Dickson alleged to have attacked Vincent Lamb outside Connelly's night club at 03.15 today. Lamb was DJ at night club where Dickson works as bouncer. Earlier incident between Lamb and Dickson during course of evening when Dickson alleged to have threatened Lamb. Witness saw Dickson strike Lamb in face several times and then drive away. Disclosure sufficient to enable me to give proper advice to Mr Dickson (although identity of witness not revealed despite request to do so)
Co-accused: If yes, details:	YES/NO
What Steps does IO take?	Interview Dickson to put allegations to him and to obtain his response.

CONSULTATION WITH CLIENT

Client's case:	Denies allegation. Says he was in bed at home at time of assault and partner will confirm this. Has no knowledge of incident and thinks someone at the night club has it in for him. Doesn't know Vincent Lamb and no knowledge of Lamb being DJ at night club that night. Denies that there was any incident earlier in the evening. Never went inside night club and spent all his time on pavement outside front.

Advice to client:	*Advised client on possible options in interview and explained possible adverse inferences from silence under ss 34, 36 and 37. Told him that disclosure was sufficient to run risk of adverse inference if he stayed silent and he should get his version of events out. Client did however appear fatigued and emotional.* *Concerned client would come across badly in interview. Advised client to hand in written statement and give no comment interview.*

OUTCOME

No further action:	YES/NO
Bail back to Police Station If yes, details:	YES/NO
Caution/Warning/Reprimand: If yes, details:	YES/NO
Charge If yes, details:	YES/NO *Client charged with assaulting Vincent Lamb on 15/12/2_ causing him actual bodily harm*
Bail Granted: Details:	YES/NO *Bail refused on grounds that Dickson would fail to appear and would commit further offences.*
Details of First Hearing:	*Chester Magistrates' Court - 10.00 am on 22/12/2_.*

TELEPHONE LOG

Date and time	Person spoken to	Details
15/12/2_ - 12.55	*PS Dunn*	*Gary Dickson arrested on suspicion of ABH and has asked that we represent him.*
15/12/2_ - 14.00	*Gary Dickson*	*Mr Dickson confirmed he wants me to represent him at the police station. Confirmed he was entitled to free legal advice and that I would attend the police station immediately. Told Mr Dickson not to talk to anyone about allegation until I arrived, and not to take part in interview/ID procedure or to give samples.*

CASE NARRATIVE

Date and times	Details
15/12/2_: 16.30-16.40	Travel from office to Chester police station.
15/12/2_: 16.40-16.50	Waiting in front office at police station.
15/12/2_: 16.50-17.00	Reading custody record and speaking to investigating officer. No problem highlighted by custody record and disclosure given was sufficient for me to advise Mr Dickson properly. Made representations about identity of witness alleged to have seen incident, but police refused to disclose this information.
15/12/2_: 17.00-18.30	Consultation with Mr Dickson and advice given (see comments above)
15/12/2_: 18.30-18.45	Attending audibly-recorded interview. No comment interview and written statement handed to interviewing officer.
15/12/2_: 18.45-19.00	Further consultation with Mr Dickson. Advised him on options open to police following interview
15/12/2_: 19.00-19.10	Attending whilst Mr Dickson charged with ABH. Made representation for bail but bail declined and Mr Dickson kept in custody pending first appearance before Chester MC on 22nd December.
15/12/2_: 19.10-19.40	Return travel to home.

8.2.2   Example application for legal aid in criminal proceedings

Reset This Page	Reset Form (All Pages)

Application for Legal Aid in Criminal Proceedings

Form
CRM14

Legal Aid Agency

ⓘ Please use the Guidance
If you do not complete the form correctly, we will return it.
You will find Guidance to help you fill in the form correctly,
at: https://www.gov.uk/government/collections/
criminal-legal-aid-application-forms
If you need more help or advice, please contact a solicitor.

MAAT Reference
(for official use)

For the Legal Representative's use

The court hearing the case

If the case is an **Appeal to the Crown Court** and there is no change in circumstances, answer **1** and then go to question **23**.

Case type
- ☐ Summary
- ☐ Either way
- ☐ Indictable
- ☐ Appeal to Crown Court and no changes
- ☐ Committal for sentence
- ☐ Appeal to Crown Court
- ☐ Trial now in Crown Court

Priority case
- ☐ Custody
- ☐ Vulnerable
- ☐ Youth
- ☐ Late application in the Crown Court for trial

Date of trial

About you: 1

1

ⓘ GUIDANCE

Mr Mrs Miss Ms Other title
☑ ☐ ☐ ☐

Your forenames or other names (in BLOCK LETTERS)
GARY

Your surname or family name (in BLOCK LETTERS)
DICKSON

Your date of birth
28/10/199_

National Insurance Number and ARC Number: give one of these only.

National Insurance Number
N	S	6	1	5	2	4	3	D

Application Registration Card (ARC) Number

☐ This is a new application.   ☐ This application relates to a change of financial circumstances.

Contacting you

2

Do you have a usual home address?

☐ No   ☑ Yes ——→ Your usual home address

17 Marsh street Chester CH3 7LW

Postcode

3

☑ 'Your solicitor's address only, if you are of 'No Fixed Abode', or not at your usual address because you are on bail or remand.

To what address should we write to you?

☑ Your usual home address (the address in 2)

☐ Your solicitor's address (see the side note)

☐ This address

Postcode

4

Your email address

Reset This Page

5 ___

Your telephone number (landline)

| 01244 431809 |

Mobile phone number

Work phone number

| 01244 531289 |

About you: 2

6 ___

✓ one box and if it is 'someone else's home', give your relationship to that person

Your usual home address is:

[✓] a Tenancy (rented)   [ ] Temporary   [ ] Your parent's home (you live with them)

[ ] Someone else's home ⟶ Your relationship [ ]

Owned by: [ ] You   [ ] Your partner   [ ] You and your partner, jointly

7 ___

Are you under 18 years old?

[✓] No   [ ] Yes ⟶ Are you charged with an adult?

[ ] No: Go to **23**   [ ] Yes: Go to **23**

8 ___

ⓘ GUIDANCE

Do you have a partner?

[ ] No: Go to **9**   [✓] Yes: Go to **10**

9 ___

✓ one box

ⓘ GUIDANCE

You are: [ ] Single: Go to **14**   [ ] Widowed: Go to **14**

[ ] Divorced or have dissolved a civil partnership: Go to **14**

[ ] Separated ⟶ Date of separation?

[ ] Go to **14**

10 ___

✓ one box

You and your partner are:

[ ] Married or in a Civil Partnership   [✓] Cohabiting or living together

About your partner

11 ___

ⓘ GUIDANCE

Your partner's details

Mr Mrs Miss Ms Other title   Your forenames or other names (in BLOCK LETTERS)

[ ] [ ] [ ] [✓] [ ] | JILL | [ ]

Surname or family name (in BLOCK LETTERS)   Date of birth

| SUMMERS | | 11/3/199_ |

National Insurance Number and ARC Number: give one of these only.

National Insurance Number

| N | S | 6 | 4 | 5 | 7 | 4 | 2 | D |

Application Registration Card (ARC) Number

12 ___

If you ✓ **Yes**, and your partner is a victim, prosecution witness, or co-defendant with a conflict of interest, do not give your partner's details for questions **13** to **22**.

Is your partner a victim, prosecution witness or a co-defendant in the case for which you require legal aid?

[✓] No   [ ] Yes ⟶ [ ] Victim: Go to **14**

[ ] Prosecution witness: Go to **14**

[ ] Co-defendant ⟶ Does your partner have a conflict of interest?

[ ] No: Go to **13** [ ] Yes: Go to **14**

13   **Is your partner's usual home address different from yours (the address at question 2)?**

☑ No   ☐ Yes ⟶ Your partner's usual home address

Postcode

Your income and your partner's income

14   **Do you or your partner receive any of the benefits listed here?**

In this form, if you answer Yes to any question which asks about you or your partner, and you can answer Yes for both of you, give details for you and your partner, not for one of you only.

☑ No   ☐ Yes ⟶ **You**   **Your Partner**

	You	Your Partner
Income Support	☐ Go to **23**	☐ Go to **23**
Income-Related Employment and Support Allowance (ESA)	☐ Go to **23**	☐ Go to **23**
Income-Based Jobseeker's Allowance (JSA)	☐ When did you last sign on?	☐ When did you last sign on?
	Go to **23**	Go to **23**
Guarantee State Pension Credit	☐ Go to **23**	☐ Go to **23**

15   **Do you or your partner, together, in a year have a total income from all sources before tax or any other deduction, of more than £12, 475 (£239.90 a week)?**

☐ No: Go to **16**   ☑ Yes ⟶ You will need to **complete form CRM15**: Go to **23**

16   **Sources of income for you and your partner. Please give details in the table:**

about:
- Employment
- Total of other benefits
- Other source of income

For all parts of this question:
- If you do not receive income from a source, put **NIL** after the '£'.

- After '**every**' put either: week, 2 weeks, 4 weeks, month, **or** year.

	You	Your Partner
Employment (wage or salary)	£ every ☐ Before tax ☐ After tax	£ every ☐ Before tax ☐ After tax
Child Benefit	£ every	£ every
Working Tax Credits and Child Tax credits	£ every	£ every
Universal Credit	£ every	£ every
Total of other benefits	£ every	£ every
Maintenance income	£ every	£ every
Pensions	£ every	£ every
Any other source of income such as: - a student grant or loan - board or rent from a family member, lodger or tenant, or rent from a property - financial support from friends and family	£ every Source:	£ every Source:

Reset This Page

17 _____ Are you or your partner self-employed, in a business partnership, or
either a company director or a shareholder in a private company?

(!)GUIDANCE ☐ No ☐ Yes ⟶ You will need to **complete form CRM15**: Go to **23**

18 _____ Do you or your partner have any income, savings or assets which
are under a restraint order or a freezing order?

☐ No ☐ Yes ⟶ You will need to **complete form CRM15**: Go to **23**

19 _____ Are you charged with a Summary offence, only?

(!)GUIDANCE ☐ No ☐ Yes: Go to **22**

20 _____ Do you or your partner own or part-own any land or property of any kind,
including **your own home**, in the United Kingdom or overseas?

☐ No ☐ Yes ⟶ You will need to **complete form CRM15**: Go to **23**

21 _____ Do you or your partner have any savings or investments,
in the United Kingdom or overseas?

(!)GUIDANCE ☐ No ☐ Yes ⟶ You will need to **complete form CRM15**: Go to **23**

22 _____ Do your answers to the previous questions tell us that you have no income from any of
the sources which we have asked about?

☐ No ☐ Yes ⟶ How do you and your partner pay your bills and daily expenses?

Information for the Interests of Justice test

23 _____ What charges have been brought against you?

(!)GUIDANCE

Describe the
charge briefly:
for instance,
'Assault on a
neighbour'.

Charge	Date of offence
1 Assault occasioning actual bodily harm contrary to s 47, OAPA 1861	15/12/202_
2	
3	
4	

24 _____ The type of offence with which you are charged

(!)GUIDANCE
✓ one box only.
If you are charged
with two or more
offences, ✓ the
most serious.

☐ Class A: Homicide and related grave offences

☐ Class B: Offences involving serious violence or damage, and serious drugs offences

✓ Class C: Lesser offences involving violence or damage, and less serious drugs offences

☐ Class D: Sexual offences and offences against children ⟶

Reset This Page

☐ Class E: Burglary etc

☐ Class F: Other offences of dishonesty (specified offences and offences where the value is £30,000 or less)

☐ Class G: Other offences of dishonesty (specified offences and offences where the value involved exceeds £30,000 but does not exceed £100,000)

☐ Class H: Miscellaneous other offences

☐ Class I: Offences against public justice and similar offences

☐ Class J: Serious sexual offences

☐ Class K: Other offences of dishonesty (high value: if the value involved exceeds £100,000)

25   **Do you have any co-defendants in this case?**

☑ No: Go to **27**   ☐ Yes ⟶ Their names

> [blank box]

26   **Is there any reason why you and your co-defendants cannot be represented by the same solicitor?**

☐ No   ☐ Yes ⟶ The reason(s)

> [blank box]

27   **Are there any other criminal cases or charges against you or your partner which are still in progress?**

☑ No   ☐ Yes ⟶ You   Your Partner

	You	Your Partner
The charges		
The Court hearing the case		
Date of the next hearing		

28   **Which Court is hearing the case for which you need legal aid?**

The Court hearing the case	Date of the hearing
Chester Magistrates' Court	22/12/202_

---

29   Why do you want legal aid?

GUIDANCE

1 to **9** are possible reasons.

We suggest you choose one or more reasons with the help of a solicitor.

For each reason you choose, say why you have chosen it.

Mention any evidence that supports your choice of a reason.

If you need more space to answer, please use a separate sheet of paper and put your full name, date of birth and 'Question 29' at the top of the sheet. Please make sure you show which part of the question (**1** to **10**) your writing refers to.

1 It is likely that I will lose my liberty if any matter in the proceedings is decided against me.

> I am charged with ABH. The guideline sentence is custody. The prosecution will allege aggravating factors - unprovoked assault with multiple blows to the head. I have previous convictions that will aggravate the seriousness of the offence if I am convicted. The CPS opposes bail.

2 I have been given a sentence that is suspended or non-custodial. If I break this, the court may be able to deal with me for the original offence.

3 It is likely that I will lose my livelihood.

> I work as a scaffolder/steeplejack and nightclub doorman. I have been told that I will lose these these jobs if I am sent to prison. A prison sentence would also prevent future employment as a doorman.

4 It is likely that I will suffer serious damage to my reputation.

5 A substantial question of law may be involved (whether arising from legislation, judicial authority or other source of law).

> I will challenge the identification evidence to be given by John Barnard, the admissibility of a police station confession, and the admissibility of my previous convictions to suggest a propensity to commit acts of violence. I will apply to exclude evidence of bad character and hearsay evidence.

6 I may not be able to understand the court proceedings or present my own case.

7 Witnesses may need to be traced or interviewed on my behalf.

> I will be calling my partner as a witness to support my alibi defence. She will need to be interviewed and a statement taken from her.

8 The proceedings may involve expert cross-examination of a prosecution witness (whether an expert or not).

> John Barnard requires expert cross-examination to undermine the credibility of his evidence. The police officer who interviewed me at the police station (PC Chambers) requires expert cross-examination to establish multiple breaches of PACE/Codes of Practice during the interview.

9 It is in the interests of another person (such as the person making a complaint or other witness) that I am represented.

> I am charged with a violent offence and it would be inappropriate for me to cross-examine the complainant in person.

10 Any other reason

> I am pleading not guilty and the case is likely to be tried in the Crown Court.

Reset This Page

Legal representation

30

The solicitor who you want to act for you

Mr   Mrs   Miss   Ms   Other title   Solicitor's initials, surname or family name (in BLOCK LETTERS)

☐ ☐ ☐ ☐   ☐   ☐

Name and address of the solicitor's firm

ULaw LLP
2 Bunhill Row
Moorgate
London EC1Y 8HQ

Postcode

Telephone (land line)   Mobile phone

Document Exchange (DX)   Fax

email address

31

Declaration by the legal representative

1 ☑ I represent the applicant. I confirm that I am authorised to provide representation under a contract issued by the Legal Aid Agency (LAA).

2 ☐ I represent the applicant. I confirm that I have been instructed to provide representation by:

☐ a firm which holds a contract issued by the Legal Aid Agency (LAA).

☐ a solicitor employed by the Legal Aid Agency (LAA) in the Public Defender Service who is authorised to provide representation.

Signed   Date   Provider's LAA Account Number

| 4 | J | 3 | 2 | 1 |

Full name (in BLOCK LETTERS)

About the information which you have provided and its protection

32

- The information which you give when you answer this question (which continues on page 8), will be treated in the strictest confidence and will not affect our decision on this application.

- We, or HM Courts and Tribunals Service, may use the information on this form and on forms CRM15 and CRM15C, for statistical monitoring or research. The information we publish will not identify you or anyone else. We will process the information according to the relevant data protection laws and other legal requirements.

1 **Are you male or female?**

☑ Male   ☐ Female   ☐ I prefer not to say

Reset This Page

2
✓ one box in the table to show the best definition of your disability.

The Equality Act 2010 defines disability as: 'A physical or mental impairment which has a substantial and long-term adverse effect on a person's ability to carry out normal day-to-day activities'.

3
✓ one box in the table of ethnic groups.

2 Do you consider that you have a disability?

[✓] No   [ ] Yes ⟶ The best definition is:

[ ] Mental health condition   [ ] Mobility impairment   [ ] Other

[ ] Learning disability or difficulty   [ ] Long-standing physical illness or health condition   [ ] I prefer not to say

[ ] Hearing impaired   [ ] Visually impaired

[ ] Deaf   [ ] Blind

3 Which of the options in the table best describes you?

White	Mixed	Asian or Asian British	Black or Black British	
[✓] British	[ ] White and Black Caribbean	[ ] Indian	[ ] Black Caribbean	[ ] Chinese
[ ] Irish	[ ] White and Black African	[ ] Pakistani	[ ] Black African	[ ] Gypsy or Traveller
[ ] White other	[ ] White and Asian	[ ] Bangladeshi	[ ] Black other	[ ] Other
	[ ] Mixed other	[ ] Asian other		[ ] I prefer not to say

Evidence to support the information which you have given

33
Have you been directed to complete a form CRM15 (see questions 15, 17, 18, 20 and 21)?

[ ] No   [✓] Yes ⟶ If you have a partner, now go to **38**. If not, go to **39**.

34
Has a court remanded you in custody?

[ ] No: Go to **36**   [ ] Yes: Go to **35**

35
Will your case be heard in a magistrates' court?

[ ] No   [ ] Yes ⟶ If you have a partner, now go to **38**. If not, go to **39**.

36
ⓘ EVIDENCE

ⓘ EVIDENCE

Are you employed?

[ ] No   [ ] Yes ⟶ ▪ **If your case will be heard in a magistrates' court, or it is a committal for sentence or appeal to the Crown Court**
We need a copy of your wage slip or salary advice. You must provide it with this form: see the guidance about evidence.

▪ **If your case will be heard in the Crown Court**
We need a copy of your wage slip or salary advice. You must provide it with this form or within 14 days of the date of your application: see the guidance about evidence.

37
If you have a partner, now go to **38**. If you do not have a partner, go to **39**.

Reset This Page

Declaration by your partner

38

ⓘGUIDANCE
If your partner is not able to sign this declaration, you must give the reason at the end of question **39**.

I declare that this form and any form CRM15 and CRM15C is a true statement of all my financial circumstances to the best of my knowledge and belief. I agree to the Legal Aid Agency and HM Courts & Tribunals Service, or my partner's solicitor, checking the information I have given, with the Department for Work and Pensions, HM Revenue and Customs or other people and organisations. I authorise those people and organisations to provide the information for which the Legal Aid Agency, HM Courts and Tribunals Service or my partner's solicitor may ask.

I have read the **Notice of Fraud** at the end of question **39**.

Signed

Date

Full name (in BLOCK LETTERS)

JILL SUMMERS

Declaration by you

39

When you read this declaration, keep in mind that some parts of it may not apply to you because the declaration is designed to cover several types of court case.

I apply for the right to representation for the purposes of criminal proceedings under the Legal Aid, Sentencing and Punishment of Offenders Act 2012.

I declare that this form and any form CRM15 and CRM15C is a true statement of my financial circumstances and those of my partner to the best of my knowledge and belief. I understand that this form must be fully completed before a Representation Order can be issued. I understand that if I tell you anything that is not true on this form or the documents I send with it, or leave anything out:

- I may be prosecuted for fraud. I understand that if I am convicted, I may be sent to prison or pay a fine.
- My legal aid may be stopped and I may be asked to pay back my costs in full to the Legal Aid Agency.
- If my case is in the Crown Court, the Legal Aid Agency may change the amount of the contribution which I must pay.

Crown Court I understand that in Crown Court proceedings the information I have given in this form will be used to determine whether I am eligible for legal aid and, if so, whether I am liable to contribute to the costs of my defence under an Income Contribution Order during my case, or if I am convicted, under a Final Contribution Order at the end of my case, or both.

I understand that if I am ordered to pay towards my legal aid under an Income Contribution Order, or if I am convicted and ordered to pay under a Final Contribution Order, but fail to pay as an Order instructs me, interest may be charged or enforcement proceedings may be brought against me, or both.

I understand that I may have to pay the costs of the enforcement proceedings in addition to the payments required under the Contribution Order, and that the enforcement proceedings could result in a charge being placed on my home.

Evidence I agree to provide, when asked, further details and evidence of my finances and those of my partner, to the Legal Aid Agency, its agents, or HM Courts & Tribunals Service to help them decide whether an Order should be made and its terms.

Changes I agree to tell the Legal Aid Agency or HM Courts & Tribunals Service if my income or capital or those of my partner, change. These changes include the sale of property, change of address, change in employment and change in capital. →

Reset This Page

It is important that you understand that by signing this declaration you agree to the Legal Aid Agency, the courts, or your solicitor, contacting your partner to check the information that you have given in this form, and in forms CRM15 and CRM15C, if you complete them.

Enquiries

I authorise such enquiries as are considered necessary to enable the Legal Aid Agency, its agents, HM Courts & Tribunals Service, or my solicitor to find out my income and capital, and those of my partner. This includes my consent for parties such as my bank, building society, the Department for Work and Pensions, the Driver and Vehicle Licensing Agency or HM Revenue and Customs to provide information to assist the Legal Aid Agency, it's agents or HM Courts & Tribunals Service with their enquiries.

I consent to the Legal Aid Agency or my solicitor contacting my partner for information and evidence about my partner's means. This includes circumstances where my partner is unable to sign or complete the form.

I understand that if the information which my partner provides is incorrect, or if my partner refuses to provide information, then: if my case is in the magistrates' court, my legal aid may be withdrawn or, if my case is in the Crown Court, I may be liable to sanctions. I understand that the sanctions may result in me paying towards the cost of my legal aid or, if I already pay, paying more towards the cost of my legal aid, or paying my legal aid costs in full.

Ending legal aid

I understand that I must tell my solicitor and write to the court if I no longer want public representation. I understand that if I decline representation I may be liable for costs incurred to the date when my solicitor and the court receive my letter.

Data sharing

I agree that, if I am convicted, the information in this form will be used by HMCTS or designated officer to determine the appropriate level of any financial penalty ordered against me, and for its collection and enforcement.

Notice on fraud

If false or inaccurate information is provided and fraud is identified, details will be passed to fraud prevention agencies to prevent fraud and money laundering.

Further details explaining how the information held by fraud prevention agencies may be used can be found in the 'Fair Processing Notice', available on the Legal Aid Agency website at: https://www.gov.uk/guidance/apply-for-legal-aid

Signed

Date

Full name (in BLOCK LETTERS)

GARY DICKSON

If your partner has not signed the declaration at **38**, please explain:

Continuing the facts of the scenario above:

Having prepared the application for legal aid, initial details of the prosecution case are supplied. These include statements from the following witnesses:

- Vincent Lamb: the victim. He gives details of the assault and the injuries he suffered (a broken nose and a laceration over the left eyebrow). Vincent will say that when he was at Connelly's night club earlier on the evening of the attack, he had been talking to someone who he now believes to be Jill, Gary's girlfriend. Gary had threatened him earlier in the evening and told him to lay off.

- John Barnard: who witnessed the attack on Vincent. Mr Barnard will also give evidence that he was handed a scrap of paper with the registration L251 CVM on it by an (unknown) passer-by. He identified Gary in an ID parade.

- Gareth Chambers: the PC who arrested Gary and interviewed him. He will also give evidence that the scrap of paper had been lost or destroyed, but that it had been noted down by another PC in his pocket notebook.

In the audibly recorded interview, Gary appeared to accept that he had assaulted Vincent Lamb.

Gary comments on these matters in his statement (**8.2.3**).

8.2.3   Gary's statement to his solicitor

STATEMENT OF GARY PAUL DICKSON

Statement of Gary Paul Dickson will say as follows:

Personal Details

My full name is Gary Paul Dickson and I reside at 17 Marsh Street, Chester CH3 7LW with my girlfriend Jill Summers. The property is owned by Jill's parents and we share a flat on the top floor.

I am 28 years old, having been born on 28th October 199_. I have two jobs. My main occupation is as a scaffolder/steeplejack. I do contract work throughout the country. Basically I am sent wherever there is work. I also do some part-time work as a doorman/bouncer on a weekend and the odd night during the week at Connelly's Nightclub in Chester.

My contact telephone numbers are:

HOME – 01244 431809

MOBILE – 05573 372537

Charge

I am charged with a s 47 assault on Vincent Lamb in the early hours of the morning of 15th December 202_. I know nothing about any assault on Mr Lamb and it is my intention to enter a not guilty plea to this charge.

Education and Employment History

I was born and brought up in York. I attended Burnholme Community College until I was 16. I left school with GCSEs in English Language, Maths, Woodwork and Art.

After leaving school I joined the army. I served as a private and latterly as a corporal with the Green Howards regiment. I left the army 5 years ago and moved to Chester to live with some former school friends.

I started doing some scaffolding work for a firm based in Chester on a part-time basis and found that I liked the work. I was never an employee of the firm, but just did contract work as and when it became available. I started doing similar work for a couple of other firms and was soon doing this work all the time. I can earn good money doing the scaffolding. The work takes me to all parts of the country and occasionally I go abroad to work.

I've been doing the work as a doorman for about three years. I'm quite a big lad and when I was having a drink in Connelly's one day, the manager asked if I'd like to do some door work. I jumped at the chance because I thought it was a way to earn some easy money.

Family Circumstances

I've been with my girlfriend Jill Summers for about 18 months. Our relationship is serious and we hope to get married at some point in the future. We are saving up money to get our own place together. Sharing a flat is fine for the moment but we'd like to start a family and need the extra space.

Health

As far as I am aware I don't have any health problems. The army gets you fairly fit and I need to stay in good physical shape to do the work as a doorman.

Previous Convictions

I have 2 convictions for threatening behaviour, one conviction for theft, one conviction for assault occasioning actual bodily harm and one conviction for common assault. I also have a conviction for failing to answer bail in a previous case.

My recent convictions for violence are all as a result of customers at the nightclub getting aggressive or drunk and needing to be ejected from the premises. Sometimes customers get a bit lippy or even try to punch you when they are being thrown out. I was only ever doing my job, but the customers occasionally complain to the police that they have been assaulted. The police don't like professional doormen and so always press charges if they can. I pleaded guilty to these offences because it was my word against the customers and a lot of their mates.

I have a conviction for theft from 4 years ago. The offence related to me walking home from work in the early hours of the morning. I noticed a crate of bottles of milk outside the back door of a restaurant. Everything was in darkness and I assumed that the milk had been thrown out. I took a couple of bottles and, as they were still in date, drank them as I walked home. The police stopped me and questioned me about the milk as they had received a telephone call to say that some had been taken from a local restaurant. I gave my explanation in interview, but was charged. I also pleaded not guilty at Court but was found guilty as my explanation was not accepted.

My last conviction was on 13th December 202_ (1 year ago) for ABH. I gave a lad a thump when he wouldn't leave the nightclub when we were closing. I pleaded guilty and got 200 hours' unpaid work. I completed this work about six months ago.

The conviction for common assault happened whilst I was still in the army. I was having a drink at a pub in York when a lad accused me of knocking his drink over. He got abusive so I pushed him away and he fell over, banging his head on a table. I pleaded guilty.

Current Offence

At about 11.00 am on 15th December 202_ I was asleep in bed with Jill at 17 Marsh Street. I had been working at the nightclub until the early hours and Jill had been out the previous evening as well. As far as I was concerned it had been a normal evening at the nightclub.

I had to deal with a couple of drunks but nothing other than that. I stayed on the door all night and didn't go into the area where the stage was.

A policeman woke me up by banging on the door. I answered the door and he asked me if I was the owner of a dark blue VW Golf registration number L251 CVM. I told him I was, but as it was parked outside the house I thought this was obvious. He then asked me to confirm my whereabouts at 3.15 am that morning. I told him I was in bed with Jill. I asked him what was going on, and he told me that there had been a complaint of an assault by a man driving a car which matched the description and registration number of my car. I told him I didn't know what he was talking about.

He asked me if I would accompany him to the police station to answer some questions. I refused to go so he arrested me. When we got to the police station I was put in a cell for several hours. I hadn't had anything to eat or drink since the previous night, but the police wouldn't give me a drink or a meal. They didn't tell me why I had been stuck in a cell.

At about 6.00 pm I was told that I was going to be interviewed. I asked to speak to a solicitor before I was taken to the interview room. They said that I had to be interviewed there and then, or wait until the following morning. I didn't want to stay there any longer than necessary and so agreed to be interviewed without a solicitor. By the time the interview started I was totally pissed off with the way I had been treated. I said some stupid things which weren't true and which I now regret. They kept asking me the same questions over and over again, and it was clear that they weren't going to believe a word I said when I told them that I knew nothing about the assault. I eventually said it was me just to get out of there.

Mitigation

I have nothing to say in mitigation because I am not guilty of this offence and I will be pleading not guilty when the charge is put to me at court. I know nothing about the attack on Mr Lamb. At the time of the attack I was asleep at home.

Matters Relevant to Bail

I intend to continue working at Connelly's because the money is good. I suppose there is always the chance of more trouble with the public, but this is an occupational hazard. All the other doormen have previous convictions. We are an easy target for the police because there is no shortage of lads who want to try it on with us and then go squealing to the police when they get a smack.

The conviction I have for failing to answer my bail was just a mix up over court dates. I thought my trial was going to be dealt with in the afternoon, and didn't appreciate that I needed to be at court for 10.00 am regardless. I did turn up at court in the afternoon, but a warrant for my arrest had already been issued. I was arrested at court. This was a genuine oversight on my part but the magistrates convicted me anyway.

I am due to go away to Kerry in the Republic of Ireland in six months' time to do some scaffolding work. Until then I will be working on a contract in the Chester area, so I will be working locally.

I understand that any bail the court grants me may be subject to conditions. Until I am due to go away with work I would be able to abide by a condition that I report to the police station daily or that I live at 17 Marsh Street.

I could afford to pay a security if required.

Signed: *Gary Dickson*

Dated: 21st December 202_

Comments on Prosecution Witness Statements

PC Gareth Chambers

This is pretty much correct. I have been arrested by PC Chambers before and he obviously has it in for me. He knows about my previous convictions. He obviously wasn't going to let me out of the interview until I said I was guilty, even though I didn't do it.

John Barnard

He must be mistaken. If he had been drinking all night as he claims, his recollection can't be reliable. He says I have short hair and a white tight-fitting T-shirt. This is the uniform worn by all the staff at Connelly's so that description could apply to any of the door staff or many of the customers as well.

He isn't very sure of the car registration number. He has either not remembered it properly or the police have told him the number. He did pick me out at the video identification, but he got that wrong as well. Perhaps the police told him who to pick.

Vincent Lamb

I don't know and have never heard of Vincent Lamb. He may have been the guest disc jockey that night. I don't really know what is going on inside the nightclub unless there is any trouble. I spend all my time at the entrance and on the street outside. I am adamant that I have never met Vincent Lamb. I'm sorry if he got his face smashed in, but I had nothing to do with it. Mr Lamb says that at one point during the evening I went over to the stage, shook my fist in his face and told him to lay off a clubber called Jill. This is untrue. I did no such thing. I spent the entire evening at the front of the nightclub. If this is meant to be a reference to my girlfriend Jill it is incorrect. Jill did not go to Connelly's that evening. Perhaps Mr Lamb has got me mixed up with another bouncer. There is another bouncer who looks a bit like me.

Peter Hansen

There is nothing I can say about this. There must be loads of dark VW Golfs on the road.

Record of audibly recorded interview

This seems to be right in terms of what was said, but the confession I made is just not true. I only said I assaulted Vincent Lamb because this was the only way I could think of to get out of the police station. Even though PC Chambers said I would be allowed to leave the police station on bail if I admitted my guilt, after I was charged the custody officer wouldn't let me have bail and I was kept in the cells overnight until court the next day.

Record of previous convictions

This is correct. As I said in my statement, you get plenty of grief on the door of the club. I sometimes gave the odd customer a smack if I thought they deserved it, but I never attacked anyone in the way I am supposed to have hit Lamb.

8.2.4   Bail appeal notice

Gary was refused bail by the magistrates' court on the basis that there were substantial grounds for believing that he would fail to surrender and would commit offences while on bail. His solicitor is instructed to appeal against that decision to the Crown Court and drafts a bail appeal notice.

DEFENDANT'S APPLICATION OR APPEAL TO THE CROWN COURT AFTER MAGISTRATES' COURT BAIL DECISION
(Criminal Procedure Rules, rule 14.8)

Case details

Name of defendant: Gary Paul Dickson

Address: c/o ULaw LLP, 2 Bunhill Row, London EC1Y 8HQ

If the defendant is in custody, give prison and prison number, if known.

Chester Remand Centre – Prison No: CRC04378

Appeal from Chester Magistrates' Court

Magistrates' court case reference number: CH000687/2_

Appeal to the Crown Court at: Chester

Crown Court case reference number: CH08001

This is an application by the defendant for the Crown Court to:

X grant bail, which the magistrates' court has withheld

☐ **vary a condition or conditions of bail, after the magistrates' court has decided an application to vary bail conditions**[1]

Which condition(s)?

Use this form ONLY for an application or appeal to the Crown Court after a magistrates' court has withheld bail or decided an application to vary a bail condition, under Criminal Procedure Rule 14.8. There is a different form for making an application about bail to the Crown Court where the Crown Court is already dealing with your case.

1. **Complete the boxes above and give the details required in the boxes below.** If you use an electronic version of this form, the boxes will expand[2]. If you use a paper version and need more space, you may attach extra sheets.

2. **Sign and date the completed form.**

3. **Send a copy of the completed form to:**
   (a) the Crown Court,
   (b) the magistrates' court,
   (c) the prosecutor, and
   (d) any surety or proposed surety who this application will affect.

---

[1] A defendant can only appeal to the Crown Court against a bail condition if:

(a) the magistrates' court has decided an application by the prosecutor or defendant to vary bail conditions; and

(b) the condition is one that the defendant must:

(i) live and sleep at a specified place (or away from a specified place),

(ii) give a surety or a security,

(iii) stay indoors between specified hours,

(iv) comply with electronic monitoring requirements, or

(v) make no contact with a specified person.

[2] Forms for use with the Rules are at: http://www.justice.gov.uk/courts/procedure-rules/criminal/formspage

You must send this form so as to reach the recipients **as soon as practicable after the magistrates' court's decision.**

The Crown Court will deal with this application no later than the business day after it was served.

A prosecutor who opposes this application must let the defendant and the Crown Court know at once, and serve on them notice of the reasons for opposing it.

1) Alleged offence(s). Give brief details of the charges against the defendant.
Charged with assault occasioning actual bodily harm contrary to s 47 Offences Against the Person Act 1861. The allegation is of an unprovoked assault causing a fractured nose and split eyebrow, which required stitches.

2) Magistrates' court bail decision. Give brief details of the magistrates' court decision you want the Crown Court to change (including the date of that decision), and the reasons which that court gave.
On 22 December 202_ the first full bail application was made at Chester Magistrates' Court and bail was refused. On 29 December 202_, a second full application was made and bail was refused on the basis that there were substantial grounds for believing that the defendant would fail to surrender and would commit offences on bail (a copy of the full argument certificate is attached).

3) Reasons for this application. Explain, as appropriate:
(a) why the Crown Court should not withhold bail,
(b) why the Crown Court should vary the conditions of bail,
(c) what further information or legal argument, if any, has become available since the magistrates' court bail decision was made.
<u>Fail to surrender to custody:</u> Mr Dickson is pleading not guilty to the one charge he faces and will come to court to clear his name. Mr Dickson has a strong defence to this charge and the evidence against him will be challenged. It will be alleged that the eye witness who purports to identify Mr Dickson as the assailant is mistaken. The admissibility of the confession evidence obtained by the police will be challenged under ss 76 & 78 of PACE 1984. An alibi witness will be called on Mr Dickson's behalf.
Mr Dickson has strong community ties. Mr Dickson resides in the Chester area with his partner. He and his partner reside in a property owned by his partner's parents. Mr Dickson has some part-time employment in the Chester area from his employment as a nightclub doorman. Mr Dickson's full-time employment as a scaffolder will require him to work on a local contract in the Chester area for the next six months.
Mr Dickson has one previous conviction for failure to surrender to custody. This failure was due to a genuine misunderstanding as to the time that Mr Dickson's case was due to start. Mr Dickson did attend court of his own volition later in the day.
<u>Commit offences on bail</u>
Mr Dickson is pleading not guilty to the current charge. He has never previously committed an offence whilst on bail, and he does not have a lengthy list of previously convictions.
Mr Dickson's last conviction was over one year ago. All of Mr Dickson's recent convictions relate to incidents when Mr Dickson was working as a nightclub doorman and was dealing with customers. The current charge relates to an alleged incident which occurred after Mr Dickson left his place of employment. There is no reason to believe that Mr Dickson will offend again whilst on bail. Mr Dickson's only other conviction was for common assault some six years ago. Mr Dickson did not re-offend for some four years after this.

4) Proposed condition(s) of bail. If the Crown Court decides to impose or vary bail conditions, what condition(s) do you propose? If the court decides to impose a condition of residence, what should that address be?

Residence at 17 Marsh Street, Chester; Reporting to Chester Police Station on a regular basis; Not to contact any prosecution witnesses; Not to enter Chester city centre other than for employment purposes; a security.

Signed[3]: *ULaw LLP* **[defendant's solicitor]**
Date: *30 December 202_*

---

[3] If you use an electronic version of this form, you may instead authenticate it electronically (e.g. by sending it from an email address recognisable to the recipient). See Criminal Procedure Rules, rule 5.3.

8.2.5 Defence statement

Gary intends to plead not guilty. His solicitor prepares a defence statement.

DEFENCE STATEMENT

(Criminal Procedure and Investigations Act 1996, section 5 & 6; Criminal Procedure and Investigations Act 1996 (Defence Disclosure Time Limits) Regulations 2011; Criminal Procedure Rules, rule 15.4)

Case details
Name of defendant: Gary Paul Dickson
Court: Chester Crown Court
Case reference number: CH090248
Charge(s): Assault occasioning actual bodily harm on Vincent Lamb on 15 December 202_.

When to use this form
If you are a defendant pleading not guilty:
(a) in a Crown Court case, you **must** give the information listed in Part 2 of this form;
(b) in a magistrates' court case, you **may** give that information but you do not have to do so. The time limit for giving the information is:
    14 days (in a magistrates' court case)
    28 days (in a Crown Court case)
after initial prosecution disclosure (or notice from the prosecutor that there is no material to disclose).
How to use this form
1. **Complete the case details box above, and Part 1 below.**
2. **Attach as many sheets as you need to give the information listed in Part 2.**
3. **Sign and date the completed form.**
4. **Send a copy of the completed form to:**
    (a) the court, and
    (b) the prosecutor
    before the time limit expires.
If you need more time, you **must** apply to the court **before** the time limit expires. You should apply in writing, but no special form is needed.

Part 1: Plea

I confirm that I intend to plead not guilty to [all the charges] [the following charges] against me:

Assault occasioning actual bodily harm – s 47 Offences Against the Person Act 1861

Part 2: Nature of the defence

Attach as many sheets as you need to give the information required.

Under section 6A of the Criminal Procedure and Investigations Act 1996, you must:

(a) set out the nature of your defence, including any particular defences on which you intend to rely;

Alibi

(b) indicate the matters of fact on which you take issue with the prosecutor, and in respect of each explain why;

(i) the allegation that the accused threatened the complainant Vincent Lamb and shook his fist in the complainant's face at Connelly's Nightclub during the evening of 14th December 202_ – as the complainant is incorrect in his allegation that the accused threatened him at Connelly's nightclub during the evening of 14th December 202_;

(ii) the allegation that the accused was in the vicinity of Connelly's nightclub in Chester city centre at or about 3.15 am on 15th December 202_ – as the prosecution witness John Barnard is mistaken in his identification of the accused as the individual who committed the assault on 15th December 202_;

(iii) the allegation that the accused's vehicle registration number L251 CXM was in the vicinity of Connelly's nightclub in Chester city centre at or about 3.15 am on 15th December 202_ – as the prosecution witness John Barnard is mistaken in his identification of the accused's vehicle as the vehicle driven by the individual who committed the assault on 15th December 202_;

(iv) the allegation that the accused assaulted the complainant Vincent Lamb causing him actual bodily harm – as the complainant is incorrect in his allegation that the accused assaulted him on 15th December 202_;

(v) the truthfulness of the confession made by the accused when questioned by the police about the assault at Chester Police Station on 15th December 202_ – as the confession is untrue and was made by the accused only as a result of the police conducting the interview with the accused at the police station in an improper manner.

(c) set out particulars of the matters of fact on which you intend to rely for the purposes of your defence;

The accused is raising an alibi defence that at 3.15 am on 15th December 202_ the accused was at his home address of 17 Marsh Street, Chester CH3 7LW.

(d) indicate any point of law that you wish to take, including any point about the admissibility of evidence or about abuse of process, and any authority relied on; and

(i) the admissibility of the identification evidence of the complainant John Barnard will be challenged under s 78 of the Police and Criminal Evidence Act 1984 because the video identification was conducted in breach of Code D of the Codes of Practice issued under s 66(1) of the Act;

(ii) if the identification evidence of the complainant is held to be admissible, the quality of this evidence will be challenged under the principles set out in R v Turnbull [1977] QB 224;

(iii) the admissibility of the confession made by the accused when interviewed under caution at Chester Police Station will be challenged under ss 76(2) and 78 of the Police and Criminal Evidence Act 1984, on the basis that the accused was dissuaded from obtaining legal advice prior to the interview commencing, and the conduct of the interview contravened Code C of the Codes of Practice issued under s 66(1) of the Act;

(iv) the prosecution have served notice that, pursuant to s 101(1)(d) of the Criminal Justice Act 2003, they intend to adduce at trial evidence of the accused's convictions for the following offences in order to demonstrate that the accused has a propensity to commit offences of the kind charged:

- *common assault – 6 years ago;*
- *threatening behaviour – 2 years and 1 year ago;*
- *assault occasioning actual bodily harm – 1 year ago.*

In addition, the offence of theft – 4 years ago – to demonstrate a propensity to be untruthful as the defendant was convicted after trial.

This notice is opposed because these offences do not demonstrate a propensity for the defendant to commit offences of this type because there is no factual similarity between such offences and the current offence (R v Hanson, Gilmore and Pickstone [2005] Crim LR 787). Also the evidential value of such convictions would be more prejudicial than probative in the eyes of the jury and it would therefore be unfair to the defendant for such convictions to be adduced in evidence (Criminal Justice Act 2003, s 101(3)). The admissibility of the conviction for common assault is also opposed under s 103(3) of the Criminal Justice Act 2003 because, as a result of the time which has elapsed since the conviction, it would be unjust for the conviction to be used in evidence. Further the single theft conviction does not demonstrate the relevant propensity.

(e) if your defence statement includes an alibi (i.e. an assertion that you were in a place, at a time, inconsistent with you having committed the offence), give particulars, including –

(i) the name, address and date of birth of any witness who you believe can give evidence in support of that alibi,

Jill Summers (date of birth: 11/03/9_). The address of the witness is 17 Marsh Street, Chester CH3 7LW.

(ii) if you do not know all of those details, any information that might help identify or find that witness.

Signed: Gary Paul Dickson   defendant / defendant's solicitor
Date: 24th February 202_

WARNING: Under section 11 of the Criminal Procedure and Investigations Act 1996, **if you (a) do not disclose what the Act requires; (b) do not give a defence statement before the time limit expires; (c) at trial, rely on a defence, or facts, that you have not disclosed; or (d) at trial, call an alibi witness whom you have not identified in advance, then the court, the prosecutor or another defendant may comment on that, and the court may draw such inferences as it thinks proper in deciding whether you are guilty.**

8.2.6 Example application to exclude hearsay evidence following notice

The prosecution intends to rely on hearsay evidence in the form of a note taken by a witness of the registration number L251 CVM (Gary's car) and serve notice to introduce hearsay evidence. Gary's solicitor prepares an application to exclude such evidence.

NOTICE TO INTRODUCE HEARSAY EVIDENCE
(Criminal Procedure Rules, rule 20.2)

Case details
Name of defendant: *Gary Paul Dickson*
Court: *Chester Crown Court*
Case reference number: *CH 090248*
Charge(s): *Assault causing actual bodily harm on 15 December 202_ on Vincent Lamb*

This notice is given by [the prosecutor]
[..........................(name of defendant)]
I want to introduce hearsay evidence on the following ground(s) in the Criminal Justice Act 2003:
☐ **the witness is unavailable to attend: s.116.**
☐ **the evidence is in a statement prepared for the purposes of criminal proceedings or for a criminal investigation and the witness is unavailable or unable to recollect: s.117(1)(c).**
☒ **the evidence is multiple hearsay: s.121.**
☒ **it is in the interests of justice for the evidence to be admissible: s.114(1)(d).**

1. **Complete the boxes above and give the details required in the boxes below.** If you use an electronic version of this form, the boxes will expand[1]. If you use a paper version and need more space, you may attach extra sheets.
2. **Sign and date the completed form.**
3. **Send a copy of the completed form and anything attached to:**
   (a) the court, and
   (b) each other party to the case.
If you are a prosecutor, you must send this form so as to reach the recipients not more than:
   (a) 28 days after the defendant pleads not guilty, in a magistrates' court, or
   (b) 14 days after the defendant pleads not guilty, in the Crown Court.
If you are a defendant, you must send this form so as to reach the recipients as soon as reasonably practicable.
The court may extend these time limits, **but if you are late you must explain why**.
A party who objects to the introduction of the evidence must apply to the court under Criminal Procedure Rule 20.3 **not more than 14 days after**:
   (a) service of this notice, or
   (b) the defendant pleads not guilty
whichever happens last.

1) Details of the hearsay evidence. If you have NOT already served the evidence, attach any statement or other document containing it. Otherwise, give enough details to identify it.
A handwritten pocket notebook entry of registration number L251 CXM. This was made by PC312 Taylor on 15 December 202_. The registration number was taken down from a piece of paper handed to PC Taylor by a witness who had received it from an unknown person who witnessed the incident surrounding the allegation of assault. A copy of the pocket notebook entry is attached and has been served on the accused, Mr Gary Dickson, through his solicitors, ULaw LLP.

---

[1] Forms for use with the Rules are at: http://www.justice.gov.uk/courts/procedure-rules/criminal/formspage

2) Facts on which you rely (if any), and how you will prove them. Set out any facts that you need to prove to make the evidence admissible. A party who objects to the introduction of the evidence must explain which, if any, of those facts are in dispute. Explain in outline on what you will then rely to prove those facts.

An unknown person witnessed the incident surrounding the assault of Mr Vincent Lamb on 15 December 202_. He noted down the registration number of a motor vehicle and handed it to another witness at the incident, Mr John Barnard. Mr Barnard handed the note to PC312 Taylor who recorded the registration number in his pocket notebook. The registration number, L251 CXM, has been linked to a dark blue XW Golf. The registered keeper of that vehicle is the defendant, Gary Dickson.

3) Reasons why the hearsay evidence is admissible. Explain why the evidence is admissible, by reference to the provisions(s) of the Criminal Justice Act 2003 on which you rely.

By virtue of section 114(1)(d) of the Criminal Justice Act 2003, it is in the interests of justice for this evidence to be admissible. The prosecution will rely upon the following factors contained in section 114(2):

  (a) the probative value of the statement as it links the defendant's XW Golf to the incident on 15 December 202_;

  (b) the witness evidence from John Barnard provides further independent evidence linking the defendant to the motor vehicle and incident on 15 December 202_;

  (c) the evidence in relation to the recording of the registration number is important because it provides further independent evidence which helps to prove the involvement of the defendant in this offence;

  (d) the note was made very shortly after the incident and John Barnard's witness statement surrounding the events of the recording was made on 18 December 202_ to Chester;

  (f) the witness evidence of John Barnard is independent evidence of the circumstances surrounding the recording of the registration number;

  (g) oral evidence of the matter stated can be given by John Barnard;

  (h) this can be challenged by the defence by cross-examining John Barnard.

In addition, under section 121(1)(c) of the Criminal Justice Act 2003 – that the value of the evidence from the police officer's notebook, taking into account how reliable the statements appear to be, is so high that the interests of justice require it to be admissible.

4) Reasons for any extension of time required. If this notice is served late, explain why. N/A

Signed[2]	J Boothroyd **[prosecutor]**
Date:	3 February 202_

---

[2] If you use an electronic version of this form, you may instead authenticate it electronically (e.g. by sending it from an email address recognisable to the recipient). See Criminal Procedure Rules, rule 5.3.

APPLICATION TO EXCLUDE HEARSAY EVIDENCE FOLLOWING NOTICE
(Criminal Procedure Rules, rule 20.3)

Case details
Name of defendant: *Gary Paul Dickson*
Court: *Chester Crown Court*
Case reference number: *CH 090248*
Charge(s): *Assault occasioning actual bodily harm on 15 December 202_ on Vincent Lamb*

This is an application by Gary Paul Dickson
I object to the introduction of the following hearsay evidence (describe the evidence to which you object):
A handwritten pocket notebook entry of registration number L251 CXM. This was made by PC312 Taylor on 15 December 202_.
of which the prosecutor served notice on 3 February 202_ because:
☐ **that evidence is not admissible, for the reason(s) explained in box 2 below.**
☐ **I object to the notice for the other reason(s) explained in box 2 below.**

How to use this form. Use this form ONLY where another party serves notice of hearsay evidence under Criminal Procedure Rule 20.2.
1. **Complete the boxes above and give the details required in the boxes below.** If you use an electronic version of this form, the boxes will expand. If you use a paper version and need more space, you may attach extra sheets.
2. **Sign and date the completed form.**
3. **Send a copy of the completed form to:**
   (a) the court, and
   (b) each other party to the case.
Note:
You must send this form so as to reach the recipients **not more than 14 days after**:
(a) service of the notice, or
(b) the defendant pleads not guilty whichever happens last.
The court may extend that time limit, **but if you are late you must explain why**.

1) Facts in dispute. Whatever reasons you have for objecting to the notice, explain which, if any, facts set out in it you dispute.
The facts relating to the evidence are all accepted.

2) Reasons for objecting. Explain, as applicable:

(a) why the hearsay evidence is not admissible, by reference to the provision(s) of the Criminal Justice Act 2003 relied on in the notice.

(b) what other objection you have to the notice.

s 114(2)(a) The probative value of the statement in proving that the defendant was directly involved in the offence is not high.

s 114(2)(b) here is direct evidence from a witness, John Barnard, who can give oral evidence at trial. His evidence as to the vehicle and possible registration number on the evening can be tested in court whereas the unknown maker of the note cannot.

s 114(2)(c) It is not accepted that the evidence contained in the note is important. It is therefore submitted that the unfairness caused to the defendant by admitting such untested evidence outweighs the prosecution's desire to put this evidence before the court.

s 114(2)(d)/(e) and (f) It is not accepted that the evidence contained within the statement is reliable. The pocket notebook entry is multiple hearsay, which is invariably less trustworthy than first hand hearsay. Whilst on the face of it the making of the pocket notebook entry appears reliable, no details of the unknown person are available to assess whether they are reliable or have a purpose of their own to serve by producing the note. In addition, there are no facts known to the prosecution or defence to assess the reliability of the unknown person's observations on the evening. The defendant will be deprived on the opportunity to question any of these matters in cross-examination.

*s 114(2)(h) **The amount of difficulty involved in challenging the statement.** If the statement is admitted, the defendant will be deprived of the opportunity to cross-examine this unknown person. This is a case in which the jury should have an opportunity to properly assess the witness's reliability on the stand. There will be limited opportunity to probe the evidence further and expose additional weaknesses in the absence of the witness.*

*s 114(2)(i) **The extent to which that difficulty would be likely to prejudice the party facing it.***

It is contended that to admit such untested evidence would be extremely prejudicial to the defendant. It is not accepted that a direction from the judge would be able to rectify such prejudice on these facts. Although it is true that the defendant can give evidence denying the truth of what the witness says, it is submitted that it would be unfair to put him in the position of having to do so, given the unreliability of the evidence.

Further, or in the alternative, the court is asked to exercise its discretionary power under s 126(1) of the Criminal Justice Act 2003 to exclude the statement on the grounds that the case for excluding the statement substantially outweighs the case for admitting it, and under s 78 of PACE 1984 on the grounds that its admission would have an adverse effect on the fairness of the trial.

3) Reasons for any extension of time required. If this application is served late, explain why. N/A

Signed: *ULaw LLP* [defendant's solicitor]
Date: 12 February 202_

8.2.7 Example application to exclude evidence of a defendant's bad character

The prosecution also intends to rely on evidence of Gary's bad character and serve notice to introduce evidence of a defendant's bad character. Gary's solicitor prepares an application to exclude such evidence.

NOTICE TO INTRODUCE EVIDENCE OF A DEFENDANT'S BAD CHARACTER
(Criminal Procedure Rules, rule 21.4(2))

Case details
Name of defendant: *Gary Paul Dickson*
Court: *Chester Crown Court*
Case reference number: *CH090248*
Charge(s): *Assault occasioning actual bodily harm on Vincent Lamb on 15 December 202_*

This notice is given by the prosecutor
I want to introduce evidence of the bad character of ...*Gary Paul Dickson*.......
(defendant's
name) **on the following ground(s) in the Criminal Justice Act 2003:**
☐ **It is important explanatory evidence: s.101(1)(c).**
☑ **It is relevant to an important matter in issue between that defendant and the prosecution: s.101(1)(d).**
☐ **It has substantial probative value in relation to an important matter in issue between that defendant and a co-defendant: s.101(1)(e).**
☐ **It is evidence to correct a false impression given by that defendant: s.101(1)(f).**
☑ **That defendant has made an attack on another person's character: s.101(1)(g).**

How to use this form
1 Complete the boxes above and give the details required in the boxes below.
If you use an electronic version of this form, the boxes will expand. If you use a paper version and need more space, you may attach extra sheets.
2 Sign and date the completed form.
3 Send a copy of the completed form to:
  (a) the court, and
  (b) each other party to the case.
Notes:
1 You must send this form so as to reach the recipients within the time prescribed by Criminal Procedure Rule 21.4 (3) or (4). The court may extend that time limit, **but if you are late you must explain why.**
2 A party who objects to the introduction of the evidence must apply to the court under Criminal Procedure Rule 21.4(5) **not more than 14 days after service of this notice.**

1) Facts of the misconduct. If the misconduct is a previous conviction, explain whether you rely on (a) the fact of that conviction, or (b) the circumstances of that offence. If (b), set out the facts on which you rely.

The defendant was convicted of theft 4 years ago having pleaded not guilty and testified. The fact of this conviction will be relied on to establish his propensity to be untruthful.

The defendant was convicted of common assault 6 years ago, s4 Public Order Act 2 years and 1 year ago and s47 ABH 1 year ago. The circumstances of both of these convictions will be relied on to establish his propensity to commit offences of violence.

The defendant's convictions for offences of common assault 6 years ago, theft 4 years ago, s4 Public Order Act 2 years and 1 year ago and s47 ABH 1 year ago. The fact of all of these convictions will be relied on when considering the character of the defendant who has made an attack on the character of others.

2) How you will prove those facts, if in dispute. A party who objects to the introduction of the evidence must explain which, if any, of the facts set out above are in dispute. Explain in outline on what you will then rely to prove those facts, eg whether you rely on (a) a certificate of conviction, (b) another official record (and if so, which), or (c) other evidence (and if so, what).

Evidence of the defendant's certificates of previous convictions (attached) will be produced. The officer in charge of the case, PC Chambers, will be called to adduce this evidence.

3) Reasons why the evidence is admissible. Explain why the evidence is admissible, by reference to the provision (s) of the Criminal Justice Act 2003 on which you rely.
s 101(1)(d) CJA 2003 - relevant to an important matter in issue between the prosecution and the defence.

Convictions recorded 6 years ago for common assault, 2 years and 1 year ago for section 4 Public Order Act 1986 and 1 year ago for causing actual bodily harm, contrary to s 47 Offences Against the Person Act 1861 as to propensity to commit offences of the type charged.

Conviction recorded 4 years ago for Theft as to propensity to be untruthful, the defendant pleaded not guilty and was convicted after trial.

S 101(1)(g) – the defendant has made an attack on the character of another.

All of the defendant's convictions on the attached list are relevant as the defendant attacked the character of another in the police interview (record of interview attached).

4) Reasons for any extension of time required. If this notice is served late, explain why.
N/A

Signed: *J. Boothroyd...*[prosecutor]
Date: *8th February 202_*

APPLICATION TO EXCLUDE EVIDENCE OF A DEFENDANT'S BAD CHARACTER
(Criminal Procedure Rules, rule 21.4(5))

Case details
Name of defendant: Gary Paul Dickson
Court: Chester Crown Court
Case reference number: CH 090248
Charge(s): Assault occasioning actual bodily harm on Vincent Lamb on 15 December 202_

This is an application by
...Gary Paul Dickson.......................................(name of defendant)
I object to the introduction of the evidence of which the prosecutor served notice on 08/02/202_ because:
☑ **that evidence is not admissible.**
☑ **I am the defendant named in that notice and it would be unfair to admit that evidence.**
☑ **I object to the notice for the other reason(s) explained below.**

How to use this form

1 Complete the boxes above and give the details required in the boxes below.

If you use an electronic version of this form, the boxes will expand. If you use a paper version and need more space, you may attach extra sheets.

2 Sign and date the completed form.

3 Send a copy of the completed form to:

(a) the court, and

(b) each other party to the case.

Notes:

1 You must send this form so as to reach the recipients not more than 14 days after service of the notice to which you object. The court may extend that time limit, **but if you are late you must explain why.**

1) Facts of the misconduct in dispute. Whatever the reasons you have for objecting to the notice, explain (a) which, if any, facts of the misconduct set out in it you dispute, and (b) what, if any, facts you admit instead.

The facts relating to this misconduct are all accepted.

2) Reasons for objecting to the notice. Explain, as applicable:

(a) why the bad character evidence is not admissible, by reference to the provision(s) of the Criminal Justice Act 2003 relied on in the notice.

Convictions for common assault 6 years ago, s4 2 years and 1 year ago, and s47 ABH 1 year ago do not demonstrate a propensity to commit offences of the kind charged since the factual circumstances of these offences are very different to the facts of the current offence charged but would be very prejudicial in the eyes of the jury if they were to learn of these convictions.

In relation to the attack on the character of others, the admissibility of the interview record will be challenged at trial.

(b) if you are the defendant named in the notice, why it would be unfair to admit the evidence. (You can object on this ground under section 101(3) of the Criminal Justice Act 2003 only if the notice gives as grounds for admitting the evidence (i) that it is relevant to an important matter in issue between you and the prosecution, or (ii) that you have made an attack on another person's character.)

If the interview record is admitted, then in the alternative, the defendant was forced to make an attack on the character of the witness, Lamb, as a result of the officer's style of questioning and it would therefore be unfair to admit evidence of the defendant's previous convictions in such circumstances.

The conviction for common assault (6 years ago) is spent and too old now to be of any evidential value.

Conviction for theft 4 years ago not relevant to demonstrate a propensity to be untruthful since there is a single offence only [R v Hanson]. The evidential value of the conviction would be very prejudicial in the eyes of the jury if they were to learn of the conviction.

(c) what other objection you have to the notice.

In relation to propensity to commit offences of the type charged, by reason of the length of time since the conviction for common assault 6 years ago it would be unjust for it to apply in this case by virtue of Section 103(3).

3) Reasons for any extension of time required. If this application is served late, explain why.

N/A

Signed: *ULaw LLP*   **[defendant's solicitor]**

Date: 15/02/202_

8.3 Wills and Intestacy, Probate Administration and Practice

8.3.1 Example simple will

The example below is based on the following scenario.

Carl Leghorn is a retired engineer and lives at Magnolia Villas, The Lane, Bridport. He recalls making a will a long time ago but would like this new will to replace it entirely. He wishes to appoint his friend, Peter Singh, to be his executor. He wishes to leave his canteen of silver cutlery to his niece Mary Bell (age 25), and the sum of £20,000 to the charity Age Plus. Once these legacies and other debts have been paid, he wants to leave everything else he owns to his daughter, Hannah Leghorn. If Hannah dies before him, or shortly after him, he would like her son, John James (age 21), to inherit in her place.

This is the last will and testament of me, Carl Leghorn, retired engineer, of Magnolia Villas, The Lane, Bridport which I make this 3rd day of August 2022.

1. I revoke all former wills, codicils and testamentary dispositions.

2. I appoint Peter Singh of 4 Lime Yard, Bridport to be my executor ('my Executor').

3. I give my canteen of silver cutlery to my niece Mary Bell.

4. (a) I give £20,000 to Age Plus (Charity Registration number 4430098) ('the Charity') for its general charitable purposes.

   (b) If at my death the Charity has ceased to exist or has amalgamated with another charity or has changed its name my Executor shall pay it to the charitable organisation which they consider most nearly fulfils the objects of the Charity.

   (c) The receipt of a person who appears to be a proper officer of the Charity or any substituted charity shall be a sufficient discharge to my Executor.

5. I give all the rest of my property after deducting debts, testamentary expenses and legacies to my daughter Hannah Leghorn if she survives me by 28 days, but if she does not so survive me then to my grandson John James.

Signed by Carl Leghorn in our joint presence and then by us in his

CARL LEGHORN ——————————

JEAN FLORE————————————

BRIGITTE FLORE————————————

8.3.2 Example codicil

The example below is based on the following scenario.

Having executed the will above, Carl Leghorn has now decided that instead of leaving the sum of £20,000 to the charity Age Plus he wants to leave this amount to the charity Cats for Life UK. He does not want to make any other changes to his will. The same witnesses will be available to witness his signature.

Codicil

1. I am Carl Leghorn, retired engineer, of Magnolia Villas, The Lane, Bridport.

2. This is the first codicil to my will dated 3rd August 2022 ('my Will').

3. I make the following amendments to my Will. I replace clause 4 with the following clause

'4. (a) I give £20,000 to Cats for Life UK (Charity registration number: 07896) ('the Charity') for its general charitable purposes

(b) If at my death the Charity has ceased to exist or has amalgamated with another charity or has changed its name my Executor shall pay it to the charitable organisation which they consider most nearly fulfils the objects of the Charity.

(c) The receipt of a person who appears to be a proper officer of the Charity or any substituted charity shall be a sufficient discharge to my Executor.'

4. I confirm the rest of my Will.

Dated

Signed by Carl Leghorn in our joint presence and then by us in his

CARL LEGHORN ————

JEAN FLORE————

BRIGITTE FLORE————

8.3.3 Example affidavit of due execution

The example below is based on the following scenario.

John Roberts of The Rectory, Newton, Hampshire died on 20 June 2021. He left a will dated 20 September 1991, appointing his sisters Faith Peters and Imelda Howard as executrixes. Faith and Imelda have applied for the grant of probate from the Brighton Registry. The registrar has noticed that John signed the will in an unusual place (under the signatures of the witnesses, Jakob and Magda Nowak) and has asked the executrixes to obtain evidence of execution. One of the witnesses, Magda Nowak, can give evidence that John executed the will correctly.

IN THE BRIGHTON DISTRICT PROBATE REGISTRY

Extracting solicitor:

Address

DX

Ref

IN THE ESTATE OF JOHN ROBERTS

I, Magda Nowak of 5 Popes Lane, Newton, Hampshire make oath and say as follows:

1. I am one of the two subscribing witnesses to the will of John Roberts of The Rectory, Newton, Hampshire deceased ('the Testator'). The other subscribing witness to the will is Jakob Nowak. The will is dated 20 September 1991. The will is now produced to me and is marked MN1.

2. The Testator executed the will on 20 September 1991 by signing his name as that name now appears on the will in the presence of me and Jakob Nowak, with both of us present at the same time. After the Testator had signed the will we each attested and signed the will in the presence of the Testator.

Sworn by the above-named deponent   [SIGNATURE OF DEPONENT]

At [insert name] [Solicitors OR Commissioners for oaths]

this [DATE] day of [MONTH] [YEAR]

before me: [SIGNATURE OF SOLICITOR OR COMMISSIONER FOR OATHS]

[Solicitor OR Commissioner for oaths]

8.3.4 Example deed of variation

Continuing with the same facts as above, John Roberts left a legacy of £100,000 to his son Alan Roberts by clause 7 of his will dated 20 September 1991. John has now died, and the executors have obtained the grant. Alan wishes to redirect the legacy to his daughter Kate Roberts (age 23). John's executors, Faith Peters and Imelda Howard are in agreement.

This DEED OF VARIATION is made the day of 2022

BETWEEN

(1) Alan Roberts of The Rectory, Newton, Hampshire ('the Original Beneficiary')

(2) Kate Roberts of The Rectory, Newton, Hampshire ('the New Beneficiary')

SUPPLEMENTAL to the will dated 20th September 1991 ('the Will') of John Roberts late of The Rectory, Newton, Hampshire who died on 20th June 2021.

WHEREAS:

(A) Under clause 7 of the Will the Original Beneficiary was given a pecuniary legacy of £100,000 ('the Legacy')

(B) The Original Beneficiary wishes to vary the dispositions effected by the Will in relation to the Legacy in the following manner

NOW THIS DEED IRREVOCABLY WITNESSES as follows:

1. By way of variation of the disposition made by the Will the Original Beneficiary declares that the Will shall have effect as if the following clause appeared in place of clause 7:

    I give the sum of £100,000 to Kate Roberts of The Rectory, Newton, Hampshire

2. The provisions of the Inheritance Act 1984, s.142 (1) and of the Taxation of Chargeable Gains Act 1992, s.62 (6) shall apply to this variation.

Signed as a deed by Alan Roberts

Signature

In the presence of

Signature of witness

Name (in BLOCK CAPITALS)

Address

8.4 Property Practice

8.4.1 Example contract

The example below is based on the following scenario.

Roger Evans is selling his freehold property, 47 Queens Road, Loamster, Maradon, Cornshire CS1 5TY to Catherine and Joanna Reade of 24 Leeming Road, Bridgeton, Cornshire CS3 4DD. Title to the property is registered with absolute title and the title number is LM12037. The purchase price is £350,000 and various items of garden furniture, a washer drier and a fridge freezer are being sold for an additional £500. A £20,000 deposit has been agreed. The property is to be sold with vacant possession. The seller is the original covenantor in respect of the covenants in entry 1 of the charges register.

Entry 1 of the charges register for LM12037 reads:

> The Purchaser with the intent and so as to bind the property hereby conveyed and to benefit and protect the retained land of the Vendor lying to the west of the land hereby conveyed hereby covenants with the Vendor that he and his successors in title will at all times observe and perform the stipulations and conditions set out in the schedule hereto.

THE SCHEDULE ABOVE REFERRED TO

'1. Not to use the property other than as a single private dwelling house; and

2. Not to build or allow to be built any new building on the property nor alter or allow to be altered any building currently erected on the property without the written consent of the Vendor or his successors in title.'

Entry 2 of the charges register shows that there is a charge over the property in favour of the Humberside and Counties Bank. This is to be discharged on completion.

The Standard Conditions of Sale (5th edition – 2018 Revision) are to apply to the contract.

For conveyancer's use only

Buyer's conveyancer: ....

Seller's conveyancer: ....

Law Society Formula: [A / B / C / Personal exchange]

CONTRACT

Incorporating the Standard Conditions of Sale (Fifth Edition–2018 Revision)

Date	
Seller	: ROGER EVANS of 47, Queens' Road, Loamster, Maradon, Cornshire, CS1 5TY
Buyer	: CATHERINE READE and JOANNE READE both of 24, Leeming Road, Bridgeton, Cornshire, CS3 4DD
Property (freehold/~~leasehold~~)	: 47, Queens' Road, Loamster, Maradon, Cornshire CS1 5TY
Title number/~~root of title~~	: LM 12037 (Absolute Title)
Specified incumbrances	: The covenants referred to in entry No. 1 of the Charges Register
Title guarantee (full/limited)	: Full
Completion date	:
Contract rate	: The Law Society's interest rate from time to time
Purchase price	: £350,000
Deposit	: £20,000
Contents price (if separate)	: £500
Balance	: £330,500

The seller will sell and the buyer will buy the property for the purchase price.

WARNING
This is a formal
document, designed to
create legal rights and
legal obligations. Take
advice before using it.

Signed

Seller/Buyer

SPECIAL CONDITIONS

1. (a) This contract incorporates the Standard Conditions of Sale (Fifth Edition–2018 Revision).

    (b) The terms used in this contract have the same meaning when used in the Conditions.

2. Subject to the terms of this contract and to the Standard Conditions of Sale, the seller is to transfer the property with either full title guarantee or limited title guarantee, as specified on the front page.

3. (a) The sale includes those contents which are indicated on the attached list as included in the sale and the buyer is to pay the contents price for them.[1]

    (b) The Sale excludes those fixtures which are at the property and are indicated on the attached list as excluded from the sale.

4. The property is sold with vacant possession.

(or) 4. The property is sold subject to the following leases or tenancies.

5. Conditions 6.1.2 and 6.1.3 shall take effect as if the time specified in them were 12 noon rather than 2.00 p.m.

6. **Representations**

    Neither party can rely on any representation made by the other, unless made in writing by the other or his conveyancer, but this does not exclude liability for fraud or recklessness.

7. **Occupier's consent**

    Each occupier identified below agrees with the seller and the buyer, in consideration of their entering into this contract, that the occupier concurs in the sale of the property on the terms of this contract, undertakes to vacate the property on or before the completion date and releases the property and any included fixtures and contents from any right or interest that the occupier may have.

    Note: this condition does not apply to occupiers under leases or tenancies subject to which the property is sold

    Name(s) and signature(s) of the occupier(s) (if any):

    Name ....

    Signature ....

    Notices may be sent to:

    Seller's conveyancer's name: *ULaw LLP*

    E-mail address:*

    Buyer's conveyancer's name: *SLT Solicitors*

    E-mail address:*

* Adding an e-mail address authorises service by e-mail: see condition 1.3.3(b)

---

[1] *Author's note*: Not attached for the purposes of this example.

161

Commentary

The following points should be noted.

Date

The contract is left undated at the draft stage. The date is inserted on actual exchange of contracts.

Parties

The full names and addresses of the parties, as they will later appear on the transfer, should be inserted. Note the inclusion of postcodes in the parties' addresses.

Property

The property is freehold, so the word 'leasehold' can be deleted. Since the property is registered with an absolute title and is a suburban property with well-defined boundaries, it will suffice to describe it merely by its postal address. No plan is needed in this case. Note the inclusion of the postcode in the description of the property; it is Land Registry practice to include this on the register.

Title

The property is registered, therefore the reference to 'root of title' is irrelevant and can be deleted. The title number and confirmation that the class of title is absolute should be inserted here.

Incumbrances

As the mortgage is to be discharged on completion there is no need to mention it. The restrictive covenants must be stated to comply with SC 3. These can be identified by reference to the official copy. There is no need, however, to set out the covenants verbatim as long as a copy is provided; in this case as it is registered land, official copies will be supplied in any event.

Title guarantee

The seller is a sole owner and will give full title guarantee. It is customary to insert this on the front page of the contract form, even though in this case the words inserted repeat SC 4.6.2.

Completion date

The completion date is left blank at this stage and inserted on actual exchange.

Contract rate

Even though it is not intended to vary SC 1.1.1(e), confirmation of that fact is included on the front page of the contract form. Unless there are special circumstances, the solicitor would normally decide on the rate of interest to be included in the contract and this is not a matter on which the client's instructions are sought.

Price

The price, amount of deposit, amount (if any) payable for contents and balance due on completion are inserted in the appropriate space towards the bottom of the front page of the contract form. Note that the deposit is normally calculated as being 10% of the price for a property. [This is to comply with SC 2.2.1]. However, here the instructions indicate that a deposit of £20,000 has been agreed.

Agreement for sale

The words 'The seller will sell and the buyer will buy the property for the purchase price' above the two boxes at the bottom of the front page of the contract form constitute the agreement for sale. A box is provided for the seller and buyer to sign. This is left blank at this stage and will be signed by the client close to exchange.

Printed Special Condition 1

Printed Special Condition 1 incorporates the text of the Standard Conditions of Sale (Fifth Edition – 2018 Revision) from the centre pages of the contract form. These pages are not reproduced in this example. This Condition should not be deleted, since to remove it is to remove the effect of the Standard Conditions.

Printed Special Condition 2

This Condition refers to the implied covenants which are given to the buyer under the Law of Property (Miscellaneous Provisions) Act 1994. In this case, the seller is selling with full title guarantee, and this fact is included on the front page of the contract form.

Printed Special Condition 3

This is necessary to ensure the contents are included in the sale. A list of the relevant items needs to be attached.

Printed Special Condition 4

This Condition provides two options, depending whether the property is to be sold with vacant possession (as here) or is subject to tenancies. In the latter case the details of the tenancies would be given in the condition.

Printed Special Condition 5

This clause has been deleted. It will be relevant where the time for completion has been altered by agreement.

Printed Special Condition 7

This has been deleted as there are no occupiers other than the seller in this property.

Conveyancers

The names (and if desired the addresses and references) of the parties' conveyancers are inserted at the foot of the back page of the contract form.

8.4.2 Example Transfer [Land Registry Form TR1]

The example below is based on the same transaction.

HM Land Registry

Transfer of whole of registered title[s]

TR1

Any parts of the form that are not typed should be completed in black ink and in block capitals.

If you need more room than is provided for in a panel, and your software allows, you can expand any panel in the form. Alternatively use continuation sheet CS and attach it to this form.

For information on how HM Land Registry processes your personal information, see our Personal Information Charter.

Leave blank if not yet registered.	1	Title number(s) of the property: LM12037
Insert address including postcode (if any) or other description of the property, for example 'land adjoining 2 Acacia Avenue'.	2	Property: 47, Queen's Road, Loamster, Maradon, Cornshire CS1 5TY
Remember to date this deed with the day of completion, but not before it has been signed and witnessed.	3	Date: [blank]

Give full name(s) of **all** the persons transferring the property. Complete as appropriate where the transferor is a company. Enter the overseas entity ID issued by Companies House for the transferor pursuant to the Economic Crime (Transparency and Enforcement) Act 2022. If the ID is not required, you may instead state 'not required'. Further details on overseas entities can be found in <u>practice guide 78: overseas entities</u>.	4	Transferor: ROGER EVANS <u>For UK incorporated companies/LLPs</u> Registered number of company or limited liability partnership including any prefix: <u>For overseas companies</u> (a) Territory of incorporation or formation: (b) Overseas entity ID issued by Companies House, including any prefix: (c) Where the entity is a company with a place of business in the United Kingdom, the registered number, if any, issued by Companies House, including any prefix:
Give full name(s) of **all** the persons to be shown as registered proprietors. Complete as appropriate where the transferee is a company. Also, for an overseas company, unless an arrangement with HM Land Registry exists, lodge either a certificate in Form 7 in Schedule 3 to the Land Registration Rules 2003 or a certified copy of the constitution in English or Welsh, or other evidence permitted by rule 183 of the Land Registration Rules 2003. Enter the overseas entity ID issued by Companies House for the transferor pursuant to the Economic Crime (Transparency and Enforcement) Act 2022. If the ID is not required, you may instead state 'not required'. Further details on overseas entities can be found in <u>practice guide 78: overseas entities</u>.	5	Transferee for entry in the register: Catherine Reade and Joanne Reade <u>For UK incorporated companies/LLPs</u> Registered number of company or limited liability partnership including any prefix: <u>For overseas companies</u> (a) Territory of incorporation or formation: (b) Overseas entity ID issued by Companies House, including any prefix: (c) Where the entity is a company with a place of business in the United Kingdom, the registered number, if any, issued by Companies House, including any prefix:
Each transferee may give up to three addresses for service, one of which must be a postal address whether or not in the UK (including the postcode, if any). The others can be any combination of a postal address, a UK DX box number or an electronic address.	6	Transferee's intended address(es) for service for entry in the register: 47, Queen's Road, Loamster, Maradon, Cornshire CS1 5TY
	7	The transferor transfers the property to the transferee
Place 'X' in the appropriate box. State the currency unit if other than sterling. If none of the boxes apply, insert an appropriate memorandum in panel 11.	8	Consideration ☒ The transferor has received from the transferee for the property the following sum (in words and figures): three hundred and fifty thousand pounds £350,000.00 ☐ The transfer is not for money or anything that has a monetary value ☐ Insert other receipt as appropriate:

Place 'X' in any box that applies. Add any modifications.	9	The transferor transfers ☒ with full title guarantee ☐ limited title guarantee

Where the transferee is more than one person, place 'X' in the appropriate box.
 	
Complete as necessary.
 	
The registrar will enter a Form A restriction in the register *unless*:
- an 'X' is placed:
  - in the first box, or
  - in the third box and the details of the trust or of the trust instrument show that the transferees are to hold the property on trust for themselves alone as joint tenants, *or*
  - it is clear from completion of a form JO lodged with this application that the transferees are to hold the property on trust for themselves alone as joint tenants.
Please refer to *Joint property ownership* *and practice guide* *24: private trusts of* *land* for further guidance. These are both available on the GOV.UK website.
	10	Declaration of trust. The transferee is more than one person and
		☐ they are to hold the property on trust for themselves as joint tenants
		☒ they are to hold the property on trust for themselves as tenants in common in equal shares
		☐ they are to hold the property on trust:

Insert here any required or permitted statement, certificate or application and any agreed covenants, declarations and so on.	11	Additional provisions The transferees jointly and severally covenant with the transferor to: 11.1 (by way of indemnity only) observe and perform the covenants referred to in Entry No 1 of the charges register of the title referred to above ('the Covenants') so far as they are subsisting and capable of taking effect; and 11.2 indemnify the transferor against any liability incurred for any breach or non-observance of the Covenants occurring after the date of this transfer.

The transferor must execute this transfer as a deed using the space opposite. If there is more than one transferor, all must execute. Forms of execution are given in Schedule 9 to the Land Registration Rules 2003. If the transfer contains transferee's covenants or declarations or contains an application by the transferee (such as for a restriction), it must also be executed by the transferee. If there is more than one transferee and panel 10 has been completed, each transferee must also execute this transfer to comply with the requirements in section 53(1)(b) of the Law of Property Act 1925 relating to the declaration of a trust of land. Please refer to *Joint property ownership* and *practice guide 24: private trusts of land* for further guidance. Examples of the correct form of execution are set out in *practice guide 8: execution of deeds*. Execution as a deed usually means that a witness must also sign, and add their name and address.	12	Execution Signed as a deed by ROGER EVANS in the presence of .... Signature of witness .... Name (in BLOCK CAPITALS) .... Address .... Signed as a deed by Catherine Reade in the presence of .... Signature of witness .... Name (in BLOCK CAPITALS) .... Address .... Signed as a deed by Joanne Reade in the presence of .... Signature of witness .... Name (in BLOCK CAPITALS) .... Address ....
Remember to date this deed in panel 3.		

Commentary

The following points should be noted:

Panels 1 and 2: the title number and the address of the property should be checked against the details in the contract and the official copies. The description should include the postcode.

Panel 3: the transfer will only be dated upon completion.

Panels 4 and 5: the names of the parties should be checked against the details in the contract and, in the case of the transferor, the official copies.

Panel 6: If the buyers intend to live in this property they will want communications to go to their new address, not their old address. If the property will be tenanted, the buyer may want communications sent to another address, such as a registered office in the case of a company.

Panel 7: this is the operative part of the deed and it should not be amended.

Panel 8: the purchase price should be written in figures as well as words. It should be the total amount payable for the property (i.e. not just the balance due upon completion) but should exclude any amount payable in respect of contents. If contents are being purchased for an additional sum, a separate receipt will be needed to prepare for this amount. Where VAT is payable, the amount stated should include VAT, as this forms part of the consideration for the property).

Panel 9: on the front page of the contract the seller has stated they are selling with full title guarantee. In addition, SC 4.6.2 states the seller is selling with full title guarantee. There is space in this box to include any modifications to the covenants that may have been agreed in the contract.

Panel 10: this panel is only relevant where there is more than one transferee. It requires them to declare whether they will hold the land as joint tenants or tenants in common. If they are to hold as tenants in common other than in equal shares it is necessary for the precise shares to be set out.

Panel 11: this is a box into which any other agreed clauses can be inserted. The most common will be an indemnity covenant, as in this example. Remember that additional clauses can be included only if they were agreed in the contract, so the contract should be consulted when completing this panel. Where the sale is subject to any obligation on which the seller will remain liable after the sale, S.C. 4.6.4 will provide that the buyer should enter into an indemnity covenant.

Panel 12: the signature of the seller, being an individual, must be witnessed

Panel 12: the buyers should also execute the transfer as they are entering into an indemnity covenant.

8.4.3 Example undertaking for costs

The example below is based on the following facts.

Ulaw LLP act for Fabrice Limited which has applied for consent from its Landlord, Patricks plc, to alter the leasehold premises. Under the terms of the lease Fabrice Limited is liable to pay the costs of Patricks plc, incurred in connection with the application for licence to alter. Their solicitors have written to request an undertaking from Ulaw LLP to pay their costs in relation to the proposed alterations, whether or not the matter proceeds to completion. They say that their costs are unlikely to exceed £550 exclusive of VAT.

Fabrice Limited have instructed Ulaw LLP that they are willing to meet the costs up to a limit of £550 plus VAT. Ulaw LLP have therefore drafted a letter of undertaking to the solicitors acting for Patricks plc.

Dear Sir/Madam,

COSTS UNDERTAKING IN RESPECT OF APPLICATION FOR LICENCE TO ALTER LEASE DATED 15 MAY 2006 BETWEEN PATRICKS PLC AND FABRICE LIMITED

We act for Fabrice Limited ('the Tenant') in connection with its application for consent from Patricks plc ('the Landlord') to alter the property demised by the lease dated 15 May 2006 ('the Property').

We undertake to pay your reasonable legal costs (subject to a cap of £550 plus VAT) in connection with our client's application for a licence to alter the Property whether or not the matter proceeds to completion and provided that your client does not unreasonably revoke or refuse to give such licence.

Yours faithfully,

[ULAW LLP]

8.5 Business Organisations, Rules and Procedures

The examples below are based on the following scenario.

Latimer Boats Limited (LBL) was formed in 2004 under the Companies Act 1985 and its articles are in the form of Table A under Companies (Tables A to F) Regulations 1985. LBL has two directors, Stuart Latimer (MD and chairman of board of directors) and Margaret Lafitte. The shareholders are Stuart Latimer, Margaret Lafitte and Robert Stonebridge, each of whom holds 1000 £1 shares. LBL wants to change its name to Richmond Vessels Limited and to update the articles of association to the model articles. The shareholders all agree to these proposals. A board meeting and general meeting are held and the necessary documents are drafted to achieve these purposes.

8.5.1 Example notice of a general meeting

LATIMER BOATS LIMITED ('the Company')

COMPANY NUMBER: 05030879

NOTICE OF GENERAL MEETING

NOTICE is given that a general meeting of the Company will be held on *[date]* at 2pm at Studio 3, Auriol Court, Richmond, TW9 3DF for the following purposes:

SPECIAL RESOLUTIONS

To consider and, if thought fit, approve the following resolutions that will be proposed as special resolutions:

1. That the name of the Company be changed to Richmond Vessels Limited.

2. That the articles of association in the form attached to this notice[1] be adopted in their entirety in substitution for the current articles of association of the Company.

By order of the board

Chairman

Studio 3, Auriol Court, Richmond, TW9 3DF

Date: [   ]

NOTE

A shareholder is entitled to appoint another person as that shareholder's proxy to exercise all or any of that shareholder's rights to attend and to speak and vote at the meeting. A shareholder may appoint more than one proxy in relation to the meeting, provided that each proxy is appointed to exercise the rights attached to a different share or shares held by that shareholder. A proxy does not need to be a shareholder of the Company.

[1] Not attached.

8.5.2   Example agreement to short notice of a general meeting

LATIMER BOATS LIMITED ('the Company')

COMPANY NUMBER: 05030879

AGREEMENT OF MEMBERS TO SHORT NOTICE OF A GENERAL MEETING

We, the undersigned, being all the members and together holding not less than 95% in nominal value of the shares giving the right to attend and vote at the general meeting of the Company to be held at 2pm on *[date]* at Studio 3, Auriol Court, Richmond, TW9 3DF agree that the meeting (including any adjournment) shall be deemed to have been duly called and the resolutions set out in the notice convening the meeting may be proposed and passed notwithstanding that shorter notice than that specified in the Companies Act 2006 or in the Company's articles of association has been given.

Dated: *[date]*   ....

Signature of Stuart Latimer   ....

Signature of Margaret Laffite   ....

Signature of Robert Stonebridge   ....

8.5.3   Example written resolutions

COMPANY NUMBER: 05030879

THE COMPANIES ACT 2006

PRIVATE COMPANY LIMITED BY SHARES

Written resolutions of LATIMER BOATS LIMITED ('the Company')

CIRCULATED ON [*date*]

Pursuant to Chapter 2 of Part 13 of the Companies Act 2006, the directors of the Company propose that the following resolutions be passed as special resolutions:

SPECIAL RESOLUTIONS

1.   That the name of the Company be changed to Richmond Vessels Limited.

2.   That the articles of association in the form attached to this written resolution be adopted in their entirety in substitution for the current articles of association of the Company.

Please read the explanatory notes at the end of this document before signifying your agreement to the resolutions.

We, the undersigned, were at the time the resolutions were circulated entitled to vote on the resolutions and irrevocably agree to the resolutions.

Signed..   Date................................
Stuart Latimer

Signed..   Date................................
Margaret Lafitte

Signed..   Date................................
Robert Stonebridge

EXPLANATORY NOTES FOR SHAREHOLDERS

If you agree to the resolutions, please signify your agreement by signing and dating this document where indicated above and returning it to the Company using one of the following methods:

a)   **BY HAND**: By delivering the signed copy to Stuart Latimer, Studio 3, Auriol Court, Richmond, TW9 3DF;

b)   **BY POST**: By returning the signed copy by post to Stuart Latimer, Studio 3, Auriol Court, Richmond, TW9 3DF;

c)   **BY FAX**: By faxing the signed copy to 0870 350 1562, marked 'For the attention of Stuart Latimer, Latimer Boats Limited'; or

d)   **BY E-MAIL**: By attaching a scanned copy of the signed document to an e-mail and sending it to stuart@Latimerboats.co.uk. Please enter 'Written Resolution' in the e-mail subject box.

If you do not agree to the above resolutions, you do not need to do anything.

Once you have signified your agreement to the resolutions, you may not revoke your agreement.

Unless, by *[date]*, sufficient agreement has been received for the resolutions to be passed, they will lapse. If you agree to the resolutions, please ensure that signification of your agreement reaches us before or on this date.

8.5.4   Example minutes of a board meeting

LATIMER BOATS LIMITED ('the Company')

Minutes of a meeting of the Board of Directors of the Company held at Studio 3, Auriol Court, Richmond, TW9 3DF on [*date*] at 1:50pm.

Present:	Stuart Latimer (Chairman)
	Margaret Laffite
In attendance:	Robert Stonebridge

1. PRELIMINARY

The Chairman noted that the meeting had been duly convened, reported that a quorum of two directors was present in accordance with the Articles of Association and declared the meeting open.

2. CHANGES TO THE COMPANY'S NAME AND ARTICLES

The Chairman proposed that the name of the Company be changed to Richmond Vessels Limited.

The Chairman also explained that, after discussions with the Company's lawyers, it was felt appropriate to modify the Company's Articles of Association to bring them into line with the changes already brought about by the Companies Act 2006.

3. TABLING OF DOCUMENTS

The board had been advised that the proposals in paragraph 2 would need resolutions of the members. Accordingly, there were produced to the meeting:

(a) a draft form of the proposed Articles of Association ('the Articles');

(b) a form of notice convening a General Meeting of the Company ('the Notice') to pass two special resolutions to give effect to the proposals in paragraph 2; and

(c) a form of consent to short notice for the General Meeting.

4. RESOLUTIONS AND CALLING OF GENERAL MEETING

IT WAS RESOLVED THAT a General Meeting of the Company be convened and held forthwith for the purpose of considering and, if thought fit, passing the resolutions set out in the Notice.

The Chairman instructed the Company's solicitors to send the Notice and form of consent to short notice to everyone entitled to receive them. The meeting was then adjourned at 1:55pm for the purpose of holding the General Meeting.

5.   POST-GM MATTERS AND ADMINISTRATION

Upon resumption of the meeting, the Chairman reported that the necessary consents to short notice for the General Meeting had been obtained, the General Meeting had been duly held and the resolutions set out in the Notice duly passed.

The Chairman instructed:

(a)   the Company's solicitors to notify the Registrar of Companies of the change of name and articles in the prescribed manner, including filing the special resolutions;

(b)   the Company's solicitors to make all necessary and appropriate entries in the books and registers of the Company; and

(c)   Margaret Laffite to ensure that all notices, signs, stationery, websites, emails and similar notifications and publications which bear the Company's name are amended to reflect the new name from the date when the change of name is confirmed by the Registrar of Companies.

6.   CLOSE

There being no further business, the meeting then closed.

....

Chairman

8.5.5   Example minutes of a general meeting

LATIMER BOATS LIMITED ('the Company')

Minutes of a General Meeting of the Company held at Studio 3, Auriol Court, Richmond, TW9 3DF on [*date*] at 2pm.

Present: Stuart Latimer (Chairman)
                       Margaret Laffite
                       Robert Stonebridge

1.   **NOTICE AND QUORUM**

It was noted that a majority in number of the members having the right to attend and vote at the meeting and together holding at least ninety-five per cent in nominal value of the shares giving that right to vote had consented to short notice of the meeting in accordance with section 307 of the Companies Act 2006 and regulation 38 of Table A.

The Chairman reported that a quorum of two members was present in accordance with the articles of association and declared the meeting open.

2. <u>CHANGE TO THE COMPANY'S NAME</u>

The Chairman proposed the following resolution as a special resolution of the Company:

That the name of the Company be changed to Richmond Vessels Limited.

The Chairman put the resolution to the meeting, took the vote on a show of hands and declared the resolution carried unanimously.

3. <u>CHANGE TO THE COMPANY'S ARTICLES OF ASSOCIATION</u>

There was produced to the meeting the notice calling the meeting, together with the attached proposed new articles of association of the Company. The Chairman proposed the following resolution as a special resolution of the Company:

That the articles of association in the form attached to this notice[1] be adopted in their entirety in substitution for the current articles of association of the Company.

The Chairman put the resolution to the meeting, took the vote on a show of hands and declared the resolution carried unanimously.

4. <u>CLOSE</u>

There being no further business the meeting then closed.

....

Chairman

---

[1] Not attached.

Conducting Legal Research

SQE2 syllabus

This chapter will help you to achieve the SQE2 Assessment Criterion of identifying and using relevant sources and information.

Learning outcomes

By the end of this chapter you should be able to:

- explain how legal research is used in a practical context;
- understand how to approach a problem presented by a client;
- identify the key stages in analysing a problem;
- describe the importance of selecting appropriate search terms; and
- understand how to access legal resources online.

9.1   Introduction

Trainees and newly qualified solicitors spend a large proportion of their time engaged in Legal Research, whether as part of a team working on a client's matter or on behalf of other fee earners. This is simply because it is more cost effective for research to be undertaken by more junior members of the firm. Carrying out Legal Research therefore presents an opportunity to impress. Strong research skills are highly valued by firms. Time and effort invested in learning how to research effectively will pay dividends from the earliest stage of a solicitor's career.

In the SQE2 Legal Research assessments candidates will be provided with relevant legal sources. Candidates are therefore not expected to carry out independent research in order to find the sources for themselves. However, given the importance of research in legal practice some basic guidance on how to conduct Legal Research is set out in this chapter. Locating the right law is but one step (albeit a very important one) in the process of finding a solution to the client's problem. Other steps in that process, as mentioned in this chapter, will arise in the SQE2 assessments.

Chapter 10 will consider research sources and **Chapter 11** will focus on the SQE2 assessments.

This chapter looks at:

- the importance of legal research;
- problem solving;
- principles of legal research;
- accessing online databases;
- guidelines for searching online databases; and
- using the free internet.

9.2   The importance of legal research

Law firms exist to make money. They generate fees by selling the time that lawyers spend on solving clients' problems. Legal Research is a particularly important step in this larger process.

In a law firm, Legal Research entails the ability to produce work that is:

- accurate;
- timely;
- up to date;
- carried out efficiently;
- commercially aware; and
- presented in an appropriate and succinct form.

The focus on timeliness and efficiency in the commercial world requires a shift in mindset for many from the academic environment, where students often have several weeks to complete a piece of research. For practising lawyers, time really is money.

9.3   Problem-solving

At any one time, a solicitor is likely to deal with a variety of case files presented by clients who are diverse in background and personality. Unsurprisingly, the issues that clients present to solicitors tend to be complex and difficult. They may have multiple strands. Often there will be a range of possible solutions, some legal and some non-legal. Each client's circumstances will generate a different set of time pressures. For all these reasons, when presented with a client's matter, a solicitor needs to adopt a logical approach.

The main purpose of a lawyer's skills and knowledge is to bridge the gap between a client's actual circumstances and what the client wants them to be: in other words, to solve clients' problems. Conducting Legal Research is, in essence, an exercise in problem-solving.

The model below is intended to set out a logical framework for problem-solving. It is in effect an expanded version of *IRAC* model referred to in **Chapter 4** on Case and Matter Analysis. Expanded because it incorporates the process of gathering the information required to enable the solicitor to identify the *Issues* and conducting the research necessary to find the *Rules*. The model is as applicable to solving the problem presented in the SQE2 Legal Research assessments as it is to solving a client's problem in legal practice.

The research process underpins all of the stages in the problem-solving model. It entails finding and reporting the material that is relevant to solving a legal problem in the quickest possible time.

Problem-solving model

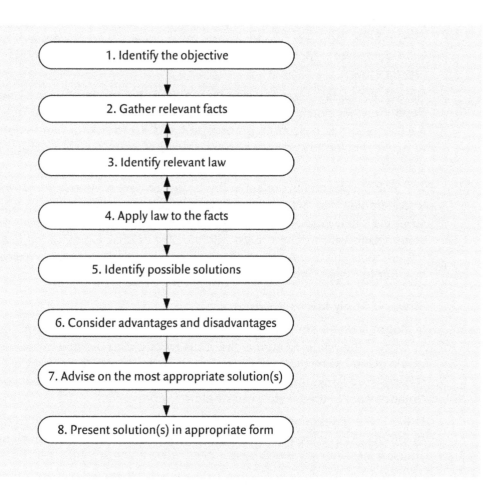

1. Identify the objective
2. Gather relevant facts
3. Identify relevant law
4. Apply law to the facts
5. Identify possible solutions
6. Consider advantages and disadvantages
7. Advise on the most appropriate solution(s)
8. Present solution(s) in appropriate form

Stage 1. Identify the objective

The first step is to clearly establish the client's objectives. What the client wants to achieve must drive a solicitor's approach to solving legal problems (in so far, of course, as regulatory and professional conduct rules allow). In legal practice a solicitor will establish the client's objectives by discussing the circumstances that prompted them to seek legal advice. In the SEQ2 assessments candidates must identify the client's objectives from a careful reading of the instructions.

Stage 2. Gather relevant facts

The main source of information is the client. A solicitor will question the client to obtain all the facts that may be relevant to tackle the problem in order to achieve their objectives. A solicitor may also need to gather more facts from a range of other sources, such as:

- other participants in the matter (such as witnesses or police officers);
- documents (such as witness statements, contracts or photographs); and
- experts (such as surveyors, doctors or forensic scientists).

In the SQE2 assessments the facts will be presented in the instructions. Candidates will need to analyse the information in order to distinguish the facts which are key, important or peripheral.

Stage 3. Identify relevant law

A number of legal issues will arise from the key facts. These may be issues of substantive law, procedure or a combination of the two. The solicitor may already have a good grasp of the general area of law in question and so be able to point immediately to some relevant law. However, the facts may raise novel issues or points of detail in which case it will be necessary for the solicitor to carry out some focused research in order to find the relevant law.

Note that double arrows link stages 2 and 3 in the model. This is because they are inter-dependent. Researching the relevant law may well prompt further questions, so that it may be necessary for the solicitor to go back to the client to ask for more information. It is important to avoid jumping to conclusions on the basis of insufficient knowledge of either the facts or the law.

The SQE2 assessments are set in the broad context of areas of law which will be familiar to candidates from SQE1. Beyond that candidates will be provided with the law required to solve the client's problem. However, just as in legal practice where research may produce some results which do not assist with the client's case, some of the law provided in the SQE2 assessments will be irrelevant. Candidates will therefore need to assess the sources provided in order to identify the relevant law.

Stage 4. Apply law to the facts

In stages 2 and 3 the aim is to build a full picture of all the possibilities of both fact and law. In stage 4 the aim is to narrow the focus by applying the law to the material facts. Note once again in the model that a double arrow links this stage to the previous one. A solicitor must reassess regularly and be prepared to be flexible as they work between facts and law; it may be necessary to take a step back before progressing.

In the SQE2 assessments candidates will demonstrate their ability to apply the law to the facts by producing a written note setting out the legal reasoning by which they have arrived at their conclusions.

Stage 5. Identify possible solutions

Having established clearly the relationship of facts and law, a range of potential solutions should begin to emerge. This phase is again one of expanding options: a solicitor should not focus on the first option that emerges; instead, they should try to ensure that no alternative is missed.

In the SQE2 assessments, as in legal practice, the advice to the client should not be confined to locating the right law. The law must be used to find a solution which takes account of the client's objectives and circumstances. The possible solutions may be legal, practical or a combination of the two.

Often solutions involve taking positive action. However, it is important to consider the possibility of doing nothing. For example, it may be worth waiting to see what action another party may take first, or it may even be worth ignoring the problem if there is reason to expect that it will resolve itself.

Stage 6. Consider advantages and disadvantages

Having listed all possible solutions, it is necessary to weigh each in terms of potential rewards and potential risks. The client's circumstances will clearly influence the solicitor's analysis. Different options may carry different financial or emotional costs (for example the stress of going to court). The requirements of external regulators and the rules of professional conduct should also determine the solicitor's thinking. Some options may be eliminated at once as wholly unworkable or inappropriate. For others, this process of evaluation may be more technically demanding or complex.

Stage 7. Advise on the most appropriate solution(s)

The solicitor should now be in a position to advise on which one or more solutions will best fulfil the client's objectives. The solicitor should be prepared to outline the varying costs and benefits in detail, especially the risks of things going wrong, the consequences of that outcome, and options for limiting risk.

In the SQE2 assessments candidates are required to produce a written note setting out their advice to the client.

Stage 8. Present solution(s) in appropriate form

To end the process, the solicitor will need to report their findings. It is usual and preferrable to present the results of the research in writing. Firms usually have their own preferred style for research reports.

The report must be tailored to the recipient. This may be the client in person. If so, the client will not need all the details of the research. They will be more concerned with practical solutions. For junior solicitors it is more likely that they will be carrying out research for their supervisor or senior solicitors in the firm who will then use the research to advise the client.

The SQE2 assessments will be presented as research to be carried out for a partner.

9.4   Principles of legal research

9.4.1   Knowing where to look

Legal information is available in paper and online versions. Sometimes the same resource is available in both formats. Increasingly, lawyers rely on online versions via subscription databases such as *Westlaw* or *Lexis+ Legal Research* (see **9.5**) which enable a search to be carried out quickly and the results printed or downloaded. However, printed materials continue to play a role in research carried out in legal practice. Cost may be a limiting factor, particularly for smaller firms, as subscriptions to databases are expensive.

As a general rule, it is sensible to begin with a source which gives a general overview of the law in a certain area. Useful starting points are *Halsbury's Laws of England* and relevant practitioner works. These commentaries on the law are referred to as secondary sources (see **Chapter 10**). Having obtained a broad grasp of the relevant law, it is then easier to drill down into a further layer of research tools: those which contain the primary sources. Primary sources are the raw materials of the law, such as statutes, statutory instruments and case law (see

Chapter 10). They are essential to research because they contain authoritative statements of what the law actually is, rather than a commentator's opinion on the law.

Some lawyers prefer the speed and flexibility of online research; others prefer the convenience of paper resources. In reality both formats have their advantages and disadvantages. Quality of information content is the most important consideration. It can be useful to combine the two. For example, starting perhaps with a printed secondary resource (such as *Halsbury's Laws of England* or practitioner works) which can help to structure the research, give an overview of a subject and identify the key legislation and cases. Then move on to an online database to find and update those primary sources. Online resources are considered in more detail **9.5**.

9.4.2 Search terms

Devising appropriate search terms is essential in order to exploit any legal resource. These are often known as 'keywords'. They are words or phrases that enable the researcher to find the relevant law to help find a solution to the client's legal problem. These keywords can be looked up in a printed index or typed into a database search engine. Effective keywords help to pinpoint the relevant area of law, thereby saving time.

9.4.3 Using indexes

The most effective way to access the information content in a source is to use an index. Most sources (paper and online) will have one or more 'tables of primary sources', and a 'subject index'. A table of primary sources is an index that helps to locate cases, statutes or statutory instruments appearing in a work. Arrangement may be alphabetical or chronological. A subject index helps to locate commentary on specific areas of the law. Often this commentary will refer to primary sources, either in the text itself or in footnotes.

When using a subject index in a paper source it is necessary to look at how it is arranged. There may be tiered entries in this form:

county court

> jurisdiction

> > extent

The broad topic, **county court**, appears first. Subsequent entries are progressively more specific. To make best use of the index, it is necessary to look up the most specific keyword that will lead to the answer to the client's problem. A good index will offer a variety of terms, including cross references (that is, references between terms of similar meaning). However, choosing the right term will always involve a process of elimination.

Online databases often allow a search for terms appearing anywhere in a source. In other words, their 'subject index' is not a separate component as in a book. Instead, it comprises every word appearing in the source. Relying on this facility, known as a 'free text' search can generate large numbers of irrelevant results. It is usually more effective to search within a particular field of the search form in an online source, such as 'case name' or 'keywords' in a database of law reports.

9.4.4 Recording the research trail

When conducting research in legal practice, it is vital to record the progress of the research and the methods used to locate information carefully. This is because the facts available might change, requiring the conclusions drawn from a piece of research to be reviewed. Or it may be that someone else in the firm (e.g. a supervisor) may wish to check or repeat part of the research.

Recording the trail requires that at each stage of the research, as well as recording the information discovered, the researcher should make a note of what they do and when they do it. The record should include:

(a) the date the research was carried out (especially important with Internet sources, where content may change daily);

(b) full citations for legislation, case law and other primary sources consulted;

(c) for books: the author, title, edition, year and publisher;

(d) for journal articles: the title of the journal, title of the article, author, year and volume number;

(e) for databases: the name of the database, and the name of the section of the database (for example, *UK Parliament Acts* on *Lexis + Legal Research*);

(f) keywords used during searches;

(g) page references or website addresses for key pieces of information;

(h) dates of publication (including the date of the latest release for a loose-leaf source); and

(i) any dates to which the law as stated is claimed to be up to date by the publisher.

The following is an example of a good research trail for a simple research query:

Topic	What are the penalties for importing cocaine into the UK?
Date of research	6 December 2022
Source used	*Halsbury's Laws of England* (via *Lexis+ Legal Research*)
Keywords used	'Controlled drug' – offences – import and export
Result	Directed to paragraph 561 of volume 75 (2021 edition) for a summary of the penalties upon conviction for import of a Class A drug (including cocaine)
How updated	Update note lists amendments in SI 2015/664 and Sentencing Council guideline, Fraudulent Evasion of a Prohibition by Bringing into or Taking out of the United Kingdom a Controlled Drug (effective from 1 April 2021)

Note that it is *not* necessary to produce a research trail in the SQE2 Legal Research assessments.

9.4.5 Updating

The law changes constantly. A new Act of Parliament or a judgment of the Supreme Court can reverse lawyers' received wisdom on an issue overnight. It is therefore essential to take steps to make sure that the law cited in the course of research is as up to date as possible.

9.5 Accessing online databases

Legal information (including case law and legislation) may be accessed online via both freely available and subscription (paid for) sources. Freely available sources include government websites, such as http://www.legislation.gov.uk, and the website of the British and Irish

Legal Information Institute, http://www.bailii.org. Reputable free sites can be extremely useful; however, it is important to exercise caution and judgement when using some of these resources (see **9.7**).

The two major subscription sources in the UK are the online databases *Lexis+ Legal Research* and *Westlaw*. There is some overlap between the content of the two (for example, both contain the full text of the authoritative *Law Reports*), but they are in competition, so most journal and case reports appear in full text on one or the other.

Despite the cost, many firms will decide that a subscription to a database is a sound commercial investment. A key advantage of databases such as *Westlaw* or *Lexis+ Legal Research* is the amount of added value content they provide. For example, they update legislation to show any amendments and give guidance on whether cases are still good law. They also offer access to commentary on the law, through either journal articles or legal texts such as *Civil Procedure*, also known as *The White Book* (via *Westlaw*), or *Blackstone's Criminal Practice* (via *Lexis+ Legal Research*). *Lexis+ Legal Research* also gives access to two substantial complementary encyclopaedias of legal precedents: *Atkin's Court Forms* and the *Encyclopaedia of Forms and Precedents*.

9.6   Guidelines for searching online databases

Searching online involves thinking of keywords that are likely to feature in documents relevant to a legal problem, then typing these keywords into a database search engine. Planning in advance how to formulate and carry out searches of databases is vitally important. Typing a string of words into a database is rarely an efficient use of time and may not produce the required results. This is a significant issue in the context of legal practice where time is a valuable commodity, and a solicitor has a professional duty of care in advice given to a client. To add to the problem, publishers of online databases use different versions of software, so the rules for searching them may differ. However, most databases feature an on-screen 'help' facility, and some even offer on-screen tutorials.

A number of simple techniques can be applied to make the searching of online databases more structured and precise. For example, it may be possible to use advanced search options which offer specific search fields to narrow the search using certain criteria, such as date range or level of court. In addition, certain symbols are widely understood across databases to stand for certain letters, or to combine or exclude words. These symbols can either widen a search or narrow it as necessary.

To search effectively, bear in mind the following techniques:

Truncation

A search with a truncated word will search for different word endings. In most databases, typing in the word **negligent** will retrieve only documents that feature exactly that word; it will not pick up occurrences of 'negligence' or 'negligently', words which might equally well be used in the case or statute sought in the search. Using a truncated form of the word to perform the search will widen the trawl. The symbol used to truncate varies between databases but can be found using the 'help' facility.

Truncation can be particularly useful for finding singulars and plurals. So, for example, searching *Lexis+ Legal Research* using **pollut!** will retrieve 'pollute', 'pollutes', 'polluting', 'pollution', 'pollutants', etc., in fact any word which begins with these six letters.

Wild card characters

These function within a word as a truncation symbol does at the end of a word. The symbol varies between databases, but as with truncation it can be found using the 'help' facility. So, for example, searching *Lexis+ Legal Research* using **wom*n** will retrieve instances of 'woman' and 'women'.

Connectors

The commands **and**, **or** and **not** are sometimes known as Boolean operators or connectors. They function as follows:

Connector	Effect	Function
and e.g. **Donoghue and Stevenson**	The computer will retrieve only those documents where both the first term and the second term appear	Narrows a search – to improve precision of results
or e.g. **fence or boundary**	The computer will retrieve all documents where the first term appears and also all documents where the second term appears	Expands a search – to search for possible synonyms, etc.
not e.g. **pollution not air**	The computer will retrieve documents that contain the first term but do not contain the second term	Narrows a search – eliminates terms not relevant to your topic

Field searching

Most databases divide documents into a number of separate fields. Searches can be confined to a specified field or a combination of fields. For example, in a search for cases on a particular topic, confining the search to the 'subject/keywords' field should produce fewer, more relevant results than using the same term in a 'free text' search.

It is usually possible to search across the entire database (cases, legislation, commentary, journal articles) using a 'free text' search from the home page. Whilst this is comprehensive, it is likely to generate a large proportion of irrelevant results. A more effective technique is to narrow the search to a particular area (cases, legislation, practice areas, journal articles) and then use links from the result to link to other relevant documents.

Phrase searching

How systems search for phrases varies. In some databases a phrase can be entered just as it is, e.g. **infringement of human rights**, and will be found; others, however, will assume that the **and** connector is to be placed between each word, and retrieve the words separately. This will probably undermine the effectiveness of the search. The most common way of searching for a phrase is to include it within double quotation marks, for example **"breach of contract"**.

Avoiding stop words

Databases tend to have a list of common words (such as 'is' and 'have') that are ignored in the process of searching. Such words should be avoided; the 'help' facility will usually identify them in that particular database.

Refining the outcome

If an initial search retrieves a large number of results rather than going back to square one, it is usually preferrable to edit the search. This might be achieved by adding an extra keyword and then searching again within the results. Or there may be the option to rearrange the results so the most relevant appear at the top of the results list.

9.7 Using the free internet

Quality of information is a crucial consideration when using free sites on the internet. Anyone can publish on free sites. Unlike subscription databases, no one is responsible for ensuring the currency or impartiality of content. So, it is always necessary to assess whether the information found online is authoritative, accurate and up to date.

9.7.1 Search engines

Search engines do not publish information on the internet; they work as a finding tool. There are various search engines available, the most popular being Google (www.google.co.uk). Search engines do not search all websites or databases, so much online legal information is not accessible via this route.

9.7.2 Official websites

The EU, Parliament, the courts and government all publish authoritative information on their websites. Useful official websites are:

- British and Irish Institute of Legal Information (www.bailii.org)
- legislation.gov (www.legislation.gov.uk)
- Ministry of Justice (www.gov.uk/government/organisations/ministry-of-justice)
- UK Parliament (www.parliament.uk)
- UK Supreme Court (www.supremecourt.uk)
- EUR-Lex (eur-lex.europa.eu/homepage.html)

However, whilst the information on official sites can be treated as reliable and authoritative, caution may still be needed. For example, not all the legislation on the legislation.gov site is available in an updated form.

9.7.3 Portals and directories

Portals and directories are gateways to selected free online legal information. They are useful for helping to find authoritative sites and can provide a quicker, more efficient route than search engines. A good example is www.venables.co.uk.

9.7.4 Social media and Web 2.0

Web 2.0 is an umbrella term used to describe collaborative internet tools such as blogs, wikis and social media sites.

Wikis are collaborative websites, which allow users to create and edit information.

Blogs are online journals containing the personal opinions of the author. Over recent years many law firms, practising lawyers and law teachers have published blogs. A useful directory of UK legal blogs is available at www.infolaw.co.uk/lawfinder.

Some content on blogs may be serious and useful (for example, a barrister may report recent developments in their specialist area of practice). Other content (even within the same blog) may be more frivolous. Therefore, while they may be worthwhile sources of comment about the law and legal practice, their content should not be relied upon uncritically when carrying out legal research. This same caution should be applied to all information found on social media and free websites.

9.7.5 Collections

Some websites act as research collections. It may be necessary to register or provide the firm's details in order to access the materials. Some examples are:

- Law.com (www.law.com/resources/) is an extensive digital library of white papers, research, legal insights and press releases aimed at in-house and private practice lawyers. It provides access to a free digital library containing almost 10,000 executive insights, many of which are written by the world's leading law firms and companies. The content is organised by category, so it is possible to locate information that is relevant to a practice area, sector or jurisdiction.

- ResearchGate (www.researchgate.net) is a wide-ranging collection of UK and international business and legal research materials with more of an academic focus.

- SSRN provides access to research materials (www.ssrn.com/index.cfm/en/lsn/), covering over 30 disciplines including law and management.

9.7.6 Finding business information

In legal practice undertaking research may involve finding information on companies and markets. There are some extremely useful and authoritative free resources available, such as:

- *The Financial Times* (www.ft.com). A search of this site can provide information on a specific company or on general commercial sectors such as banking or retail. Some of the content is freely available and some is restricted to those with a subscription. Subscribers can access profile information for the company selected, details of directors, financial data, share prices and news articles on the company published by the FT.

- Companies House (www.gov.uk/government/organisations/companies-house). This site provides access to a range of information on companies, forms and guidance.

- *The Gazette* (www.thegazette.co.uk). This site publishes online profiles of every UK business registered with Companies House. It also contains a useful section called Companies Resources which includes articles and guidance on relevant topics.

10 | Research Sources

SQE2 syllabus

This chapter will help you to achieve the SQE2 Assessment Criterion of identifying and using relevant sources and information.

Learning outcomes

By the end of this chapter you should be able to:

- explain the difference between primary and secondary sources;
- select appropriate primary sources for research;
- locate legislation and case reports; and
- understand how to cite legislation and case law.

10.1 Introduction

In the SQE2 assessments candidates will not be required to find sources for themselves. The relevant sources (along with some irrelevant ones) will be provided. Nevertheless, it is essential to be able to identify what the sources are, where they come from and the status given to them. In many ways the sources should be approached as if they were the product of your own research.

The sources retrieved via effective Legal Research fall into two types: primary and secondary. Primary sources, that is legislation and cases, are the raw materials of the law. The advice given to the client will be based on these primary sources.

Secondary sources state what a commentator believes the law to be. They offer valuable introductions and summaries, written by authors who are experts in their field and whose names may carry authority; but the statements of law they contain are still second-hand.

When conducting a piece of Legal Research, rather than going straight to primary sources, it is often advisable to start with secondary sources such as a general legal encyclopaedia or a good practitioner work. These are a useful first step because they provide an overview of the law and highlight any key legislation and case law. For this reason, secondary sources will be considered first in this chapter.

Chapter 9 dealt with conducting Legal Research and **Chapter 11** focuses on the SQE2 assessments.

This chapter looks at:

- secondary sources;
- legislation;
- case law; and
- EU law.

10.2 Secondary sources

10.2.1 *Halsbury's Laws of England*

Halsbury's Laws of England provides the only complete narrative statement of the law in England and Wales. The printed version runs to around 100 volumes. The same content is available online on the *Lexis+ Legal Research* subscription database.

Halsbury's Laws of England provides commentary upon the present state of all areas of English law. It is arranged alphabetically by subject. Each subject is divided into numbered paragraphs that summarise the law in a particular area. Footnotes direct the reader to related cases and legislation (the primary sources).

10.2.1.1 The paper version

Finding the law using the paper version requires separate sections to be consulted in a four-stage process:

- **Consolidated index**

The first step is to search for relevant keywords in the index volumes. The index refers on from those keywords to discussion of the law in one or more of the main volumes. Each reference indicates the context in which the keyword is being discussed, followed by the number in bold of the main volume where the discussion appears, then the edition to which this main volume belongs, and then one or more paragraph number(s). If the paragraph number is followed by 'n', the reference is to a footnote to that paragraph.

- **Main volume**

The 'main volumes' give statements of the law of England and Wales, arranged by subject. Each self-contained subject is known as a 'title'. Each volume has its own subject index at the back. This may be useful if the main volume was reissued after publication of the annual consolidated index, since reissue of a volume may mean reordering of paragraph numbers.

- **Cumulative supplement**

Over the years, the main volumes are reissued on a rolling programme. As time goes by, some information contained in older volumes will be superseded. So, it is necessary to check that the information in the main volume is up to date.

The first stage of updating is to consult the annual, two-volume 'cumulative supplement'. There will be a note at the front which gives the date to which the content has been updated. Any developments affecting the selected area of law since publication of the main volume and the date of the cumulative supplement will be noted. Entries appear under the same volume and paragraph references as in the main volumes.

- **Noter-Up**

The 'Noter-Up' booklet is replaced monthly. Looking under the volume and paragraph number of the original reference will reveal any very recent changes in the law.

10.2.1.2 The online version

The full text of *Halsbury's Laws of England* online can be accessed on *Lexis+ Legal Research*. This includes the updating material contained in the latest annual Cumulative Supplement and monthly Noter-Up.

It is possible to browse the contents list or to enter search terms. In either case, the basic building blocks are numbered paragraphs. Each describes the law in a narrow area and corresponds exactly to the numbered paragraphs in the equivalent printed volume of *Halsbury's Laws*.

Browsing the contents list allows the researcher to drill down to information on a topic, via a hierarchy of contents lists arranged by subject. Using the + (plus) symbol next to headings in the list enables more specific entries to be seen; the − (minus) symbol shows broader entries. A numbered heading without a + or − symbol corresponds to a paragraph. Alternatively, the researcher can search the whole encyclopaedia by entering search term(s) to retrieve a list of paragraphs where they occur.

Browsing the contents list or searching will produce a list of numbered paragraphs. The list of results can be arranged by source order or relevance. Selecting the relevance option will list the results which contain the most hits on the search terms first. Individual items on the list can then be opened to view the full text.

The online version of *Halsbury's Laws* is updated weekly. Lexis has started updating volumes online by integrating the legal changes into the core content in the numbered paragraphs, but it has not yet completed this work. An update icon contains links for any outstanding updates to the law relating to the main paragraph.

10.2.2 Practitioner databases

10.2.2.1 *Practical Law*

Practical Law is published by the same company that publishes *Westlaw* but is aimed at practitioners. It is possible to search from the home page using the search box or search a topic by browsing by practice area.

The 'overview documents' are often a good place to start research as they summarise the law. These documents provide a commentary, and so are secondary sources, but they will provide links to other relevant materials, including legislation and cases.

Practical Law also has precedents and know-how services across a wide variety of practice areas. Each service combines a bank of standard documents with commentary and analysis, email updates, and practice notes and checklists.

10.2.2.2 *Lexis+ Practical Guidance*

Lexis+ Practical Guidance is published by the same company that publishes *Lexis+ Legal Research*, and like *Practical Law* it is aimed at legal practitioners and so arranges its content by subject area. Drop down options enable the relevant area to be selected and then it is possible to browse all the topics covered.

Selecting *Read Overview* will provide a summary of the law. This overview document again contains links to key cases and legislation.

Lexis+ Practical Guidance also has a wide range of useful precedents for legal transactions and procedures in each practice area.

10.2.3 Practitioner works

Practitioner works are written for, and usually by, practising lawyers. They give detailed and comprehensive coverage of an area of the law, with special emphasis on practice and procedure. They may also reproduce selected primary sources. As well as a printed edition (often in loose-leaf format) many practitioner works have online versions.

Although the original author may be long dead, their authority is such that practitioner works often continue to be known by their name rather than the name of the current editor. For example, *Chitty on Contracts* was originally written by Joseph Chitty (1796–1838).

There are a number of access points depending on the nature of the research. The overall table of contents can be used to plot the layout of the work as a whole. Tables of cases and statutes can be used to locate a discussion of particular court decision, statute or statutory instrument. The subject index identifies discussions of particular topics.

It is important to check that the content is up to date. At the beginning of a paper version there will be a note of the cut-off date to which the publisher affirms that the law expressed is current. Some paper versions of practitioner works are replaced by a new edition every year (for example, *Archbold: Criminal Pleading, Evidence and Practice*). Paperback supplements may appear during the lifetime of an edition; these accumulate updates to particular sections in the main work (for example, *Chitty on Contracts*). Loose-leaf format allows individual pages to be replaced, so that changes to the law are integrated regularly into the text (for example, *Kemp and Kemp: Quantum of Damages*). Titles may additionally be supplemented by a brief bulletin or newsletter, giving notes on recent cases or pieces of legislation.

Online versions of practitioner works will be updated as frequently as the editors can manage. This may be daily, but it may be monthly or even quarterly. When looking at an online version, using the information icon will reveal the date to which it is up to date.

10.3 Legislation

10.3.1 Sources of legislation

There are two major classes of legislation in the UK:

(a) *Primary legislation* is passed by Parliament in the form of Acts (also known as statutes)

(b) *Secondary legislation* is made under powers delegated by Parliament, usually to government ministers; it almost always takes the form of statutory instruments (also known as regulations or orders).

It is vital to check that the version of any legislation referred to is actually in force. Some provisions do not come into force for some time after they have been passed by Parliament. The last section of a statute usually deals with arrangements for its own commencement. A specific date may be given; a specific period after the date of Royal Assent may be stipulated; or the commencement may be delayed until such time as the Secretary of State makes a commencement order (usually by way of a statutory instrument). Many are then amended over time, or even repealed altogether.

The official versions of both Acts and statutory instruments are published by Her Majesty's Stationery Office. They appear in paper form and also on the website www.legislation.gov. uk. Although the website is a useful resource, some caution must be exercised as many of the texts are not subsequently amended to show the effects of later legislation (this is flagged on screen).

There are many different sources of legislation, in paper and online form. The best printed sources are *Halsbury's Statutes* and *Halsbury's Statutory Instruments*. Online alternatives are *Westlaw* and *Lexis+ Legal Research*.

10.3.2   Citing legislation

A statute is usually cited by its 'short title' (which should include the year it was passed), e.g. 'Human Rights Act 1998'. Sometimes citations appear by 'chapter number', for example the Human Rights Act 1998 may be cited as 'c 42 1998' (because it was the 42nd Act to be passed in 1998). Prior to 1963, statutes were referred to by the year of the monarch's reign. However, for convenience surviving old statutes are now referred to by a subsequently adopted short title, for example the Criminal Libel Act 1819 rather than its formal citation '60 Geo 3 & 1 Geo 4 c. 8'.

The body of a statute is divided into numbered sections, each containing a different rule of law. It is usual to abbreviate 'section' to 's', so that 's 1' refers to section 1. Sections are sub-divided into subsections, e.g. s 1(1); paragraphs, e.g. s 1(2)(a); and even sub-paragraphs. In larger statutes, sections may be grouped together into different parts, each dealing with a separate area of law.

Some statutes have one or more schedules at the end. The content of schedules varies; for example, some may contain detailed provisions which are not found in the main body of the Act, or they may expand or define phrases in the Act or contain detailed amendments of earlier legislation. The last schedule will normally say which earlier statutes the present Act repeals. References to schedules are often abbreviated as 'sched' or 'sch' and the divisions are known as 'paragraphs', often abbreviated to 'para'.

A statutory instrument is cited by its title and also by the form 'SI [year]/[serial number]', e.g., SI 1998/3132, which was the first published form of the Civil Procedure Rules 1998. The serial numbering reverts to '1' at the start of each calendar year.

The body of a statutory instrument is divided. The names of these divisions depend on the form of the title. If it is called an 'Order', the divisions are known as articles. If it is entitled 'Regulations', the divisions are also known as regulations. If it is entitled 'Rules', the divisions are also known as rules. A subdivision is always known as a paragraph.

10.3.3   Searching for legislation

10.3.3.1   *Current Law Statutes*

Current Law Statutes is a print resource which publishes statutes chronologically. They first appear as loose-leaf booklets. These are later republished as several hardback volumes each year. This original version of the statute is then 'frozen' permanently: subsequent amendments and repeals are not incorporated.

10.3.3.2 *Halsbury's Statutes*

Halsbury's Statutes contains an annotated version of all statutes in force in England and Wales. Amendments are incorporated; repealed provisions are excluded. The arrangement is alphabetical by subject. It is the best printed source for consulting up-to-date versions of statutes.

Finding the law using the paper version of *Halsbury's Statutes* involves the same four stages as when using *Halsbury's Laws* (see **10.2.1**):

- Consolidated index
- Main volumes
- Cumulative Supplement
- Noter-Up

10.3.3.3 *Lexis+ Legal Research*

The subscription database *Lexis+ Legal Research* contains the full, amended text of UK primary and secondary legislation in force. Legislation that has been recently enacted but is not yet in force is also included.

A named piece of legislation can be found narrowing the home page search field to *Legislation* and then entering search terms. It is also possible to use Advanced Search to specify a *Year* and a particular *Provision* (section or schedule number) or add search terms.

Legislation
Select a different content type ⌄

Document segments/fields

While these segments apply to the majority of documents, they may not apply to all documents.

Title

[   ]

Provision, Part or Schedule

[   ]

Terms

All of these terms

[Enter terms that you want to add to your search, this is the same as using AND between each word. Click Add]   [**Add**]

© Reproduced with kind permission of RELX (UK) Limited t/a LexisNexis

Legislation on a topic can be located by entering a keyword(s) in the *Search terms* box. Using *Search* will retrieve a list of sections of legislation where these occur. The list can be sorted by relevance or refined by entering another keyword using the *search within results* option.

When viewing the full text amendments appears in square brackets; text that has been repealed appears as '...'; text that will be amended or repealed at a future date appears in *italics*. Search terms are highlighted. Footnotes provide brief details about commencement and sources of amending legislation.

The *Supporting Materials* option accesses information about commencement, repeals and amendments via a source called *Status Snapshot,* and *Related Documents* links to commentary, cases or journal articles relating to the section on the screen.

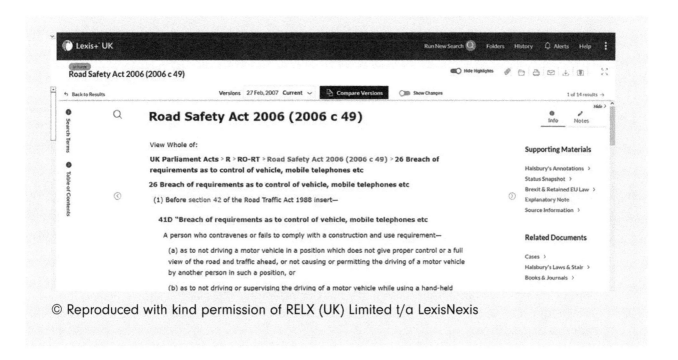

A statutory instrument can be found by entering its title or year and series number or using the search terms field.

10.3.3.4 *Westlaw*

Legislation is available via this subscription database. The *Basic Search* screen in *Legislation* allows a search of the text of UK Acts and SIs, as amended. It is possible to search either by *Title* and *Provision Number* or, to find material about a topic, by *Free Text*.

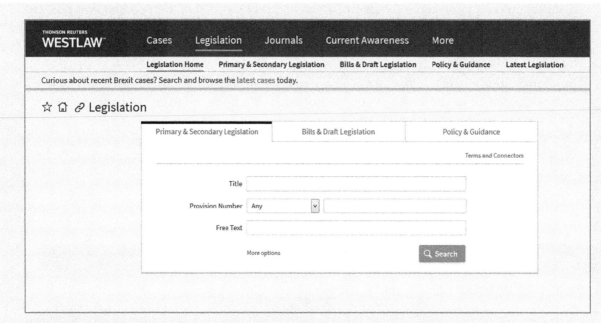

© Reproduced with kind permission of Westlaw UK

From the Legislation search screen, there are three tabs offering different search options. First, a search for primary and secondary legislation (i.e. Acts of Parliament and statutory instruments currently in force). Second, a search for draft Bills currently before Parliament. Third, a search for policy and guidance material relating to legislation (e.g. Codes of Practice, Consultations and HMRC Manuals).

There is also the facility to browse content arranged by year or title.

When viewing a piece of legislation firstly the arrangement of the Act is shown (listing the individual parts, sections, Schedules etc.). Each section has a symbol alongside it showing the status of that section.

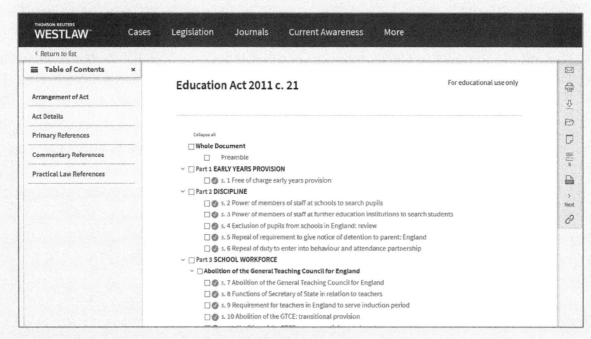

© Reproduced with kind permission of Westlaw UK

From the *Table of Contents, Act Details* provides details of any changes which are planned, commencement information, details of any legislation which has already modified the Act, links to definitions of terms contained in the legislation and any statutory instruments which have been made under the Act. *Primary References* gives details of any other legislation which mentions the Act. *Commentary References* provides information on relevant journal articles and topic overviews available on *Westlaw*.

10.3.4 Updating legislation

Legislative updates, usually in the form of later amending legislation, happen from time to time. Therefore, it is important to check for any changes to the legal status of legislation.

Legislation on *Westlaw* and *Lexis+ Legal Research* is generally updated daily, in the sense that the editors add new material every day. However, it does not follow that the content is current to today. Incorporating all the effects of new legislation is a complex and time-consuming task. Where recent legislation materially changes earlier legislation, but the editors have not yet incorporated the amendments, each affected section will feature a warning symbol.

The consolidated versions in *Halsbury's Statutes* and *Halsbury's Statutory Instruments* in paper format are current to within a month or so, provided all the updating steps have been followed through properly.

10.4 Case law

10.4.1 Publication of cases

Judgments delivered in court are published via a number of channels. Many can be accessed online soon after the judgment is given. For example, Supreme Court judgments are published on the Court's website on the day they are handed down. A large archive of transcripts of judgments can also be accessed via subscription databases such as *Westlaw* and *Lexis+ Legal Research*.

10.4.1.1 Transcripts

Transcripts are simply a written and verbatim record of the court's judgment. In straightforward cases, the court may be able to give judgment as soon as the hearing finishes. The judge gives a verbal judgment (ex tempore judgment) which is recorded and/or taken down by a short-hand stenographer. The transcript of the judgment will not be available until it has been transcribed by the court stenographers and approved by the judge. In more complex cases the court will reserve judgment. This means that judgment will be handed down at a later date, usually in the form of a written judgment. The transcript will generally be an exact copy of that which was handed down.

10.4.1.2 Law reports

Law reports are written by law reporters (barristers and solicitors) and are usually produced when the case makes a change to or develops the law. Law reports have all the information contained in a transcript along with other important elements of content such as summaries ('headnotes') and tables of cases and legislation referred to.

Law reports are published as a series and are usually available in both paper and online formats. Three general series feature the most significant cases across the law:

- The *Law Reports* (AC, QB, Ch and Fam)
- The *Weekly Law Reports* (WLR)
- The *All England Law Reports* (All ER)

Some series of reports are intended to cover cases in specialist areas (e.g., the *Road Traffic Reports* and the *Family Law Reports*). Brief reports are published regularly in *The Times* newspaper. Case notes also appear in weekly practitioners' journals, such as the *New Law Journal* and the *Law Society Gazette*.

Cases that are not selected for inclusion in such publications are termed 'unreported'. The internet has facilitated widespread access to unreported decisions, in the form of case transcripts. However, they should be treated with caution as foundations for legal advice. The courts will permit an advocate to cite an unreported case only if it 'contains a relevant statement of legal principle not found in reported authority' (*Practice Direction (Citation of Authorities) (Senior Courts)* [2012] 1 WLR 780).

10.4.2 Authority

The *Law Reports* published by the Incorporated Council of Law Reporting for England and Wales (ICLR) have the most authority. They are the nearest to an official series of case reports for England and Wales. Uniquely, they include arguments presented by counsel and are checked by the presiding judge before publication. For these reasons, and by direction of the judiciary, an advocate citing a case before a court is required to use the version in the *Law Reports* in preference to any alternatives (see *Practice Direction (Citation of Authorities) (Senior Courts)* [2012] 1 WLR 780).

The *Law Reports* have been published continuously in various parallel series since 1865. The names of these series have changed frequently over the years, in line with the shifting structure of divisions of the courts. There are currently four separate series: Appeal Cases (abbreviated to AC); Chancery Division (Ch); Family Division (Fam); and Queen's Bench Division (QB). These reports are available in printed format and online via *Westlaw* and *Lexis+ Legal Research*. If a case is reported in the *Law Reports*, it will usually be the first citation listed (after any neutral citation – see **10.4.3**).

10.4.3 Citing cases

Citations identify cases by notation, referring to a volume and page in a particular series of law reports. A typical citation for an English case is:

Jordan v Burgoyne [1963] 2 QB 744

This identifies that the report of the case of *Jordan v Burgoyne* starts at page 744 of vol 2 of the Queen's Bench series of the *Law Reports* for 1963.

Certain conventions underpin the system of citation:

- Party names appear in italics.
- Year of publication appears in [square] or (round) brackets:
  - in the example above, the year appears in square brackets because it is essential for locating the case; volumes of the *Law Reports* are consecutively numbered within each year only;
  - by contrast, the case of *Bowker v Rose* is reported at (1977) 121 SJ 274; volumes of the *Solicitors' Journal* are consecutively numbered from year to year; the case can be found in volume 121; the year is strictly superfluous, so it appears in round brackets.

- The number of the volume in which the report appears comes before the (abbreviated) title of the series, and the number of the first page of the report comes after.

- References to different series of reports are ordered in a hierarchy: the neutral citation (if it exists – see below) comes first; then any reference to the *Law Reports*; the *Weekly Law Reports*; the *All England Law Reports*; other specialist series of law reports; newspaper law reports.

In January 2001 the neutral citation of judgments was introduced (see *Practice Note (Judgments: Neutral Citation)* [2001] 1 WLR 194). The system is 'neutral' as regards format and publisher. In other words, it identifies cases by a unique reference, independent of the series of reports in which they are reproduced and independent of whether they appear online or in print. The purpose is to enable reports of cases to be published and accessed more easily online.

All cases heard in the Supreme Court, the Court of Appeal and the High Court are now covered by these arrangements. A neutral citation is allocated by the court to every judgment. This is intended to feature in every subsequent publication of that judgment. It takes the form of year (in square brackets), abbreviation of the name of the court, and running serial number (the serial number reverts to 1 at the start of each calendar year). For example:

Supreme Court [2021] UKSC 1, 2, 3, etc.

Court of Appeal (Civil Division) [2021] EWCA Civ 1, 2, 3, etc.

Court of Appeal (Criminal Division) [2021] EWCA Crim 1, 2, 3, etc.

High Court (Administrative Division) [2021] EWHC 1, 2, 3, etc. (Admin)

Since 2001, judgments have also been set out in numbered paragraphs, which are easier to locate within electronic law reports than page references. The citation of the authority from a particular decision might thus be in the form: *Smith v Jones* [2001] EWCA Civ 10 at [59], i.e. paragraph 59 in the judgment of *Smith v Jones*, the 10th judgment of the year 2001 in the Civil Division of the Court of Appeal of England and Wales.

10.4.4 Searching for cases

The report of an individual case can be located in paper form and online using its citation. The citation to a series of law reports should be enough to locate a case, even without the names of the parties concerned.

Without the citation, it is possible to search an online database by typing in the party name. However, the more common the surname, the less efficient this approach is likely to be. The *Current Law Case Citator* is an index of cases by party. Coverage is comprehensive, beginning in 1947. It is published in paper form. The printed set comprises several volumes covering different date ranges. The same content is available online via *Westlaw*. *Case Overview* is a case citator that is available in online form only, via *Lexis+ Legal Research*.

Online subscription databases such as *Lexis+ Legal Research* and *Westlaw* are very useful for searching for cases on a particular subject since they offer the facility to search for occurrences of keywords anywhere in the text of documents. However, they can generate large numbers of results, many of which may be irrelevant.

Most online versions of single series of law reports, such as *All England Law Reports* on *Lexis+ Legal Research* or *Weekly Law Reports* on *Westlaw*, permit free text subject searching using keywords. It is also possible to search across all case reports by limiting the date, or court or even cases heard by a particular judge. Another way of finding the most relevant cases from a large list of results is to use the *Sort by Relevance* option offered by both *Lexis+ Legal Research* and *Westlaw*. This works by reordering the results so that those cases with the most mentions of your search term are listed first.

10.4.5   Updating case law

Having found a case, it is necessary to check whether it is still good law. The decision may, for example, have been reversed on appeal or overruled by a later case.

Updating online is relatively straightforward. Having carried out an online search for a case, the results screen will show the name of the case, details of the court and date of the hearing and a symbol indicating the type of subsequent judicial treatment the case has received. For example, an icon featuring a no entry sign or a white cross on a red background signifies negative judicial treatment and warns that at least one point of law in the case has been overruled or reversed. *Case Overview* (part of *Lexis+ Legal Research*) is an alternative online citator for researching subsequent judicial consideration again status icons to show the treatment the case has received.

For paper reports the best source for checking the subsequent judicial treatment of a case is a citator, such as the *Current Law Case Citator*. Using the printed version, the procedure is to find the latest reference to the case in an annual volume (entries in these volumes are cumulative), so it is necessary to work backwards from the most recent citator until a reference to the case is found. The reference will indicate where else in the volumes the case has been commented on and the treatment received.

10.5   EU law

Despite the UK's departure from the European Union, EU law cannot be completely ignored. An explanation of how EU legislation impacts upon UK law appears at www.legislation.gov.uk/eu-legislation-and-uk-law:

> EU legislation which applied directly or indirectly to the UK before 11.00 p.m. on 31 December 2020 has been retained in UK law as a form of domestic legislation known as 'retained EU legislation'. This is set out in sections 2 and 3 of the European Union (Withdrawal) Act 2018 (c. 16). Section 4 of the 2018 Act ensures that any remaining EU rights and obligations, including directly effective rights within EU treaties, continue to be recognised and available in domestic law after exit.

> The European Union (Future Relationship) Act 2020 (c. 29) implements the arrangements for the relationship between the UK and the EU after the implementation period, as agreed on 24 December 2020. These arrangements include the Trade and Cooperation Agreement, the Agreement on Nuclear Cooperation and the Agreement on Security Procedures for Exchanging and Protecting Classified Information. The Act provides for the application of these, and any supplementary, agreements in domestic law. It also provides for the interpretation of domestic laws in light of these agreements.

Therefore, any researcher will still need to consider the potential impact of EU law on the area being considered, even if these considerations conclude that the area is now wholly covered by domestic legislation.

The *Official Journal of the European Union* (OJ) is the official publication of record for the EU. The EU itself publishes a vast amount of information, including primary legal materials, freely on the Internet. The major sites are *Europa* and *EUR-Lex*. EU information can also be accessed on some subscription databases, including *Westlaw* and *Lexis+ Legal Research*.

EUR-Lex is the legal portal within the *Europa* website. It offers free access to EU law, including the *Official Journal of the European Union* L-series (Legislation) and C-series (Information and Notices), treaties, legislation, international agreements, preparatory acts and parliamentary questions. Case-law coverage includes judgments of the Court of Justice and the General Court of the European Union. Also available are the Commission documents (the 'COM' series), a collection of consolidated legislation, and the texts of treaties.

11

Legal Research

SQE2 syllabus

This chapter will help you to achieve the SQE2 Assessment Objective of demonstrating that you are able to conduct Legal Research from a variety of resources provided and produce a written report.

Learning outcomes

By the end of this chapter you should be able to:

- identify and utilise relevant legal sources;
- provide client-focused advice; and
- report research clearly and effectively.

11.1   Introduction

Legal Research is an integral part of the work of a solicitor. No solicitor, however experienced, can be expected to know every element of the law. Added to which the law is constantly changing. As a matter of professional conduct solicitors are subject to the requirement that 'you maintain your competence to carry out your role and keep your professional knowledge and skills up to date' (Paragraph 3.3 SRA Code of Conduct for Solicitors, RELs and RFLs).

General written communication skills were considered in **Chapter 2**. **Chapter 9** considered conducting research and **Chapter 10** looked at research sources. This chapter considers the specific requirements of the SQE2 Legal Research assessments.

This chapter looks at:

- the assessments;

- reading and analysing;

- sources; and

- written notes.

11.2   The SQE2 assessments

11.2.1   Form

In the SQE2 assessments candidates are required to investigate a problem for a client and produce a written note explaining their legal reasoning and the key sources they rely on and setting out the advice that the partner should give to the client.

Candidates will sit a total of three Legal Research assessments in the practice areas below. Questions in these practice areas may draw on underlying black letter law in the Functioning Legal Knowledge shown in brackets next to each one:

- one in the context of either Dispute Resolution (*Contract Law and Tort*) or Criminal Litigation (*Criminal Liability*);

- one in the context of either Property Practice (*Land Law*) or Wills and Intestacy, Probate Administration and Practice (*Trusts*); and

- one in the context of Business Organisations, Rules and Procedures (including money laundering and financial services) (*Contract Law*).

Remember that questions on ethics and professional conduct will be pervasive throughout SQE2.

(See the SRA website for the full syllabus.)

It is important to note that whilst the assessments will be set in the context of these practice areas, the purpose of the assessment is research. This means that the specific subject matter of the assessments may be outside the scope of the Functioning Legal Knowledge.

Candidates will receive their instructions for the SQE2 assessments in the form of an email from a partner asking the candidate to research an issue or issues, so that the partner can report back to the client. The email will set out the facts and explain what the candidate is required to do. The instructions will be accompanied by a number of legal sources.

The email/instructions will be provided electronically. Candidates will have 60 minutes in which to complete their answer.

11.2.2   Criteria

In the SQE2 assessments candidates will be assessed against the following Assessment Criteria:

Skills

(1) Identify and use relevant sources and information.

(2) Provide advice which is client-focused and addresses the client's problem.

(3) Use clear, precise, concise and acceptable language.

Application of law

(1) Apply the law correctly to the client's situation.

(2) Apply the law comprehensively to the client's situation, identifying any ethical and professional conduct issues and exercising judgment to resolve them honestly and with integrity.

You can read more about the SQE2 assessments in **Chapter 1**. In the appendix to that chapter, you can see how the Statement of Solicitor Competence applies to the skill of Legal Research.

11.2.3 The practicalities

In the SQE2 assessments you will be provided with electronic instructions which comprise an email from a partner accompanied by a number of legal sources. You will be asked to produce a written note for the partner setting out your advice for the client and your legal reasoning including key sources and authorities that you rely upon and which you have selected from the sources provided.

Note that you will not have access to any legal databases. Consequently, you will not be required to undertake any independent research. The task, therefore, is to identify the key issues, locate the relevant law amongst the sources provided and then apply the law to the facts before you.

In the SQE2 assessments, you will have 60 minutes to complete the task in its entirety. It is likely that you will need to spend the majority of the time dealing with the sources provided. The remainder of the time will obviously be spent on a combination of reading, planning and writing.

There is no absolute rule on how to divide your time. A useful rule of thumb may be to allow up to 40 minutes for the sources. However, you may feel that you will need more time for writing. In reality it is a matter of practising in order to find a time allocation that you can comfortably work with. Having that time allocation in mind will help to ensure that you do not feel under pressure to start to write prematurely in the assessment.

Bear in mind that you may be presented with a scenario in which there are several issues to be addressed. You will need to split your time between them efficiently as all issues will need to be covered in your written note.

11.3 Reading and analysing

Obviously, the starting point in the SQE2 assessment is to read the email and any additional instructions provided.

You should look out for any instructions given about the assessment itself. This may take the form of setting out any issues that you do not need to consider. This may be in the email from the partner (e.g. 'I only want you to report on whether the client has a claim. Don't worry about the level of damages at this stage') or in a separate note to candidates (e.g. 'Candidates are not required to deal with Inheritance Tax'). There may be instructions on what you are permitted to do, for example to cite primary sources referred to in a secondary source even though the full text of the primary source has not been provided. (For primary and secondary sources see **Chapter 10**.)

It is easy for candidates to skim over such instructions in their anxiety to get to the substance of the matter. However, it is important to follow them. You will waste time in the assessment and receive no credit, for example, for addressing issues which do not need to be considered.

You will then need to read the facts presented in the email from the partner. You may need to do this more than once. This will immediately alert you to the subject matter of the assessment. The nature of the Legal Research assessments is such that you may have no knowledge of the particular topic covered. Do not panic. Remember that the test in Legal Research is not whether you know the answer, but whether you can find it.

You will then need to analyse the facts in order to identify the issues which arise and which the partner wishes you to address in your written note. One way to do this is to formulate a question or questions that need to be answered through your 'research' in order to provide the client with the advice they require. The email may provide some assistance with this by effectively setting the main question, for example, 'the client wants to know whether he can dismiss the director'. Alternatively, the wording of the email may be quite wide, for example, 'the client wants to know how to proceed'. Whether you are given the main question or have to identify it for yourself, you will probably also need to formulate and answer a series of more specific questions.

Formulating the questions to be answered should enable you to then plan for the shape that your written note will take. A detailed plan is not required but you should have an outline in mind of the points that will need to be covered and the order in which to deal with them. However, you should also be prepared to be flexible; as you begin to look at the sources provided, further questions may occur to you or certain facts/issues may assume greater or lesser significance than appeared at first sight.

11.4 Sources

Once you have formulated your questions you can then turn your attention for the first time to the sources provided in order to find the answers. There is, of course, nothing to prevent a candidate turning to the sources at an earlier stage. A candidate may wish to take an 'early' look at some of them, for example, to gain an indication of what issues are likely to arise if the subject matter of the assessment is completely new. However, the risk in looking at the sources first is that the candidate may begin to 'bend' the facts to fit the law that they have looked at, rather than matching the right law to the relevant facts.

In the SQE2 assessments candidates will be provided with a range of sources in electronic form. They are likely to be a combination of primary and secondary sources taken from a variety of legal resources (e.g. *Lexis+ Legal Research*, *Westlaw*, law reports and practitioner works – see **Chapter 10**).

Some of the sources provided will *not* be relevant. Part of your task is to distinguish those sources which are relevant from those which are not. Remember that one of the criteria that you will be assessed against is your ability to 'identify and use relevant sources and information'.

There is likely to be an index and the sources will probably be presented in alphabetical order. The index is a good starting point as it will give an overview of the range of materials and help you to navigate around them.

The volume of material provided means that you will not have time in the 60 minutes available to read everything in detail. Nevertheless, it is necessary to interpret and evaluate the sources provided. You will therefore need to skim the texts by just looking at headings, sub-headings and key sentences in order to gain an overview of the contents and where you are going to be able to find the answers to your questions. This should also enable you to identify those sources which are not relevant.

You should then be in a position to read the relevant sources. Again, in the assessments time is short so you are unlikely to be able to read through them in detail more than once. When conducting a piece of Legal Research, a secondary source (for example, *Halsbury's Laws*) is a good starting point (see **10.2.1**). Secondary sources are useful in providing the researcher with an overview of the topic before they drill down into the detail of the primary sources. This may also be the case in the SQE2 assessment, unless, of course, you have been provided with a secondary source which is in fact not relevant.

You will need to come back to the sources for the purposes of writing your note. So, you will need to ensure that you are able to do so easily when the time comes, perhaps by making a note or, if you have the facility to do so, highlighting the relevant text as you are reading through.

11.5 Written notes

11.5.1 Form

There is no standard way of presenting the results of a piece of Legal Research. In legal practice firms tend to have their own preferred house style for research reports. In the SQE2 assessments you are required to produce a 'note'. You will be given a template for the note, but this is likely to be simply divided into two sections by headings: one for legal advice and one for legal reasoning.

When conducting a piece of research in legal practice it usually essential to produce a research trail setting out in detail how the research has been conducted (see **9.4.4**). This enables the research to be easily checked, repeated or varied if necessary. However, note that a research trail is *not* required in the SQE2 assessments.

The note is, in essence, an example of a piece of Legal Writing. You must therefore take care with its tone, style etc. (see **Chapter 5**) and ensure that the spelling, punctuation and grammar is correct (see **Chapter 2**). One of the Assessment Criteria that you will be assessed against is your ability to 'use clear, precise, concise and acceptable language'.

Your note must set out the advice clearly. It may, for example, be helpful to add your own sub-headings to the note if, say, there are several issues to be addressed.

11.5.2 Advice

The purpose of the 'research' is to enable the partner to go on to advise. So, in this part of the note you must set out the advice which the partner will pass on to the client. It is a matter of stating the relevant facts and applying the law. It must be a combination of the two. The Assessment Criteria for skills require candidates not only to identify the relevant law, but also to use it.

The recipient of the note is the partner rather than the client, so as a piece of Legal Writing the appropriate tone and language is that for a partner (see **5.6.4**). The partner, for example, will not need to have legal terms or basic principles explained to them. Nevertheless, you should aim to make the partner's task as easy as possible. Keep the eventual recipient of the advice in mind and present the advice in a client focused manner. For example, if the client has raised a particular question, provide the answer clearly and simply so that the partner could copy it into a letter/email to the client if necessary.

There is no need to include a section repeating the facts. It is more a matter of identifying the issues and weaving the relevant facts into the advice.

The law must be applied correctly and comprehensively to the facts. It is easy to fall into the trap of seeing Legal Research as an academic challenge to 'find the right piece of law'. However, in the SQE2 assessments, as in legal practice, the true task is to use the law to provide a solution to the client's problem. It is therefore necessary to take account of the client's particular circumstances as well as practical and commercial considerations. You should not stop at the law. You may need to include suggestions on practical steps that the client could take.

As part of your analysis of the facts you should have identified whether ethical or conduct issues arise. Any such issues must be addressed as part of your advice. It may be, for example, that the client should be advised that the firm cannot continue to act if the client is determined to pursue their proposed course of action.

11.5.3 Legal reasoning

In this part of the note, you will need to set out your legal reasoning so that it is clear to the partner how and why you have arrived at your advice for the client. The content of this part of the note is for the partner alone and will not be passed onto the client. Its purpose is to enable the partner to check the process that you have followed in order to arrive at your advice.

In this section you will need to refer to the key sources and authorities that you have relied on in formulating your advice. You should cite the case or legislation (including specific sections). Consider whether it is better to copy the text of the source/authority or to paraphrase it. If you decide to copy the text, make sure that you only include the relevant extracts.

11.5.4 Example

The example of a written note below is based on the following scenario:

Ten years ago, Mr Howarth planted a row of three cypress trees at the end of his garden. He planted the trees in order to screen the view of a new housing development which was being built just over the boundary wall of Mr Howarth's property. The trees have now grown to a height of five metres and their foliage has grown sideways and has become interwoven.

The house situated immediately next to the boundary wall was sold recently. Yesterday the new owner went to see Mr Haworth and complained that the trees were preventing the sunlight getting to the vegetable patch in his garden with the result that nothing will grow. The exchange became rather heated and ended with Mr Haworth stating that he would not remove the trees, and the neighbour responding by saying that he was going to make a complaint about the trees to the local authority.

Mr Howarth wants to know whether his neighbour would be justified in making a complaint and, if so, what action the local authority could take.

Written Note

Advice to the client

We should advise Mr Howarth that it is likely that his neighbour would be justified in making a complaint to the local authority. Mr Howarth can be reassured that he cannot be forced to remove the trees, but the local authority can require him to reduce the height of the trees if the complaint is upheld.

Part 8 of the Anti-Social Behaviour Act 2003 provides a procedure for complaints to be made to the local authority about high hedges adversely affecting the reasonable enjoyment of a neighbouring property.

Section 66 of the Act defines a high hedge as a barrier to light or access caused by a line of two or more evergreens rising to a height of two metres. 'Evergreen' is further defined as an evergreen or semi-evergreen tree or shrub. There is case law on the meaning of 'hedge' which says that the question is fact specific; the alignment and proximity of the trees is important, as well as a common sense approach to what constitutes a hedge.

Mr Howarth's cypress trees are evergreens and there is a line of three of them rising to five metres in height. The trees are close together and form a line with inter-mingling foliage and so would probably be considered a hedge for the purposes of the Act. The trees are preventing sunlight getting to the neighbour's vegetable patch and so are likely to be considered a barrier to light and a high hedge such as to justify a complaint.

If the local authority decide that the trees are adversely affecting the neighbour's reasonable enjoyment of his property, under s 69 of the Act they will issue a remedial notice. The notice will specify what action which Mr Howarth must take in relation to the hedge. The notice cannot require the hedge to be removed or reduced to a height of less than two metres.

We should warn Mr Howarth that failure to comply with a remedial notice is a criminal offence which carries a penalty of a fine of up to £1,000 on conviction.

The likelihood is that if the neighbour makes a complaint it will be upheld by the local authority with the result that Mr Howarth will have to take some action with regard to the trees. Rather than wait for that action to be imposed on him, it would be preferable to try to come to a compromise with the neighbour. As Mr Howarth has already experienced, neighbour disputes can be unpleasant. It is likely that some reduction in the height of the trees is all that will be required. It may be that an agreement can be reached on the extent of the remedial action which meets the need of both Mr Howarth and the neighbour.

Legal Reasoning mentioning any key sources or authorities

Anti-Social Behaviour Act 2003, s 65:

(1) This Part applies to a complaint which–

   (a) is made for the purposes of this Part by an owner or occupier of a domestic property; and

   (b) alleges that his reasonable enjoyment of that property is being adversely affected by the height of a high hedge situated on land owned or occupied by another person.

High hedge is defined by s 66 of the Act

(1) In this Part *'high hedge'* means so much of a barrier to light or access as–

   (a) is formed wholly or predominantly by a line of two or more evergreens; and

   (b) rises to a height of more than two metres above ground level.

(3) In this section *'evergreen'* means an evergreen tree or shrub or a semi-evergreen tree or shrub.

R (on the application of Castelli) v London Borough of Merton [2013] EWHC 602 (Admin):
'The concept of a line of two or more evergreens raises, to my mind, issues not only of the degree of alignment of the plants complained of, but also of their proximity' and 'indeed a decision-maker should, I would suggest (in agreement with the thrust of his submission) take his or her decision in the light of common sense. It seems to me that in applying the criteria of section 66, and, in particular, the concept of a line of evergreens, a decision-maker should keep it in the back of his or her mind that this is a test for identifying a hedge' (per Nicholas Paines QC (Sitting as a Deputy High Court Judge) at [21] and [22])

Anti-Social Behaviour Act 2003, s 69:

(1) For the purposes of this Part a remedial notice is a notice–

   (a) issued by the relevant authority in respect of a complaint to which this Part applies; and

   (b) stating the matters mentioned in subsection (2).

(2) Those matters are–

   (a) that a complaint has been made to the authority under this Part about a high hedge specified in the notice which is situated on land so specified;

   (b) that the authority have decided that the height of that hedge is adversely affecting the complainant's reasonable enjoyment of the domestic property specified in the notice;

   (c) the initial action that must be taken in relation to that hedge before the end of the compliance period;

   (d) any preventative action that they consider must be taken in relation to that hedge at times following the end of that period while the hedge remains on the land; and

   (e) the consequences under section 75 and 77 of a failure to comply with the notice.

(3) The action specified in a remedial notice is not to require or involve–

   (a) a reduction in the height of the hedge to less than two metres above ground level; or

   (b) the removal of the hedge.

The penalties for failure to comply with a remedial notice are set out in s75 of the Act:

(1) Where–

   (a) a remedial notice requires the taking of any action, and

   (b) that action is not taken in accordance with that notice within the compliance period or (as the case may be) by the subsequent time by which it is required to be taken, every person who, at a relevant time, is an owner or occupier of the neighbouring land is guilty of an offence and shall be liable, on summary conviction, to a fine not exceeding level 3 on the standard scale.

Section 122 Sentencing Act 2020 sets out the standard scale. The maximum fine for level 3 is £1,000.

Index